A Short History of Cultural Studies

A Short History of Cultural Studies

John Hartley

SAGE Publications
London · Thousand Oaks · New Delhi

SAGE Publications Ltd
6 Bonhill Street
London EC2A 4PU

SAGE Publications Inc
2455 Teller Road
Thousand Oaks, California 91320

SAGE Publications India Pvt Ltd
32, M-Block Market
Greater Kailash – I
New Delhi 110 048

British Library Cataloguing in Publication data

A catalogue record for this book is
available from the British Library

ISBN 0 7619 5027 3
ISBN 0 7619 5028 1 (pbk)

Library of Congress Control Number: 2002108288

Typeset by M Rules
Printed in Great Britain by The Cromwell Press Ltd,
Trowbridge, Wiltshire

To Tina Horton
and to
Karri, Rhiannon and Sophie Hartley

Iti sapis potanda tinone

Contents

Illustrations

Acknowledgements

Thanks to

- Chris Rojek for putting me up to this;
- Olga Tobreluts for the cover image;
- Tina Horton, Charlotte Brunsdon, Terence Hawkes, Graeme Turner, Alan McKee, Joke Hermes, Stuart Cunningham and Lawrence Grossberg for reading it;
- my family for giving me space and encouragement to get on with it during testing times for all of us;
- my colleagues at Cardiff University, especially Ian Hargreaves and others in the Tom Hopkinson Centre for Media Research, for a stimulating four years;
- my colleagues at QUT, especially Peter Coaldrake and Elaine Harding, for letting me think about this when there was work to be done;
- all the folk in, round and against cultural studies who made me want to be part of it;
- and you, 'dear reader'.

As the man on the radio used to say: 'If you have been, thanks for listening.'

John Hartley
Brisbane

Introduction – A Philosophy of Plenty
A new *Endeavour*?

Cultural studies as an object of study

Somewhere buried in the endless British TV cop show *The Bill* is a bit of dialogue where a detective speculates on his possible future outside of the police force. I can't remember why; perhaps he'd been a naughty boy. In answer to a polite inquiry about what he planned to do next, he mused for a moment, then came up with the most ridiculous scenario he could think of. Evidently the scriptwriters wanted something so unlikely that viewers would realise that the character saw no future for himself other than as a policeman. 'Oh I dunno,' he says, deadpan, 'maybe I'll go to college and do a degree in cultural studies.' Laughter all round.

Cultural studies has come of age; it has achieved sufficiently wide popular recognition to become a butt of jokes in the media, and denunciation in the daily press. But its demonisation as the latest successor of poststructuralism, postmodernism and political correctness suggests that it has touched a nerve somewhere in the body politic. As a field of academic, intellectual and activist inquiry, analysis and criticism, it's not the sort of thing you'd normally expect to crop up on *The Bill*.

Even within intellectual communities and academic institutions, there is little agreement about what counts as cultural studies, either as a critical practice or as an institutional apparatus. On the contrary, the field is riven by fundamental disagreements about what cultural studies is for, in whose interests it is done, what theories, methods and objects of study are proper to it, and where to set its limits.

Cultural studies is attacked by some because (they say) it has abandoned belief in the real and commitment to the truth. But others worry that it is all too directly connected with contemporary realities. As a field (they say) that celebrates the popular, it is too close to the agenda of corporate capitalist expansionism to achieve critical distance. In fact cultural studies has been criticised from all sides over a number of issues:

- Some say that it is too political. Others that it is not political enough.
- It has no method. It has no object of study. It has no discipline. Or – it is too institutionalised academically.

- It belongs in low-prestige teaching colleges, not high-end research universities. Or – it can only be practised by researchers who already know about the politics of knowledge in an established discipline.
- It's undergraduate consciousness-raising. Or – it's the name given to the latest enthusiasm of senior writers in half a dozen different fields.
- It is too English. Or too American.
- Too academic; not activist enough. Or – too activist; not scholarly enough.
- It celebrates when it should criticise. Or – it criticises when it should undertake policy research for external clients.

At stake in such debates are important questions about the power of intellectual work in society and in the development of public policy. Can thinking, analysing and criticising stuff, change the world? If not, why would anyone, a retired detective say, want to bother with it? And should intellectual horsepower be applied to banal activities, leisure pursuits, fun and games, everyday life? If so, further questions ensue about the politics of developing a contentious field with an unworthy object of study that is also an examinable academic subject, expanding at a rapid rate around the world. There are even questions about the nature of the real, which continues to baffle philosophers and scientists, even though it comes over as pretty obvious on a week-to-week basis to your bluff, blokeish, no-nonsense cockney detective (so obvious, in fact, that it is as well to remember that it's the *detective* who's unreal here).

Cultural studies can't supply definitive answers to the intellectual, cultural and philosophical questions of the day, but it has proven a lively field of debate and dialogue. People from many different academic backgrounds, political persuasions and philosophical speaking positions have tried to address them in such a way that practical strategies and ways of acting in the world – whether that's the academic or the real world – can be improvised and implemented, as well as theorised and thought through.

Because of its position as a crossroads or bazaar for the exchange of ideas from many directions, cultural studies has been at one and the same time a motley confusion of difference, and an ambitious intellectual enterprise, seeking nothing less than to rethink received truths and remake inherited frameworks of explanation. On the ground of difference, debate and disagreement, it has sought to build a new consciousness.

Cultural studies is itself a symptom – not least in having such an ambition – of widespread doubt and disillusion about the continuing ability of inherited truths to command assent. The wonderful promises of the *modern* era – progress, science, truth, reason, plenty, comfort, security – looked very battered indeed in the years after the Second World War. Holocaust, Cold War, Mutually Assured Destruction, police states, Stalinism, Vietnam: no one was innocent, nothing was plain and simple, fear and desire infested reason and truth, progress created its own terrorists. Cultural studies was a symptom of the urgent and profound need to think seriously and in a sustained way about such matters, and how they connected with unprecedented personal freedoms and affluence at least in the developed world, new opportunities in education and cultural expression, and expanded horizons of experience for young people, women, gays and lesbians, people of colour, and many other social groups and identities.

How to teach a new generation of students to engage ethically with their own culture, *without* relying on the discredited master narratives of nationalism, racial supremacy, patriarchy or imperialism? The question was sharpened by the fact that the students themselves were also largely a new phenomenon, certainly in Britain and Australia, where higher education until the 1960s remained very much a minority pursuit. Students then were preparing for officer-class jobs in the professions like the law, the military, the Church or medicine, or functionary positions in the industrial landscape of applied science, business and management, and government administration. The idea that intellectual emancipation should be extended to the poor, to women, to *everyone*, was novel and threatening.

Education, knowledge, ideas, critique, were all thought to be *scarce* – you simply couldn't share them out too widely, on the grounds that more means worse. This was the 'if everyone has an MA then nobody does' school of thought. It wanted to *ration* education, culture and power. Cultural studies was in part a symptom of the effort to oppose such arguments and to democratise higher education as well as the cultural domain itself.

Cultural studies was from the very beginning interested in knowledge and ideas and culture as part of what Michel Foucault later called the 'plenitude of the possible' (Foucault, 1984: 267). Culture, knowledge, theory, ideas and – after Foucault – power itself, were not scarce at all, but *plentiful*, and part of the project of cultural studies was to study and practise not just the traditional aesthetics and pursuits of the governors, but to include in and as culture as much as possible, indeed everything – the 'whole way of life' of a people (as Raymond Williams put it). Cultural studies was a philosophy of plenty, of inclusion, and of renewal.

It was a bit 1960s in this – it had some of the self-delusion of flower power, thinking that its own goodwill was freedom for others; that mind expansion and the intense experience of the self *were* political liberation; that music, sex, lifestyle, desire and consumption were *more* important than politics, war, jobs and GDP.

This ambition for inclusiveness extended to culture itself, of course. The philosophy of plenty rejected the idea that culture should remain confined to the horizons inherited from philosophies of scarcity that reduced culture to a zero-sum game, where someone's gain was another's loss. Modernism was one such philosophy. Marx and Engels themselves, most influential of the modernist philosophers of power and history, had declared that works of wonder for the rich entailed prostitution and poverty for the poor. But what if they didn't? What if culture wasn't a scare resource at all, but plentiful and abundant, suffusing every nook and cranny of everyone's life? Cultural studies set about finding culture in places where it was hitherto unlooked for. In the context of the time this meant looking for it in demographic locations other than those of the rich. So working-class culture, women's culture, youth culture, gay and lesbian culture, postcolonial culture, third world culture, and the culture of everyday life were all quickly discovered and described.

But there was no established method or discipline, no corpus of work, no precedent or provenance, for the study of the culture of what a philosophy of scarcity could only identify as the dispossessed. If industrial workers, women, the poor, young people, third world and colonised people were dispossessed, it necessarily seemed to follow that they didn't have any culture, because they didn't have any power. But this was clearly nonsense. Culture was evident everywhere, from Samoa to the San Fernando Valley, even to Sun Hill (fictional South London location of *The Bill*).

As a philosophy of plenty, cultural studies also sought to address its own constituency. It did not want to be confined to dealing with ideas and phenomena only. It wanted to take seriously the culture(s) of those it taught, and talk about them as part of its project of inclusion and renewal. Increasingly folk from right across the spectrum of difference would turn up in class, enrolled on Cultural Studies 101, wondering, it was to be hoped, what was going on. What now?

The only tools to hand belonged to anthropology, literary criticism, political economy and other existing disciplines. These were themselves based on philosophies of scarcity. They were devoted to the study of *other* peoples, *great* literature, *powerful* economies. They were not dedicated to inclusiveness, nor to the emancipation or empowerment of those who studied them (not directly as part of their own method). But cultural studies did harbour this desire. It wanted to be an agent of social and political change, and for its own student-readers to be part of that process, armed with a self-reflexive understanding of how their culture connected with others, and with existing arrangements of power and privilege. As a philosophy of plenty, cultural studies introduced into the academy the novel idea that you might not have to choose between high and low culture, or even between the rich and the dispossessed, but instead you needed to find out what connected, drove, and separated these differences. 'More' meant not 'worse', as in the slogan, but something both simpler and harder to analyse. More meant . . . more.

Once that line of investigation was embarked upon, not least as a dialogue between teachers and students, authors and readers, it did begin to seem to have both *implications* and *applications*.

The *implications* for the literary and artistic imagination were that the philosophy of plenty soon overwhelmed the canon of great works of literature, opera, music and art. The philosophy of plenty exposed this regime as a restrictive practice, designed to preserve scarcity and therefore value (price) in a market not only of works like paintings, but also of repute, symbolic power and representativeness (cultural capital). Indeed, so firmly did this implication take hold in the collective unconscious of cultural studies that eventually one of its own senior practitioners was provoked into protest:

> As an Afro-Caribbean student of mine said, referring to the whole sweep of modern art, 'We were not taught about this at school. Why have we been excluded?' . . . The exclusive insistence on mass culture as the only form relevant to the masses implies . . . that the mass audience is incapable of understanding high art. (Wilson, 2001: 11).

Elizabeth Wilson was right to scold cultural studies. Confining the masses to mass culture was not a generous act of inclusion, but tended to perpetuate 'the very racism and elitism that such well-meaning gestures aim to eliminate'. Cultural studies needed to remain a philosophy of plenty. Folk needed to learn what they didn't know, as much as they needed to affirm in knowledge their own identity, subjectivity and culture. The *implication* of cultural studies for the literary and artistic imagination is therefore to focus on the expansion of difference, not on vanquishing outmoded cultural forms.

Its *application* to the field of political economy required that attention be paid to consumption and usage as well as to production, profit and power. Bringing consumers into the conversation – including directly, in the form of students and readers – was itself a novel extension of established practice. But the implications of taking seriously the agency and culture of consumers would eventually have profound consequences on the mode of production itself. In an economy of scarcity, consumers are in a sort of adversarial relation with producers – they're a somewhat dehumanised mass market whose behaviour has to be manipulated and modified by aggressively competitive corporations who are out in the end to take power *over* consumers. But in an economy of plenty, consumers are partners, clients, occasionally suppliers and competitors. They have a determining influence on new products and directions. They're part of the force and energy of productive development, not its passive victims. Their culture and taste will determine the success or otherwise of new products.

What happened in practice to this philosophy that wanted to explore the 'plenitude of the possible' is the subject of this book. Some of the people whose work, ideas or views are discussed here would not self-identify as proponents or exponents of cultural studies: opponents, maybe. However, in a lively and argumentative field with a post-disciplinary reach and cross-over tendencies, many voices have contributed to the enterprise, and some of those voices have certainly been poached from neighbouring bands.

Endeavour replica?

The present short history of cultural studies, done by one who has served before the mast since the late 1970s, cannot therefore claim to be exploring *terra incognita*. This book is not *Voyage of the Beagle*, more *Endeavour Replica*. It seeks to ply modestly and in many directions up and down the coast of cultural studies, charting how things connected, and where they didn't, and showing newcomers the ropes as it goes along. But it doesn't forget that modest colliers can have ambitious purposes, can wander far afield, and can be present at the discovery of wonders. That truth is forever encapsulated in the name of the *Endeavour* – not a starship or space shuttle, but the little wooden Whitby collier that was converted to serve as Captain Cook's vessel for the voyage in which he discovered (for modern Western culture), among other wonders, Australia. It's also the name of the modern replica of that ship, built in Fremantle of local jarrah and karri, initially bankrolled by disgraced media, brewing and property tycoon Alan Bond, a ship that is both seriously real and not real at all, a globetrotting simulacrum that purports to be what it analyses, and takes paying guests for rigorously authentic and not very comfortable cruises. Sometimes these guests are accompanied – not to say goaded – by media crews, who film them suffering the reality of life aboard an extinct species of vessel in the latest of media sports and reality TV: 'extreme history.' Such a series was filmed by the BBC on the *Endeavour* itself in 2001, with, among others, historian Iain McCalman (president of the Australian Academy of the Humanities) on board. The (media) crew ensured that conditions were as trying as possible. His discomfort as a person was duly contrasted with his status as historian of the period in which the original *Endeavour* sailed. Apparently the message to the viewing public was that those interested in the past should beware, or at least should experience what it felt like at the time.

Well, this new *endeavour* seeks to explore the strange and fascinating landscape of cultural studies, as unsentimentally as possible. Like Australia, it may seem low, featureless and unprepossessing to the newcomer, but also like Australia, its history is one way of thinking about the adventure – for good and ill – of the modern. Like the replica *Endeavour*, it may occasionally be difficult to determine whether what you're looking at is real or constructed, original or replay, substance or style, reality or reality TV. But that's cultural studies. Astute reading is its number one skill.

Despite my involvement in cultural studies as a participant observer (during which time I've experienced a fair amount of cold water, often poured by those who sought to test my ideas thoroughly in public), the book is not offered as a personal position, nor does it seek to argue towards positions with which I agree. I've tried to be a reliable witness as a historian. The treatment of cultural studies presented in the ensuing chapters if anything underplays its author's preferences, predilections and prejudices (though occasional prating may be encountered, and easily skipped). Chief among my own passions have been the media – television, the press and popular (fashion/style) magazines in particular – on which topic I have authored or co-authored quite a few books and not a few articles, starting in the 1970s. The books include

- *Reading Television,*
- *Understanding News,*
- *Making Sense of the Media,*
- *Tele-ology,*
- *The Politics of Pictures,*

- *Popular Reality,*
- *Uses of Television,*
- *American Cultural Studies: A Reader,*
- *The Indigenous Public Sphere,*
- *Communication, Cultural and Media Studies: The Key Concepts.*

Many of them are still in print (as I write), so interested readers may refer to them directly for coverage of those media from a cultural studies perspective.

And while, in those books, I have developed a specialist interest in textual analysis as opposed to a political economy approach, the present book does not seek to reproduce that imbalance, which is a product of my training and expertise, not a desire to promote one approach at the expense of others (my own academic training was in literary not economic studies). So much so that there's no chapter devoted specifically to textual analysis in the present book, but there is one on the connection between culture and economy (Chapter 4). At the end of that chapter I describe what could be a new manifesto for cultural studies, but it is not one of my own making – it arises from a policy document published by a British government department. Other interests of mine receive scant attention here: e.g. journalism studies and history, especially non-news journalism; the creation of modern popular readerships; media literacy and citizenship; suburbia; media history, especially that of popular content in the photo-press and visual media; girls in news and fashion media; radio and democracy; the fashion/art interface; Indigenous media; creative industries policy and industry research. The fact is, in relating this history I've been guided by the field, rather than by my own position in it.

However, there are still gaps. Some important topics within cultural studies are all too briefly or glancingly dealt with. Chief among these are its internationalisation beyond the triple-A axis of the Anglo-American-Australian region. Cultural studies has begun to burgeon in China, Taiwan, Hong Kong and Singapore; in South Africa; Latin America; South East Asia; and Scandinavia. Occasional interested glances even come out of Germany (e.g. from Ruhr-Universität Bochum), though of course France remains convinced of the adequacy of its own versions of these matters. I've done my own bit to encourage the internationalising process as Editor of the *International Journal of Cultural Studies*. This is not only because I am an economic migrant – in fact I'm a serial emigrant, having moved, *en famille*, successively from England to Wales, Wales to Australia, and back, and back again (to date). More to the point, the multinational uptake and appropriation of new intellectual currents indicates a new and exciting set of concerns, and new voices too, for cultural studies. This book underplays these developments, along with work coming out of the postcolonial studies area, for instance that of Paul Gilroy, Ien Ang, Dipesh Chakrabarty (subaltern studies), Homi Bhabha, and others. As they begin to bed down into established patterns, such omissions ought to be rectified in later editions.

A genealogy of cultural studies

The main body of *A Short History of Cultural Studies* is written in the past tense, precisely because the field has reached the point of having a history. It is not located in the endless present tense of disciplinary methods or universal truth. And each chapter sets off in pursuit of a *different* cultural studies; six of them in all. Given the peculiarities of cultural studies it would be unwise to impose upon it the false unity of a linear history.

The object of study in cultural studies changed over time and took different forms depending on who was investigating it and why. This was not only a matter of deciding what was meant by culture in general and in specific instances, but also a question of the analytical agenda – which shifted from class to gender and then to ethnicity and postcolonial matters, for instance. Nevertheless, some continuities and patterns did emerge. Cultural studies was of necessity an interdisciplinary field of inquiry. It drew widely from the humanities and social sciences, from anthropology, textual theory, social and political theory and media studies, with some contributions from history, geography, the visual and performative arts. Psychology tended to figure more as an opponent and a symptom than as a useful framework of explanation.

Cultural studies was committed to self-reflexivity in its mode of intellectual production, denying innocence or transparency to its own practices. It specialised in margins and boundaries, both discursive and social, and that included its own intellectual and academic status, methods and corpus. Self-reflexivity extended to a perennial reluctance to accept disciplinary authority of any kind. No orthodoxy was allowed uncontested. Nothing about cultural studies got away with being standardised, including the:

- **definition** of culture;
- **scope** of cultural studies as a field of inquiry;
- **methods** appropriate to that task;
- **history** of cultural studies itself.

This book too seeks to show what discussions were afoot in relation to these issues, not to produce a definitive text.

Cultural studies wasn't interested in definitive texts, least of all about itself. A rhetoric of disavowal grew up around the genre of writing associated with the history of cultural studies. Even as they told the story, authors proclaimed that the usual history (Hoggart, Hall, Williams) was itself a bit of a myth. They described and simultaneously decentred the crucial position of the Centre for Contemporary Cultural Studies at the University of Birmingham in England. They complained about the Anglo-American-Australian Anglophone bias of cultural studies, but quoted mainly from such sources. This strange behaviour was not very helpful for students who wanted to know what was what and when, but it was inevitable, because cultural studies was a critical not a disciplinary enterprise.

Any orthodoxy, *especially* in its own practices, was suspect. Perhaps this explains why cultural studies is relatively well endowed with histories of itself, and why publishers remain interested in commissioning more, including this one. Neighbouring fields, such as media and communication studies, for instance, seemed less anxious about their provenance.

Despite anxieties about itself, cultural studies drew strength from this radical refusal to naturalise the hegemonic positions within its own practice, even though it necessarily established a hierarchy of concerns, personalities and publications in the very act of returning constantly to them. By refusing disciplinary orthodoxy, cultural studies kept the door open to innovation from the margins, in line with its longstanding interest in difference and marginality. This also helped to preserve the idea that cultural studies was not wholly academic, certainly in its longer term aims. It was committed to engagement in cultural politics, not only to establishing an object of study and a disciplinary method.

Another strength was that, as part of cultural criticism more widely, cultural studies had gone into the analytical world armed with various rhetorical ploys that were designed to reveal or disrupt the speaking position of the analyst. No concession was made to universalism in its own enunciation: there was no authoritative position from which it could survey, order and evaluate its own or anyone else's being. Its published form was always 'adorned with the props of the argument's staging,' as Homi Bhabha put it (Bhabha, 1998: 29).

But there was a down side to this indeterminacy, both intellectual and practical. Intellectually, cultural studies was so hybrid that it was hard to tell what it was and where it ended. Anyone could join in, and many did, resulting in discomfort for those whose sense of what was necessary didn't coincide with the interests of others. But because of its refusal to professionalise its disciplinary form, cultural studies had no institutional means to deal with bad practice, bad faith, or bad politics done in its name.

And – hence – cultural studies was slow to set up a practical machinery for the conduct of its affairs and the promotion of its objectives. An attempt by Pertti Alasuutari, Joke Hermes, Ann Gray (and myself) to set up an international Association for Cultural Studies demonstrated how difficult it was to agree anything. A determined critique of the whole idea was led by Larry Grossberg, for whom the spectre of academic associations on the American model loomed large. He didn't want cultural studies to develop big hegemonic organisations like the ICA, APA or MLA. The debate rumbled on for several years and across several continents over email and at the biannual Crossroads in Cultural Studies conferences at Tampere and Birmingham. For some it was simply a matter of networking and perhaps getting discounts on journals; for others this was subjugating the field to dominant institutions and commercial publishers. For some it was a chance to organise interventions in public debate; for others it reeked of careerism and opportunism. For some it was a good way to inform folk from other countries what was happening elsewhere; for others it was another Euro-American (and Australian) take-over. It was hedged about with *must be* rather than *can do* rhetoric, so it floundered where it might have flourished, and had to wait several years before it was finally launched in modified form at the 2002 Crossroads conference at Tampere. Even then, its structure was more ideologically representative than practically useful, skewing regional representation towards what some thought the international map ought to look like, as opposed to following the contours of cultural studies' actual strength in different regions, thereby over-representing Latin America, for instance, and under-representing Australasia, where cultural studies was well established.

But there were institutional gains. In the UK cultural studies achieved visibility in one of the RAE (Research Assessment Exercise) panels that determined research strength in all UK universities in assessment exercises in 1992, 1996 and 2001. Panel 65, chaired by Philip Schlesinger, was devoted to Communication and Cultural Studies, although many senior figures in the field, including some people serving as assessors on that panel, returned their own research to a different one (usually Sociology). In the event, the sector's gain was wellspring's loss. Birmingham's department of cultural studies and sociology, successor to Hoggart's CCCS, scored a modest '3A' in the 2001 RAE. Despite perfect teaching scores and high undergraduate demand, it was promptly closed by the university. By a quirk of timing this decision was announced – to international bewilderment – at the opening of the 2002 Crossroads Conference in Tampere, and the first act of the newly constituted Association for Cultural Studies was to protest it.

What was cultural studies?

It was a **philosophy of plenty**. It was:

- Dedicated to the study of the **expansion of difference** in human affairs (during an era of increasing globalisation, corporate concentration and technological integration of those affairs);
- An assemblage of **intellectual** concerns about power, meaning, identity and subjectivity in modern societies;
- An attempt to recover and promote **marginal**, unworthy or despised regions, identities, practices and media (it was a profane pursuit);
- A **critical** enterprise devoted to displacing, decentring, demystifying and deconstructing the common sense of dominant discourses;
- An activist commitment to **intellectual politics** – making a difference with ideas, to ideas, by ideas.

It was also a **publishing** enterprise, partly defined by cultural entrepreneurs in both the academy and the publishing industry. Cultural studies was what its practitioners and publishers said it was.

Cultural studies showed a marked tendency to concentrate on the relations between addresser and addressee in modernity. It produced nuanced and interesting work on the practices of sense-making in various textual and social contexts, especially the inequalities of those relations, the media they were conducted through, and the possibility of changes to them. There was a steady interest in popular culture, class (sub)cultures, popular media (drama, journalism, music), everyday life, cities and suburbs, subjectivity, ideology, hegemony, discourse, power, visuality (and other non-speech semiosis), the body, the body and technology, the relations between public and private and between institutional and personal, the politics of culture, the circumstances of marginal people and practices, transnational knowledge and image flows, colonial and imperial residue among non-metropolitan cultures, for instance.

The study of cultural studies itself has a history. Early in the field were some of the founding practitioners. Richard Hoggart (cultural studies as the democratised literary imagination) and Stuart Hall (cultural studies as the political theory of popular resistance and change) both wrote about it, as did Hall's successor at Birmingham, the historian Richard Johnson (cultural studies as bemused materialism). The first book-length history of (British) cultural studies was written by (Australian) Graeme Turner; a careful working through of theories and theorists, books and arguments, concepts and controversies (Turner, 1990; 2nd edn 1996; 3rd edn 2002). It's still the best treatment of the topic. Many introductory books about cultural studies – by, say, John Storey (1999), Nick Couldry (2000), Chris Barker (2000) – incorporated historical accounts into their exposition of methodology and their analytical and conceptual exegesis. Senior figures of cultural studies – say, Charlotte Brunsdon, Paul Gilroy, Elizabeth Wilson, Angela McRobbie, David Morley – included historical accounts in their own unfolding *oeuvres*. Critics who marched to the beat of a different drum, but still called the tune cultural studies, such as Fred Inglis and Ioan Davies, did it their way. Because cultural studies was something of a come all ye festival, and one to which many did indeed turn up, both students and teachers, there was no shortage of storytelling going on all around. There were always different ways of telling the tales, and many voices were needed to do them justice.

Kindness and unknowing: Caveat lector

Winston Churchill was reputed to have quipped that 'history will be kind to us: I intend to write it'. Whether he said it or not, there was truth in the remark. Those who have participated in various events, great or small, political or intellectual, have a vested interest in two opposing aims: they want history to come across as accurate (i.e. to appear as history, not propaganda or self-aggrandisement), and they want it to be kind.

There's clearly scope here for an author to succumb to the temptation of cooking the books; laying out the relevant facts in such a way that a reader may imagine that the world belongs to the winners as a natural outcome of those facts. This risk is especially strong in the case of histories told by participants in the events described. So – *caveat lector*.

But participants are not in full possession of knowledge about themselves, and cannot know what information may prove relevant. So there's another view of lived history, this one propounded not for political gain by a national war leader, but by Raymond Williams, at the end of *Culture and Society*:

> A culture, while it is being lived, is always in part unknown, in part unrealised. The making of a community is always an exploration, for consciousness cannot precede creation, and there is no formula for unknown experience. A good community, a living culture, will, because of this, not only make room for but actively encourage all and any who can contribute to the advance in consciousness which is the common need . . . for we do not know the future, we may never be certain of what may enrich it. (Williams, 1961: 334)

Terry Eagleton made the same point about intercultural communication. 'Every culture,' he wrote, 'has an internal blindspot where it fails to grasp or be at one with itself, and to discern this . . . is to understand that culture more fully' (Eagleton, 2000: 96). From that insight (which he attributed to Slavoj Žižek), Eagleton suggested that analysis of other cultures, or 'the Other', can be useful not only to the analysis but also to the culture in question:

> It is at the point where the Other is dislocated in itself, not wholly bound by its context, that we can encounter it most deeply, since this self-opaqueness is also true of ourselves. I understand the Other when I become aware that what troubles me about it, its enigmatic nature, is a problem for it too. (Eagleton, 2000: 96)

In short, participant analysts ought to be open to their own self-ignorance, and to the unknown parts of both their own and other cultures. Readers for their part ought to beware of seductive narratives taking the form of relevant facts.

One of the facts about the history of ideas is that ideas rarely have a birth, life and death in the way that biological organisms do. Ideas don't have a single origin – they aren't worthy of the name unless they're widely shared, used, revamped, re-versioned and revised. As Yuri Lotman has written, 'the individual human intellect does not have a monopoly in the work of thinking.' Intellectual operations are also carried out by 'semiotic systems', and by social institutions and agencies, which 'preserve, rework, and increase the store of information' (Lotman, 1990: 273). Cultural studies is one such 'semiotic system', and its institutionalisation in publishing houses, universities and colleges, and in various more or less fugitive practices, means that it is both collective and dispersed, with multiple origins, subjectivities and uses. It is a thinking machine that has a life of its own, sometimes at cross-purposes with those of the individuals who thought they had made it.

The history of cultural studies can't be other than sensitive to the volatile and fugitive nature of ideas about it. Once released, ideas tend to dart about like quarks in the cosmos – everywhere and nowhere at once; hard to identify but important to understand. It might be possible to measure their impact without understanding their origin. So in the realm of ideas, history isn't 'one damn thing after another' (as the saying goes); it's not as simple as tracing causal sequence in phenomena (Thorstein Veblen's phrase). But that is what makes ideas fascinating to follow, not least because studying their history helps to 'contribute to the advance in consciousness which is the common need,' as Williams put it. And, as Eagleton argued, studying what has bothered others is a way of thinking about what bothers the self.

What was cultural studies? For the purposes of this book (i.e. its sequence of chapters), the philosophy of plenty was a series of endeavours, enterprises, essays, not quite mutually commensurate, as follows:

- **Cultural studies and literary criticism:** Why was culture seen as so important by literary writers, critics and publishers? Why was studying culture seen as political (Chapter 1)?
- **Cultural studies and mass society theory:** In a climate (or typology) of opposition between popular and high culture, what was the possibility of popular culture carrying serious content, from Shakespeare to contemporary music and media (Chapter 2)?
- **Cultural studies and art history:** How were the ingredients of realism, constructivism, civic humanism and art combined in the cultural studies recipe (Chapter 3)?
- **Cultural studies and political economy:** What was the nexus between economy and culture; what determined the economic, political and cultural spheres (Chapter 4)?
- **Cultural studies and feminism, anthropology, sociology:** If 'culture is ordinary', then how to study banal, everyday activities – for example travel, walking, shopping, eating (Chapter 5)?
- **Cultural studies and teaching:** How did cultural studies address its own readers? How did it create a large, transnational, multidisciplinary readership, and bring both astute peers and uncommitted entry-level readers along to share its interests (Chapter 6)?
- **Cultural studies and publishing:** Routledge, Sage, Arnold, Duke, Minnesota, Oxford, Cambridge . . . they were there (References)!

These different histories, topics and questions underlie the six main chapters of the book (and the bibliography). Each brings a slightly different object of study into view. Together they add up to a history of ideas about culture, power, difference and identity that amounts only to what Graeme Turner wisely calls a 'provisional map' (1990: 6). It may be of use among readers – including newly retired detectives – who wish to undertake their own explorations, whether they want to travel just up the coast or across the wide ocean.

1

The Intelligent Co–ed's Guide to Cultural Studies

From Virginia Woolf to Tom Wolfe (destination O'Hare)

Cultural studies and literary criticism

Cultural studies was the 'yoking by violence together', to use Dr Johnson's phrase about the construction of metaphors, of literary and political writing. To be more exact, it was writing *about* literature and politics, literary-critical writing that wanted to be taken as *political*, rather than the writing of literary fiction or political oratory as such. This form of cultural studies has quite a long history, going back to the beginnings of political modernity and liberal humanism, i.e. to the period when political sovereignty passed from monarch to people in the eighteenth century. It was a product of Enlightenment journalism.

In the two or three centuries after that, this mode of writing branched. Some of it continued to splutter and rage from the back half of broadsheet newspapers, especially their weekend editions or literary supplements. Here the technology of gentlemanly, amateur criticism of society in the name of the arts, and of the arts in the name of public values, continued almost unchanged from the 1700s. Even the parade of canonical literary luminaries was the same: the names 'twitter and gleam like celebrities arriving by limousine,' as Tom Wolfe once put it (2000: 27). Writers in this arena tended not to identify themselves with cultural studies – indeed, cultural studies often featured as one of the evils of the post-modern world against which they spluttered and raged.

The other branch of literary writing about society retreated somewhat from journals addressed to a politically active public, or dedicated to calling such a public into being, into the more specialised world of the academy. Here the reading public was reduced to the reader of literary fiction, and politics to moral protest. Of this branch, cultural studies (as we know it) was but one strand. Even back in the 1960s Wolfe thought the literary-intellectual essay 'superannuated'. But 'books and moral protest' in the 'British polite-essay form' were the prehistoric form of cultural studies:

> The literary-intellectual mode that still survives in the United States and England today [the 1960s] was fashioned more than 150 years ago in Regency England with the founding of magazines such as the *Edinburgh Review*, the *Quarterly*, *Blackwood's*, the *London Magazine*, the *Examiner* and the *Westminster Review*. They became platforms for

educated gentlemen-amateurs to pass judgement in a learned way on two subjects: books and politics. This seemed a natural combination at the time, because so many literati were excited by the French Revolution and its aftermath. . . . Remarkably, the literary-intellectual has remained locked for more than a century and a half in precisely that format: of books and moral protest, by gentlemen amateurs, in the British polite essay form. (Wolfe, 2000: 28)

However, Wolfe's criticism of the form didn't prevent him from being one of its best exponents. He used it to scorn what he saw as its own inconsequentiality.

A Wolfe at the door; a Woolf in her room

'What If He Is Right?' was Wolfe's own celebrated essay on McLuhan. It was originally published *as* literary-political journalism, in the Sunday magazine section of the New York *World Journal Tribune* (Wolfe, 2000: 22–31). Herbert Marshall McLuhan was a Canadian professor of English. In the 1960s he achieved cult status for his pronouncements on new communications media, and television in particular. Remarking on the difference between McLuhan's obscure origins and his new status as an intellectual celebrity in fashionable New York, Wolfe characterised the world of the literary intellectual thus:

McLuhan rose up from out of a world more obscure, more invisible, more unknown to the great majority of mankind than a Bantu village or the Southeast Bronx. Namely, the EngLit academic life. Tongaland and the Puerto Rican slums may at least reek, in the imagination, of bloodlust and loins oozing after sundown. EngLit academia, so far as the outside world is concerned, neither reeks, nor blooms; an occasional whiff of rotting tweeds, perhaps: otherwise, a redolence of nothing. (Wolfe, 2000: 27)

It was out of this world that contemporary cultural studies arose. Perhaps its own denizens wanted – or for Wolfe, at least, *ought* to have wanted – a little more visibility; more reek, ooze and bloom. It was that or 'practically nothing':

In effect, the graduate-school scholar settles down at an early age, when the sap is still rising, to a life of little cubicles, little money, little journals in which his insights, if he is extremely diligent, may someday be recorded. A Volkswagen, a too-small apartment, Department Store Danish furniture with dowel legs – before he is 30 his wife will have begun to despise him as a particularly sad sort of failure, once the cultural charisma of *literature* has lost its charm. How much better to have failed at oil prospecting or the diaper-service game than at . . . practically nothing! (Wolfe, 2000: 27)

Of course this was a fiction in itself, and forgot that many grad-school scholars, even in the 1960s, were women. For some, perhaps, Virginia Woolf's essay from forty years earlier still held great force. It showed how important money and 'a room of one's own' (even a 'too-small apartment' and a VW) might be for women (Woolf, 1945: 5). A sufficient income, and a 'door with a lock on it,' afforded release. Without those, bitterness and fear. With them:

> . . . I need not hate any man; he cannot hurt me. I need not flatter any man; he has nothing to give me. . . . By degrees fear and bitterness modified themselves into pity and toleration; and then in a year or two, pity and toleration went, and the greatest release of all came, which is freedom to think of things in themselves. That building, for example, do I like it or not? Is that picture beautiful or not? Is that in my opinion a good book or a bad? (Woolf: 33–4)

For Tom Wolfe, EngLit as a career held out the promise of little public cachet, and less private desire, for all its 'insights'. This was the 'superannuated target' that McLuhan had rendered 'irrelevant' with his aphorisms about media. But for Virginia Woolf, that same obscurity was the best that could be hoped for. She concluded *A Room of One's Own* with her vision of 'Shakespeare's sister' – the female equivalent of Shakespeare's genius, which would emerge from the work of generations of women writers if 'women generally . . . took to writing':

> For my belief is that if we live another century or so – I am speaking of the common life which is the real life and not of the little separate lives which we live as individuals – and have five hundred a year each of us and rooms of our own . . . then the opportunity will come and the dead poet who was Shakespeare's sister will put on the body which she has so often laid down. . . . I maintain that she would come if we worked for her, and that so to work, even in poverty and obscurity, is worth while. (Woolf: 94)

Woolf wrote of the importance of the anonymous 'common life' (although she sometimes used common *people* for what John Carey called 'a stimulus to fury, loathing and fear' (Carey, 1992: 209–10)). She valued the *freedom* that came from thinking of 'things in themselves' (not about people's relations with each other). She advised: 'Do not dream of influencing other people, I would say, if I knew how to make it sound exalted. Think of things in themselves' (Woolf: 91). But, she wrote:

> It matters far more than I can prove in an hour's discourse that women generally . . . took to writing. . . . For masterpieces are not single and solitary births; they are the outcome of many years of thinking in common, of thinking by the body of the people, so that the experience of the mass is behind the single voice. (Woolf: 55)

Virginia Woolf wrote this in 1928, for a lecture to women students at Cambridge University. At that time, she thought there were not sufficient numbers to make what would later be called a 'critical mass' – a sufficiency of talented work building on itself until a 'Shakespeare's sister' (a woman universal literary artist) could emerge from it. The 'century or so' she thought might be needed for 'women generally' to be emancipated into the freedom to 'think of things in themselves' has still not yet elapsed. It may be, then, that Tom Wolfe was premature – or perhaps not thinking of female subjects – in his scornful estimation that life in a *carrel* of one's own, as it were, counted for less than success in the diaper-service game. For Woolf, 'poverty and obscurity' were a small price to pay for contributing to 'thinking by the body of the people'.

There was a current in the history of cultural studies that actively sought that 'common life'; the 'experience of the mass behind the single voice'. With Virginia Woolf it knew that cumulative anonymity was no disgrace, though it may have been evidence of several millennia of material deprivation. On this point, Woolf included a lengthy quotation from Sir Arthur Quiller-Couch (known as 'Q'), originally published in 1913, which pointed out that the majority of significant poets of the previous century or so had enjoyed independent means:

> It may seem a brutal thing to say, and it is a sad thing to say: but, as a matter of hard fact, the theory that poetical genius bloweth where it listeth, and equally in poor and rich, holds little truth. . . . These are dreadful facts, but let us face them. It is – however dishonouring to us as a nation – certain that, by some fault in our commonwealth, the poor poet has not in these days, nor has had for two hundred years, a dog's chance. Believe me . . . we may prate of democracy, but actually a poor child in England has little more hope than had the son of an Athenian slave to be emancipated into that intellectual freedom of which great writings are born. (Quiller-Couch, 1946: 32–3. Quoted in Woolf, 1945: 88–9; see also Goulden and Hartley, 1982: 19)

Woolf concluded, 'That is it. Intellectual freedom depends upon material things. Poetry depends upon intellectual freedom. And women have always been poor, not for two hundred years merely, but from the beginning of time' (89).

Here was a foundational question for cultural studies; the need to bring the life of the imagination (in this case literary fiction and drama) into some sort of critical contact with socio-economic and historical realities. Wrote Woolf: 'What were the conditions in which women lived, I asked myself . . .':

> Indeed, if woman had no existence save in the fiction written by men, one would imagine her a person of the utmost importance; very various; heroic and mean; splendid and sordid; infinitely beautiful and hideous in the extreme; as great as a man, some think even greater. But this is woman in fiction. In fact, as Professor Trevelyan points out, she was locked up, beaten and flung about the room. (Woolf: 36–7)

That's why she needed a room of her own. But it was in fact Q's class analysis of intellectual freedom, not Woolf's gender analysis, that first preoccupied academic cultural studies. Q's own argument was not addressed to women, of course – the *son* of a slave held his attention. He was thinking primarily of 'the poor'. And speaking personally, I too came across Q before Woolf, and quoted this same passage in an article about the future of literary education (Goulden and Hartley, 1982). Sir Arthur's estimation was that dogs and Athenian slaves had a better chance of intellectual freedom than a poor English child. Having been one of the latter, this meant a fair bit to me. So I quoted Q, just as (unknown to me) Virginia Woolf had done half a century earlier, to reproach the unacknowledged class bias of curriculum English in the British school examination system in the 1980s. Q himself had been an Inspector of Schools. Not enough had changed during the supposedly modernising, egalitarian twentieth century.

He was right about class; Woolf about gender. Cultural studies picked up their baton.

The argument about the material basis for participation in culture and the life of the intellect applied similarly to poor people and to women (and for me personally, being 'emancipated into intellectual freedom' was a class thing). But commonalty of cause did not automatically engender fellow-feeling between the claims of a class analysis and those of gender analysis. This too became part of the internal history of cultural studies. The Birmingham Centre for Contemporary Cultural Studies was subsequently to witness a crucial argument between the women's group (*Women Take Issue*) and those who'd been working on (mostly male) working class subcultures (Hall, 1992; Brunsdon, 1996). It seemed that the world so lightly dismissed as 'practically nothing' by Tom Wolfe still held plenty of passion for those who had less secure circumstances than his.

Tom Wolfe quoted McLuhan on the outrage his own work provoked, causing McLuhan in turn to denounce the 'moralist' who 'substitutes anger for perception':

> 'The merely moralistic expression of approval or disapproval, preference or detestation, is currently being used in our world as a substitute or observation and a substitute for study. . . . Moral bitterness is a basic technique for endowing the idiot with dignity.' (McLuhan, cited in Wolfe, 2000: 29)

Here again was an interesting insight into the later career of cultural studies – its propensity to provoke moralistic side-taking among its own practitioners. It was still, evidently, without a room of its own.

One issue that Tom Wolfe did not address in his short history of the 'books and politics' form of cultural studies was the important historical shift from real gentlemen amateurs to *textual* ones – i.e. people who wrote using that persona without the social standing of the eighteenth-century pioneers of the form. By the 1960s, and throughout the subsequent history of cultural studies, the possibilities for moving freely between 'books' (writing) and 'politics' (running the country) were, for most, radically reduced. As the republic of letters was democratised, so the likelihood lessened that the people engaged in the 'polite essay form' were also significant political leaders, activists or administrators. Perhaps the latter groups were no longer to be found even among the form's readership.

The critique of culture from a politicised literary standpoint, incorporating moral protest at the evils and tyrannies of the age, became *discursively* more 'governmental' (see Chapter 4) the more removed its practitioners were from government. This seeming paradox raised the question of whether cultural studies should be a 'contemplative' or an 'activist' pursuit. Should it investigate the discourses of power, or intervene in the processes it sought to describe?

Cultural critique began in the early modern period as an attribute of men of affairs who had some direct stake in *governing the country*. That had been the *work* of the gentleman amateur since Aristotle, and the ideal of 'civic humanism' from the eighteenth century (see Barrell, 1986). Its retreat to *discourses about governmentality* (Foucault, Bennett), betokened a shift from active to contemplative mode. There was nothing inherently lesser about this mode; indeed Virginia Woolf rated the 'contemplative' novel more 'interesting' than the 'naturalist' branch of the species (Woolf, 1945: 73). But, as Tom Wolfe put it: 'Intellectuals thus become a kind of *clergy without ordination*' (2000: 29).

And so the polite essay thus became a kind of *sermon without congregation*. It soon became axiomatic among contemplative, intra-mural cultural critics that *discourses organise practices*. That is to say, the study of culture was simultaneously the study of power, and the key to understanding power was *language*. Language itself was not merely literary – it extended to non-literary forms. But it was 'textual', and textual analysis became notorious for concentrating on the 'discourses' without engagement of any direct kind with the 'practices' of power (Lucy, 1995).

The study of language for *signs* of power may still have been done in the form of the literary essay, but the content was radically expanded. It extended (using spatial axes as a metaphor) *vertically* from literature downwards through quasi-literary genres like drama, to demotic forms associated with popular entertainments, such as television shows. *Horizontally*, language extended from spoken (linguistic) and written (literary) content to describe communication by any means, including image, motion and sequence. This was where semiotics came in. Semiotics held out the promise of being able to analyse non-linguistic communication as if it were a language. Thus studies of film 'language' (Metz's eponymous book, 1978), the 'language of fashion' (Barthes's *Système de la Mode*); 'man-made' language (Dale Spender) – and so on – became all the rage.

Semiotics aspired to a scientific method – 'a science that studies the life of signs in society' (Saussure, 1974). It could claim to be a morally neutral, perceptive and rigorous method, which was handy because most of the early practitioners of semiotics were, like Barthes, on the political Left, and used this scientific method to attack the cultural power of the bourgeoisie. Semiotics promised to get its practitioners around the difficulty objected to by McLuhan: now political protest could be based on 'observation and study,' rather than upon 'moral bitterness.' Here then, the politics of cultural studies: language determined discourses, discourses organised practices, power was discursive, and so the proper study of power was . . . the semiotics of television shows.

This general tendency could be found in other cultural fields where democratisation, new literacy and massive expansion via new media could be observed. The more people watched TV cooking shows, the more they bought celebrity cookbooks, but the less they practised cookery at home (see Chapters 3 and 5). Ditto gardening: discourses supplanted practices, as literacy supplanted action. In fashion, the democratisation of *haute couture* via the fashion press and the supermodel in the late 1980s and early 90s was accompanied by a much greater literacy about fashion in the high street, resulting before too long in the supplanting of C&A Modes by The Gap, *Ladies' Home Journal* by *Elle*, and so on. But it was not accompanied by masses of new fashion designers, or by more bespoke apparel, or by more home-made fashion. On the contrary; *Vogue* stopped printing DIY patterns in the main journal, hiving them off to a specialist sibling magazine. The more that the general population knew about fashion, the more people bought branded designs off the peg, and the less they made clothes. As in broadcasting, so in fashion: *diffusion* of brand-name labels was popular, not securing. The democratisation of cultural politics and fashion alike was accompanied by a shift to consumption rather than activism, although consumption was by no means passive – indeed it was, in a word, *literate*.

But against this 'contemplative' tendency, cultural studies was itself part of the *militant* urge towards democratisation. It was a teaching regimen for civic education of individuals from among the anonymous but sovereign mass, who were experiencing in their lives (but not in traditional educational disciplines) new forms of citizenship associated with media and commercial culture. Here was a project for cultural studies – to assist in the 'emancipation into intellectual freedom' of the 'poor child in England', and the woman who had previously been, and perhaps still was, 'flung about the room'.

A Shaw thing – pick up a Penguin

This project of cultural studies was launched by George Bernard Shaw in 1937. Shaw did not, as 'Q' had challengingly put it, 'prate of *democracy*' (though he was a world-class prater), but he did have a great deal to say about socialism. *The Intelligent Woman's Guide to Socialism, Capitalism, Sovietism and Fascism* was first published in the same year – 1928 – that Virginia Woolf's lecture on women and fiction was delivered to women at Cambridge. Like her, Shaw addressed his emancipatory remarks to a female subject. But where Woolf insisted on the material basis of writing as the first thing needful for women, Shaw was more concerned with the intellectual superstructure. His was a lesson in the theory of political economy.

George Bernard Shaw (1856–1950) was a literary giant of his age. His publisher Penguin's web page credits him as 'showman, satirist, controversialist, critic, pundit, wit, intellectual buffoon and dramatist'. He is probably best remembered for his plays and their prefaces, not least owing to their sedimentation into school curricula as set texts, notably *St Joan* and *Pygmalion* (i.e. *My Fair Lady*) – both prime examples of Woolf's 'woman in fiction written by men'. Shaw was also a political polemicist and pamphleteer, one of the leading figures of the Fabian Society.

The Intelligent Woman's Guide was republished in 1937, in two volumes. These were the first books – A1 and A2 – of publisher Allen Lane's new imprint,

Pelican Books. They were so cheap that Shaw had to reassure readers they were getting the real thing:

> they have in their hands the authentic original text in full, word for word, but with the addition of two new chapters dealing with events that have occurred since its first publication in 1928. (Shaw, 1937: v)

Here was a lively combination of literary imagination, political passion and enterprising publishing – in a good democratic cause, addressed to a feminised, 'ordinary' readership. All of these ingredients prefigured cultural studies, which was perhaps most accurately named in that configuration.

Shaw was a proponent of socialism, which he saw clearly and simply as 'equality of distribution'. He wanted equal incomes: 'instead of sympathizing with the poor and abolishing the rich we must ruthlessly abolish the poor by raising their standard of life to that of the most favourably treated worker' (Shaw, 1937: v). But here was a failure of nerve: the poor were not to be 'raised' to the 'standard of life' of *the rich*.

But Shaw did advocate equality, and offered a practical definition of it that would remain both serviceable and challenging – a stretch target – for decades to come: 'Nor do I see any other test for practical as distinguished from arithmetical equality except the test of complete marriageability between all sections of the community' (Shaw, 1937: v; 66–9).

He was by no means brief in his arguments (a recent edition, published in 1995, ran to 576 pages), but he was very keen to address his reader – the 'intelligent woman' directly and plainly. He wrote:

> This book is not a compilation: it is all out of my own head. It was started by a lady asking me to write her a letter explaining Socialism. I thought of referring her to the hundreds of books which have been written on the subject; but the difficulty was that they were nearly all written in an academic jargon which . . . is unbearably dry, meaning unreadable, to women not so specialized. And then, all these books are addressed to men. . . . So I had to do it all over again in my own way and yours. (Shaw, 1937: 463)

The Shavian way was an early version of the KISS doctrine: keep it simple stupid!

> Though there were piles of books about Socialism, and one enormous book about Capitalism by Karl Marx, not one of them answered the simple question 'What is Socialism?' The other simple question, 'What is Capital?' was smothered in a mass of hopelessly wrong answers, the right one having been hit on (as far as my reading goes) only once, and that was by the British economist Stanley Jevons when he remarked casually that capital is spare money. I made a note of that. (ibid.)

Direct address to a non-specialist but feminised reader, in order to simplify but not trivialise the big issues of the epoch, as part of a project that may be named as *emancipation through reading*. That was cultural studies 101 – or in this case, A1.

Allen Lane launched Penguin Books in 1935. At that time he was a director of the publishing firm The Bodley Head. According to the story on the Penguin company history page:

> After a weekend spent with Agatha Christie in Devon, Lane searched Exeter station's bookstall for something to read on his journey back to London, but found only popular magazines and reprints of Victorian novels. Following this, he recognised the need for good quality contemporary fiction at an attractive price. Lane was determined that the new range be available not just in traditional bookshops, but also in railway stations and chain stores such as Woolworths. (http://www.penguin.co.uk)

This genesis anecdote invoked many of the tropes of modernity – mobility, mass markets, railways, chain-stores, the enterprising individual inventor who saw how to profit from the improvement of the common people, like Thomas Cook before him. Even Agatha Christie's name offered more than a pleasant whiff of the celebrity author – her crime stories combined modernist rationality (Poirot's method of detection) with popular fantasy (the country house, the Orient Express). Love of physical and social mobility, of mass communication by rail and book, associated Penguins with contemporaneousness and popular success.

Indeed, Penguins were an instant success – not least because hardback novels cost seven or eight shillings, while a Penguin book was sixpence, the price of a packet of cigarettes (a cheap and popular consumer item of those days). Lane converted 'book-borrowers' into 'book-buyers', and thereby brought 'good books cheap' into homes where they were previously scarce; three million of them in the first year.

Authors, even those on the Left, were worried. George Orwell summed up the dilemma: 'In my capacity as a reader I applaud the Penguin Books; in my capacity as a writer I pronounce them anathema.' Orwell thought that 'if other publishers follow suit, the result may be a flood of cheap reprints which will cripple the lending libraries and check the output of new novels' (*New English Weekly*, 5 March 1936). J.B. Priestley, however, sent a congratulatory note:

> Dear Lane,
>   These Penguin Books are amazingly good value for money. If you can make the series pay for itself – with such books at such price – you will have performed a great publishing feat.
>   Yours sincerely, J.B. Priestley

By 1937, Lane was ready to launch the next imprint, Pelican Books, edited by V.K. Krishna Menon, which included 'the first new and original books to be published by Penguin; all titles so far had been paperbacks of books previously published by other companies' (Penguin website). According to the back-cover blurb of A1, Pelicans were non-fiction books on 'Science, Astronomy, History, Archæology, Politics, Economics'. Lane himself explained the move in the journal *Left Review* thus:

> There are many who despair at what they regard as the low level of people's intelligence. We, however, believed in the existence in this country of a vast reading public for intelligent books at a low price. (*Left Review*, 1938)

This was a new philosophy, not more risky but certainly more bold than the Penguin imprint itself. Here was more than a venture to capture and trade in popular desire. Pelicans were directed not to the selves or the relationships of the readers, but to the realities of the modern world – Woolf's 'things in themselves'. These realities were understood as those same readers' own personal, intimate business (and see Woolf, 1945: 55–65). Pelicans were a direct and conscious contribution to the democratisation (Lane would have used the term 'popularisation') of *academic* and scientific knowledge. Series editor V.K. Krishna Menon was advised by H.L. Beales, Reader in Economic History, London University, W.E. Williams, Secretary, British Institute of Adult Education, and Sir Peter Chalmers-Mitchell, former Secretary of the Zoological Society, London.

Among its effects were to make a 'vast reading public' available for the works of the Left intelligentsia. Concomitantly it put such works into the hands of people whose trust in the Penguin/Pelican name made them curious about titles, subjects or authors they might otherwise never have seen. How did Pelicans appeal to the 'common reader'? Here's a 1938 notice advertising Freud's *Psychopathology of Everyday Life*:

> **Why do you** FORGET THINGS YOU OUGHT TO REMEMBER? MAKE SLIPS OF THE TONGUE, OF THE PEN? DO THINGS YOU DIDN'T MEAN? . . . This interpretative study of common errors is as fascinating as it is informative. Dr. Freud explains the psychological basis for everyday faults – faults which are so ordinary we rarely stop to take notice of them. . . . *Psychopathology of Everyday Life* presents an amazing insight into the lives of all of us. It tells you something of the 'you' you may have forgotten or never known. (Notice inserted in the end matter of *Totem and Taboo*)

And so the 'Freudian slip' entered the language. Was it given to the public by Dr Freud – or by Pelican Books? Was Freud's 'wide impact,' like Hoggart's, as much to do with Allen Lane's democratisation of academic publishing as with the quality of the work published?

The connection between Pelicans and cultural studies is direct. Many of the works that are now recognised as founding texts of cultural studies itself, or of one of its contributing disciplines, were published, increasingly as originals, by Pelican Books:

The Intelligent Woman's Guide to Socialism, Capitalism, Sovietism and Fascism (1) –
    Bernard Shaw: Pelican A1
The Intelligent Woman's Guide to Socialism, Capitalism, Sovietism and Fascism (2) –
    Bernard Shaw: Pelican A2
A Short History of the World – H.G. Wells: Pelican A5

Religion and the Rise of Capitalism – R.H. Tawney: Pelican A23
Psychopathology of Everyday life – Sigmund Freud: Pelican A24
Totem and Taboo – Sigmund Freud: Pelican A33
The Common Reader – Virginia Woolf: Pelican A36

All of these titles were published before the end of 1938, along with books by Sir Leonard Wooley, Julian Huxley, Harold Laski, Beatrice Webb and A.N. Whitehead among others (a total of forty books in the first year and a half).

Then, later, three of the most important founding texts of cultural studies as we know it, the ones that really got things going (the Exodus, as it were, as opposed to Genesis), were published as Pelicans:

The Uses of Literacy – Richard Hoggart: Pelican A431
Culture and Society – Raymond Williams: Pelican A520
The Making of the English Working Class – E.P. Thompson: Pelican A1000

Richard Hoggart's *The Uses of Literacy* was published in hardback by Chatto & Windus. Of its Pelican edition, Hoggart wrote:

> Allen Lane read the book very early, sitting in the sun at his place in the Balearics, and 'phoned his office or Chatto to say he wanted it for Pelican and as soon as possible. It was, he said later, exactly the kind of book he had hoped to publish when he had founded the Pelican list just before the war . . . Lane's decision . . . was the foundation of the book's wide impact. (Hoggart, 1992: 5)

Edward Thompson's *The Making of the English Working Class* was originally published by Victor Gollancz in 1963. A revised Pelican version was published in the turbulent year of 1968. The assignation to this book of Pelican number 1000 clearly signified a publishing event. It was in equal measure a great compliment to Pelicans and the acknowledgement of a great achievement by the author: it was the *thousandth*, think of that, example of this collective willingness not only to write *about* the 'English working class' but also to address its members, directly, at a price they could afford, about 'things in themselves'.

Obviously it cost more than the original Shavian sixpence, but it was still pretty much the equivalent of a packet of fags: I bought my copy in 1974 (its 4th Pelican reprint), by which time this 960-page book was £1.25. I don't know about Ms Woolf, but I could afford this *and* a room of my own, on a state scholarship. Of Allen Lane, Richard Hoggart wrote:

> I had been happy to talk to Allen Lane whenever he asked because the Penguin/Pelican idea had been part of my education, of my sense of what was needed by people like me. . . . He had created a major democratic instrument; he had believed in greater access to the world of ideas for 'the people of England / Who have not spoken yet'; he had assumed that they had the capacity to judge those ideas in spite of the barriers which made access so difficult for so many. (Hoggart, 1992: 50–1)

Given that Hoggart was born within a year of my mother, it says something for Lane, but less for British education history, that the same was true for me, a long generation later. Hoggart was 19 or 20 when Pelicans were first issued in the late 1930s. I came to them in the late sixties and early seventies, just as Allen Lane, who died in 1970, was coming to the end of his life. My house was, and remained, full of crumbling Pelicans and Penguins, procured, not always first-hand, by 'my sense of what was needed by people like me'.

Penguin Books was sold to Pearson in 1970, the year Sir Allen Lane died. Pearson rose to be a media giant, owning Longman, the *Financial Times*, Grundy Television (Australian maker of *Neighbours*), among other household names (see http://www.pearson.com/aboutus/history.htm). Hoggart's comment on the sale of Penguin, by the way, was unusually acid for the mild-mannered Clark Kent of cultural studies: 'the *Boule de Suif* argument, that the whores can protect the virtuous women, doesn't suit artistic matters' (Hoggart, 1992: 50). But per-haps his judgement was premature. Pearson wrote this 'about us' in 2002, evidently still seeing itself as a 'major democratic instrument':

> At its core, Pearson is about education and enlightenment. About helping children succeed at school or adults succeed in their work. About helping politicians consider different points of view or business people divine markets. About inspiring people to take a fresh look – or enjoy a wry smile – at the world. (http://www.pearson.com/aboutus/index.htm)

Allen Lane certainly knew what he had made. Hoggart related the story of how in 1967 'Lane became greatly exercised about the future of the remarkable insti-tution he had created. . . . He was wondering whether some sort of trust or foundation of universities might be set up to take over Penguin' (Hoggart, 1992: 49). The idea of a great publishing venture *as* a university could not at that time be accommodated within the framework of universities' view of themselves. But times and technologies changed. Publishers and booksellers became less squeamish about calling their backlist a 'university'. For instance, booksellers Barnes and Noble in the USA launched their 'own brand' university. Check out: http://www.barnesandnobleuniversity.com. The 'courses aren't accredited but the learning is real'. The 'top three courses' on a day I visited were: How To Think Like Leonardo da Vinci; Feng Shui for Your Home; The World in Your Palm (Palm handheld electronic device, not palmistry). On another day they were: The Making of Modern China – NEW!; Writing for Children; The Brain and How it Works. Naturally there were links to the B & N shopping trolley, but the courses themselves were free.

Meanwhile universities scrambled gracelessly to do deals with publishers, or their e-heirs . . . for instance, Universitas 21, a global consortium of eighteen prestige universities oriented towards e-learning, was capitalised by ThomsonLearning (http://www.universitas21.com/news.html#press1). Like Pearson, owners of Penguin, Thomson was successor to one of the best-known newspaper empires of the twentieth century. Pearson owned Westminster Press and the *Financial Times*. Thomson took over Kemsley Newspapers, the *Sunday Times* and *The Times* in the UK to add to its Canadian titles and Associated Book Publishers (including Routledge), all of which they later disposed of as they headed for the new economy:

> Pioneer in the old print economy, Thomson helped create the electronic age with early proprietary online systems and CD-ROM products. We moved aggressively to capitalize on the reach, customization, and speed of the Internet to even greater effect. We hold leading positions in the information sectors of the legal and regulatory, financial services, scientific, healthcare, education and corporate training markets on a global basis. Our indispensable content, and outstanding brands, have firmly established credibility with customers in our chosen fields. Their rapid adoption of the Internet creates a wired world of opportunity for us to build on these relationships with Web-based delivery platforms and services that make it easier for our customers to do business. That is our aim as a global e-information and solutions business. (http://www.thomson.com/About_Us/)

That's what universities began to sound like too; content-rich competitors in the learning-services industry. With e-businesses like ThomsonLearning as partner, competitor, supplier and client, they provided 'online and traditional classroom learning for individuals, learning institutions and businesses' (www.ThomsonLearning.com). Lane was well ahead of his time, but in fact his 'university' had the desired social effect without the institutional investment, acting directly on the brains of Pelican's readers, of whom there were certainly tens of thousands more than the then shamefully small UK population of university undergraduates.

Another direct connection between Penguin and cultural studies was financial. It was Allen Lane who capitalised the founding institution of British cultural studies, Hoggart's Centre for Contemporary Cultural Studies at the University of Birmingham's English Department, in 1965.

In 1960 Hoggart had appeared for the defence when Penguin was prosecuted for obscenity after publishing D.H. Lawrence's *Lady Chatterley's Lover*. Hoggart was coy about accepting a *causal* connection between this and Lane's decision to 'set us up':

> It was inevitable that some people would say he gave the money as a covert thank-you for my evidence in the *Lady Chatterley's Lover* case. I am sure I would have asked Allen Lane for funds even if I had not appeared in his defence three years before; I knew him well enough to be sure the idea would interest him. (Hoggart, 1992: 89)

Lane donated the lion's share of the start-up capital for the Centre for Contemporary Cultural Studies, topped up by small donations from Chatto & Windus, publishers of the hardback edition of *The Uses of Literacy*, and by the *Observer* newspaper. Hoggart got £2,500 a year for seven years, plus a one-off £500. With this funding, he was able afford for the Centre a room of its own, so to speak, and to offer a research fellowship to Stuart Hall. Later, after meeting him on a train, he appointed 22-year-old Michael Green too. The rest, as they say, was history; or maybe more accurately it became history as 'myth-representation'.

Richard Hoggart thought much more came of his brief encounters with Allen Lane than an institutional pay-off, momentous though that outcome proved in time to be. In the meantime, the 1960 *Chatterley* trial changed things culturally, ushering in (i.e. emblematising if not causing) the then novel idea of the 'permissive society', and adding a new word to the written, literary form of the English language:

> It was felt deep down that if the word 'fuck' were allowed to escape into free print then more than a word would have been released. Sexually explicit passages . . . do not shock the British psyche as much as that word does, when seen in print. (Hoggart, 1992: 57)

Since the whole point of Penguin books was that they were cheap enough for everyone, the case was also a trial of who should be responsible for dealing with that shock. To the surprise of the Director of Public Prosecutions the answer was that ordinary people could decide for themselves:

> The other main element in the opposition to the book's appearance was the fact that it was to be a paperback and so available to anyone who had a few bob to spare. We are back with the lack of trust, the overweening sense that 'ordinary people' have to be protected from corruption by those who know better – a comical as well as a sombre thought. (Hoggart, 1992: 58)

Unlooked for outcomes ensued. 'Years later,' recalled Hoggart, at a conference at a big American university to celebrate the fiftieth anniversary of Lawrence's death, 'the audience in the large lecture theatre seemed to be mainly nuns from liberal arts colleges. When the opening lecturer, speaking about *Lady Chatterley's Lover*, began: "Let's face it. Lady C. was fucked, sucked, buggered and blown," the nuns took notes without concern' (Hoggart, 1992: 10).

The O'Hareites

Dutiful note-taking by the co-eds of America projects this part of the history of cultural studies forward (in time) to where it began (in this chapter). In the 1960s, Tom Wolfe joined those who lectured to large audiences in the vast US universities sprawling across the plains and prairies among the corn and the cattle. It may well have been that Hoggart arrived at Chicago's O'Hare airport (busiest in the world for much of the twentieth century), on his way to talk to the very students whose minds, let's say, had begun to interest Tom Wolfe.

Although he never mentioned Bernard Shaw's *Intelligent Woman's Guide*, Wolfe was clearly playing with it in the title of his 'The Intelligent Coed's Guide to America' (1977). G.B. Shaw had addressed his 'guide' to his sister-in-law, Mary Stewart Cholmondeley (pronounced 'Chumley'). But Wolfe's 'intelligent coed' was the client, possibly the obscure object of desire, certainly not the interlocutor. The co-ed was deployed as the desirable bearer of truths that intellectuals themselves had somehow betrayed. The 'ideal reader' of cultural studies evolved from Cholmondeley to comely.

Wolfe began by asking: 'Has it even been duly noted that O'Hare . . . is now the intellectual center of the United States?' It was in fact a major entrepôt for traffic in writers: 'All the skyways to Lecture-land lead through O'Hare Airport. In short, up to one half of our intellectual establishment sits outside of Chicago between planes.' (Wolfe, 1977: 94–5). Then, like Hoggart, he headed for the lecture theatre, perhaps the very one that held those imperturbable note-taking nuns:

> Picture, if you will, a university on the Great Plains. . . . The conference is about to begin. The students come surging in like hormones. You've heard of rosy cheeks? They *have* them! Here they come, rosy-cheeked, laughing, with Shasta and 7-Up pumping through their veins, talking chipsy, flashing weather-proof smiles, bursting out of their down-filled Squaw Valley jackets and their blue jeans – O immortal denim mons veneris! – looking, all of them, boys and girls, Jocks & Buds & Freaks, as if they spent the day hang-gliding and then made a Miller commercial at dusk and are now going to taper off with a little Culture before returning to the coed dorm. (Wolfe, 1977: 96–7)

This democratic vista, as it were, of desirable, fecund, utopian richness, contrasted horribly with the message brought in by the 'bards and sages of O'Hare.' They sang not of freedom and progress but of political repression, police surveillance, economic exploitation, media manipulation, racism, authoritarianism, and ecological disaster. As Wolfe tells the story, at the end of one further such pathologisation of the American body politic, up stood a student:

> 'There's one thing I can't understand,' said the boy.
> 'What's that?' said the ecologist.
> 'Well,' said the boy. 'I'm a senior, and for four years we've been told by people like yourself and the other gentlemen that everything's in terrible shape, and it's all going to hell, and I'm willing to take your word for it, because you're all experts in your fields. But around here, at this school, for the past four years, the biggest problem, as far as I can see, has been finding a parking place near the campus.' (Wolfe, 1977: 99)

Wolfe contrasted the interior life of the *idiots-savants* of heartland America with the knowledge of the 'all-knowing savants of O'Hare, who keep warning them that this is "the worst of all possible worlds," and they know it must be true – and yet life keeps getting easier, sunnier, happier. . . . How can such things be?' (Wolfe, 1977: 99–100).

It may simply have been that the blue-jeaned and rosy-cheeked co-eds had rooms of their own, but Wolfe was making an accusation of treason – *trahison des clercs* – or, at the very least, bad faith and self-delusion, against the jet-setting cultural pessimists of the time. The job of the intellectual was not to understand the felt reality of their society (optimism of the intellect; pessimism of the car park), nor to contribute to its good government (affluence and freedom, widely distributed), but to *pathologise* that reality; to make it appear ideological, illusory or oppressive. The social, environmental, cultural and psychological sciences seemed bent on counting the human cost of modernity, not the manifold benefits it brought to those who were most visibly its beneficiaries – affluent American youth.

In fact, the ticket through 'bountiful O'Hare' *depended* on an adversarial reaction to everything contemporary America offered to its middle-class heartland. The intellectual had become 'like the medieval cleric, most of whose energies were devoted to separating himself from the mob – which in modern times . . . goes under the name of the middle class' (Wolfe, 1977: 105). The job of the O'Hareite Order was to make young people feel bad about their own lives. Like Hoggart's nuns, they were dutifully willing to oblige – but they didn't *get* what was being said to them, and wondered how old they would be when the Apocalypse hit them (Wolfe, 1977: 99, 106).

It was the intellectual's job to tell 'millions of college students in the vast fodderlands of the nation' that they could not believe the evidence of their lives. 'Young people in the U.S. – in the form of the Psychedelic or Flower Generation – were helping themselves to wild times that were the envy of children all over the world' (Wolfe, 1977: 107). But no; their freedoms and thrills were illusory. Wolfe tracked various culprits until in the end he got round to Herbert Marcuse, American successor to the German Frankfurt School. Marcuse's *One Dimensional Man* had attained cult status in dorms, and Marcuse himself had attained guru status during this time. Wolfe (true to his name) pounced:

> Freedom was in the air like a flock of birds. Just how fascist could it be? The problem led up to . . . Herbert Marcuse's doctrine of 'repressive tolerance.' Other countries had real repression? Well we had the obverse, repressive tolerance. This was an insidious system through which the government granted meaningless personal freedoms in order to narcotize the pain of class repression, which only socialism could cure. Beautiful! Well-nigh flawless! (Wolfe, 1977: 107)

As academic or intellectual cultural studies diverged further from journalistic or gentleman-amateur cultural studies, so the academic branch tended to become more ideological, adversarial, and disengaged from the everyday palaver of government. If you will, more contemplative, but like walled-up (intra-mural) clerics in the European dark ages, what they contemplated best was their own apocalyptic vision of contemporary culture as virtualised Vikings marauding all over the countryside. But now the raping and pillaging was being done, said the O'Hareites, by their own government and corporations. The lines for a sporadic low-intensity war of mutual misunderstanding and suspicion were drawn between academic and journalistic cultural commentators, both sides seeking the high ground of the public intellectual. But one side – the journalist-amateurs – wanted to occupy that ground in order to *address the public directly about public affairs.* The other – the intra-mural branch of cultural studies – argued for critical distance between everyday flux and its critique, so that positions could be properly theorised.

Higher education was so large a community that both positions were sustainable. Theorised studies of culture became standard commodities in the backlists of academic publishing houses, while in the back pages of the Sunday papers the polite essay could continue to treat literary subjects as politics. How much either of them contributed to literature, or to politics, remained unclear. With Virginia Woolf, it may need a century or so to find out.

Meanwhile, cultural studies had found 'a room of its own', in Birmingham, in 1964, with the opening of the Centre for Contemporary Cultural Studies (Hoggart, 1992: 90). At that very moment, Richard and Mary Hoggart went house-hunting. Hoggart was unable to confine cultural studies to the academy – he performed it even as he lived it: 'the search produced a fascinating cultural cameo of provincial middle-class and middle-executive life at that time. . . . Most haunting were the children's bedrooms, the overlapping pop-star posters seeming both lonely and public gestures, the children away at boarding school' (1992: 84). Hoggart probed deeper:

> In the recesses of a surprising number of such homes one came across a raffish element. The owner would swing open a door to exhibit the great size of a built-in wardrobe, and out would fall a profusion of operatic gear, amateur dramatic costumes, voluntary association uniforms, Country and Western, Civil War and pantomime outfits. Inside so many Englishmen is a woman trying to get out; inside many an Englishwoman is a little girl wanting to play at nurses, Carmen, Mrs Miniver. (Hoggart, 1992: 84)

Here then, in rooms peopled by peculiarities that connected sex and nation, desire and display, class and costume, cultural studies found room for its subject, its object, and its voice.

2
Culture from Arnold to Schwarzenegger
Imperial Literacy to Pop Culture (destination democracy?)

Cultural studies and mass society

Cultural studies was the study of mass or popular culture, especially the mass media in a mass society. It was also preoccupied with cultural politics, which in this context referred to a struggle between popular or mass culture and high or minority culture. However, that struggle was only seen as such by one side of the supposed contest. Very few individuals or organisations within the domain of popular culture itself sought actively to defeat or destroy high culture, least of all on behalf of the claims of the popular. If they took any notice, it was usually quite respectful, not to say reverential, as a viewing of almost any big-screen Shakespeare would instantly reveal. Militancy was confined to those who thought it necessary to struggle against *popular* culture on behalf of high or minority culture.

These struggles began as an imperial discourse on the governability or otherwise of the masses in Britain. The 1860s to 1880s was a period of:

- **political agitation**. The second Reform Act of 1867 extended the franchise to virtually all mature men;
- **educational reform**. The Education Acts of 1870–81 established free, compulsory, elementary schooling;
- **imperial ascendancy** (not to mention Fenian outrages). The British Empire had painted the world map red, bringing under the governance of the British crown ever more disparate, unruly and resistant subjects from all inhabited continents;
- **commercial and scientific materialism**. Coal was king, and Darwinism was coming of age;
- **population explosion**. The world's first megalopolises were growing up in London, Birmingham and the Black Country, Manchester and Glasgow.

It was in this mix that culture first became a political hot potato.

Struggle, democratisation, and the masses

Some, led by Matthew Arnold (son of Thomas Arnold, pioneering headmaster of Rugby School), who was himself both a poet and an Inspector of Schools, felt that under these pressures traditional spiritual and moral values, and cultural tastes, were under immediate threat of extinction. Even national political disintegration ('anarchy') was feared. The answer, it transpired, was to be found in high culture. The idea was not to produce more of it, but to train leaders and masses alike to respond to the existing canon of great works, as the antidote to mass society.

The 'struggle' strand

Arnold's vision found its fullest expression in the twentieth century in the works and schemes of F.R. Leavis, whose militant opposition to modern industrial life was only matched by his insistence on the 'redemptive power of English' (Mathieson, 1975: 96–7). For forty years between the 1930s and the 1960s, Leavis drummed out the same message – English Literature was the moral centre of the school curriculum; and he demonstrated in his publications how he thought literary criticism ought to be done, in the cause of preserving the language and 'fine' responses to it. Leavisite ideas proved influential in universities, schools and teacher education programmes, not least through Leavis's journal *Scrutiny*, as well as in university English departments. In schools the emphasis was not only on the practice of literary criticism, but also on militant opposition to the supposed deadening effects of mass culture (Mathieson: 96).

Later the Leavisite 'resistance' to mass society was recast as class struggle, where the enemy was still commercial media and popular culture, but the good guys were intellectuals rather than poets; political radicals rather than literary missionaries. Stuart Hall's first book, *The Popular Arts*, co-written with Paddy Whannel in 1964, is an interesting halfway house between Leavisite lit-crit and the more explicitly class-based (Marxist) analysis of popular culture for which he eventually became better known. Richard Hoggart's *Uses of Literacy* occupies the same ground, with a more explicit debt to Leavis.

Later again the notion of struggle was rejected in favour of a concern with policy, and Marxist models were supplanted by the Foucauldian notion of 'governmentality,' in a reformist cultural studies led by Tony Bennett (see Chapter 4). But there was still something oddly Arnoldian about this, despite the change in rhetoric. The idea was still to explore the cultural sector for techniques for governing mass, anonymous populations. And while Leavisite histrionics had been explicitly abandoned, along with any interest in poetry, Bennett's own longstanding interest in the history of museums meant that there was still a strong focus on the use of public cultural institutions for the formation of citizenship.

The 'democratisation' strand

Meanwhile, and alongside, another strand of cultural studies pursued an under-standing of popular culture based not on struggle but on democratisation. This strand had its antecedents in the same literary and analytical traditions as those involved above (from Arnold to Bennett), but was characterised by a non-met-ropolitan, provincial and suburban mode. It was less concerned with governability than with emancipation; less interested in class antagonism than in the productive capacity of cultural systems; less interested in governmental-ity than in the media as vehicles for the extension of 'cultural citizenship'. The work of Meaghan Morris and John Fiske, in rather different ways, came into this category, as has my own.

More recently, popular culture and high culture were reunited in the cause of national and regional economic development, recast as the 'creative industries' (http://www.creativeindustries.org.uk/; http://www.culture.gov.uk/creative/mapping.html; www.creativeindustries.qut.com). The creative industries emerged as content-providers for the new economy (Leadbeater, 1997). 'Cultural entrepreneurs' created wealth as well as culture, using 'thin-air' resources like talent and intangible assets like know-how.

As befitted a non-metropolitan or provincial mode of cultural studies, the *democratisation* branch did not so much oppose as differentiate itself from the predominant *struggle* school of thought. It trod the same path as Williams, Hall, Bennett and so on (learning from them to disagree, as it were), but saw different features in the landscape – sometimes a different vista altogether. It was more preoccupied with meanings (story, song, spectacle, speech) than with power; more optimistic in mood; more inclined to take ordinariness as an end of democ-ratisation, not as a means to power; less interested in ruling than in teaching. Its own antecedents, being non-metropolitan and therefore dispersed into mutually unacquainted provincial traditions, were rarely recorded in the standardised histories of the discipline. In my own case, as a product of the Cardiff school of cultural studies (see Turner, 1990: 83–4, and below), the important antecedents were S. L. Bethell and Terence Hawkes.

Both strands of cultural studies were interested in popular culture: the strug-gle branch in its structural position within a radically unequal class society founded on capital and inherited privilege; the democratisation branch in the possibilities of renewal from below. Both saw popular culture largely in terms of contemporary, urban, mediated leisure pursuits (i.e. not as folk culture) – centred on the popular arts like the movies and television, popular music and dancing, photography and fashion, tourism and motoring.

However, these activities did not present themselves to cultural studies as innocent pursuits undertaken by a fun-loving populace without a care in the world. Cultural studies didn't go in for the Jeremy Clarkson (presenter of the BBC's car show, *Top Gear*) provocative, opinionated but ultimately celebratory mode of address. On the contrary, popular culture came to cultural studies under a very black cloud. Popular culture presented itself not as 'popular' ('well-liked'; 'widespread'), but as *mass-cult*: manipulation of the de-individuated masses by money-crazed moguls and power-crazed demagogues. Pop culture was seen as the opposite, indeed the nemesis, of culture itself, which was defended – for the sake of the spiritual, moral or political health of the society that spurned it – by a minority of cultural intellectuals. From this perspective it was hard to see mass culture in terms of democratisation, emancipation, productive capacity, cultural citizenship, meanings, optimism, ordinariness, teaching and renewal from below. It didn't matter whether the critics were on the political Right (Leavis, T.S. Eliot, Wyndham Lewis), or on the Left (Hall, Hoggart): mass culture was a common enemy.

Indeed, the struggle school of thought was directly in line of succession to the cultural intellectuals who opposed mass culture from the start, as will be shown below. The preoccupation with governability or governmentality, class struggle, power and rule in the sphere of culture came directly from a view of the masses as a *threat* both to culture and to the good governance of the polity. Left and Right agreed on that; the Left seeing it as an opportunity to exploit – in the name of a coming restructuring of society by revolution; the Right wanting to contain it. Both also tended to agree that the masses were somehow not fully alive; that they were deadened or narcotised by their encounters with cinema, advertising and commercial fiction. Cultural studies, as an emancipatory discourse, was itself 'governed' by an intellectual tradition with sometimes alarmingly anti-democratic tendencies.

The masses

There were not always masses; they were a special product of modernity. Previously there were, of course, different kinds of collective populations, including classical plebeians, medieval laity, foreign hordes and the ever-present mob. Many words persist in English as a reminder that the view of the populace by those who wrote about them was not often very complimentary. The *OED* (1st edn) derived the word 'populace' from Latin, via Italian, with a quotation from Florio: 'the grosse, base, vile, common people, the riraffe people'. It glossed the word as: 'the mass of the people of a community, as distinguished from the titled, wealthy, or educated classes; the common people; *invidiously*, the mob, the rabble'. It traced this distinction between 'masses' and 'classes' to W.E. Gladstone (British Prime Minister) in 1886.

Used to describe large numbers – but not the *general population*, since 'the mass' was distinguished from other 'classes' – 'the mass of the people of a community' might have seemed a neutral and trans-historical description, applicable to such populations anywhere at any time. But in fact there was little neutrality even in the dictionary. 'The mass' described an amorphous, internally undifferentiated body, seen from the outside not from within; 'often with the notion of oppressive or bewildering abundance' (*OED* 'mass' 4a). When applied to human beings it referred to 'a multitude of persons mentally viewed as forming an aggregate in which their individuality is lost' (*OED* 'mass' 5a). This *'mass'* was set in *class* antagonism to the aristocratic (titled), capitalist (wealthy) and literate (educated) classes. Common people were *coterminous* with what was feared from them ('mob, rabble'), and of course they were denied title, wealth and education, even individuality, by the very definition that produced them. So 'mass' was hardly a neutral term in itself (see also Raymond Williams on 'the masses' in *Culture and Society*, 1961: 287ff.).

Moreover, its plural form, 'the masses', had already come to be applied to the 'lower orders' as opposed to 'the classes' (*OED* 'mass' 6c) – the bewilderingly over-abundant if not actually surplus 'populace' produced by modernity, industrialisation and imperial expansionism. Here of course the dictionary merely followed usage, which was itself remarkably consistent in the nineteenth and twentieth centuries about the import of these terms. In his polemical book *The Intellectuals and the Masses*, John Carey noted how the pejorative or invidious view of the masses was held right across the spectrum of the educated classes from Left to Right.

> To a degree what both [H.G.] Wells and Hitler reflect, and what they appeal to in their readers, are the hostility and loss of focus induced in modern consciousness by a world where populousness defeats the imagination. Given the multitudes by which the individual is surrounded, it is virtually impossible to regard everyone else as having an individuality equivalent to one's own. The mass, as a reductive and dismissive concept, is invented to ease this difficulty. (1992: 201)

Following Nietzsche, it seemed that fear and loathing of the masses was almost a condition of entry into the intellectual or educated class. Carey showed in detail how Hitler, as revealed in his own writings, held orthodox, even 'stereotypical' intellectual views about both high and mass art (Carey: 198–208). Carey argued that the consequent dehumanisation of 'the mass' was a prerequisite of the Holocaust:

> Contemplating the extermination of Jews was made easier by thinking of them as a mass. Mass transportation, destruction and incineration, and the mass production of fertiliser from their ashes, all acquired a certain appropriateness once the initial proposal that they were a mass – not fully alive people – was accepted. In this sense the Holocaust could be seen as the ultimate indictment of the idea of the mass and its acceptance by twentieth-century intellectuals. (Carey: 206)

Carey concluded his book with a critique of Hitler's ideas on culture – but what was sauce for the goose, he insisted, had to be sauce for the gander:

> The contention, then, that Hitler's ideas on culture were trivial, half-baked and disgusting [these terms were Hugh Trevor-Roper's] can be allowed only if the same epithets are applied to numerous cultural ideas prevalent among English intellectuals

of the first half of the twentieth century, some of which are still espoused today. The superiority of 'high' art, the eternal glory of Greek sculpture and architecture, the transcendent value of the old masters and of classical music, the supremacy of Shakespeare, Goethe and other authors acknowledged by intellectuals as great, the divine spark that animates all productions of genius and distinguishes them from the low amusements of the mass – these were among Hitler's most dearly held beliefs. (1992: 208)

Hitler's intellectually standard views on the literary and artistic canon were matched by his intellectually standard views on popular culture:

His contempt for 'gutter journalism', advertising and 'cinema bilge', his espousal of the aristocratic principle, and his comparison of the 'dunderheaded multitude' with women and children, are other features that readers . . . will have no difficulty matching in intellectual discourse. (ibid.)

For Carey, the lesson of Hitler was not that his views were 'disgusting', but that they were all too familiar: 'his various rewritings of the mass – as exterminable subhumans, as an inhibited bourgeois herd, as noble workers, as a peasant pastoral – will also be familiar intellectual devices. The tragedy of *Mein Kampf* is that it was not, in many respects, a deviant work but one firmly rooted in European intellectual orthodoxy' (ibid.).

Cultural studies inherited 'European intellectual orthodoxy' in good measure. The perennial debates about popular and high culture, and about the impact of mass media on mass society, were riddled with the prejudices of literary intellectuals who had pondered with Malthusian alarm the 'populousness' that 'defeats the imagination' as the Industrial Revolution gathered pace and produced exponentially more people. Intellectuals of the twentieth century were dogged by philosophies of scarcity: more people meant less culture in a zero-sum game. A philosophy of plenty, such as that embodied in the 'bring me your huddled masses' ideology of democratising and industrialising modern America, was just as threatening to the intellectuals of Europe as was its own home-grown totalitarianism.

But America had recognised something crucial, no matter how individualist and commercial its expression. What was peculiar about these new masses, compared to pre-modern mobs, was that although they were amorphous, unknowable and had 'lost' their individuality (viewed from the outside), they were increasingly *sovereign*. Unnumbered, anonymous, the 'masses' were also 'masters' – they could vote, consume, sustain major institutions and cultural forms (from unions to cinema), and take physical actions, from fun to fighting, that might have national or international cultural consequences. They began to win civic rights, political citizenship, and a claim on health, education and social security entitlements (see Evans, 1998, especially xii–xiii and 652–3).

Meanwhile, they were subject to scientific investigation and psychological experiment, to missionaries and educationalists, all of whom wanted to bridge the gulf of unknowability, in order to fill the gap with their own knowledge, behaviour, belief and enlightenment. As Carey put it, 'intellectuals believe in giving the public what intellectuals want; that, generally speaking is what they mean by education' (Carey, 1992: 6).

The politics of reading

But the fortress was culture itself. Mass citizenship of the domain of taste was resisted long after it had been established. Accusations of dumbing down accompanied every encroachment of popular culture into previously reserved areas. Music, drama, visual arts, literature: all were roped off from their popular counterparts – pop music, cinema and TV, fashion and photography, and journalism. Democratisation of culture proceeded apace. Newspapers, cinema, tourism, pulp fiction and music hall were all well established by the turn of the twentieth century. But each new scene of popular participation and pleasure was greeted by catcalls and boos from the intellectual balcony.

The very last bastion inside the citadel of culture was *literary reading*. This was because literary reading and response were taken to be the true test of a cultured individual. Literary culture had been promoted by Arnold and his successors as the antidote to both kinds of materialism – that of science, which was held to undermine religion, and that of consumerism, which was held to undermine morals. Literary culture was espoused with truly missionary zeal; its proponents thought it would save the nation, by making the masses (both middle-class philistines and labouring populace) more alive, more human. 'The reader' was shifted from private study and enjoyment to the centre of public life: the masses were to be taught to read, whether they liked it or not; and not for their own economic well-being, but for the soul of the nation, as it were. In a secular age, the populace were to find in poetry what they were feared to have lost in religion. If they had abandoned Bunyan and Wesley, let them read not the *News of the World* but Wordsworth.

Arnold secured the compulsory recitation of English poetry in elementary schools throughout England and Wales. Indeed, as Margaret Mathieson pointed out in her valuable study of *The Preachers of Culture*:

> Above all, it was to poetry that Arnold looked for the redemption of the middle and lower classes in a society which was not only politically disturbed but appeared to be losing religion at the same time as it was threatened by science. The religious role which he desired for poetry is clear. . . . Moral zeal, therefore, which was a characteristic both of the Victorian headmasters concerned about the development of their pupils into leaders of society, and of the evangelicals anxious to protect the newly literate masses against corrupting reading matter, is clearly an important part of Arnold's support for literature. (Mathieson, 1975: 39–40)

The terms set by Arnold determined the approach to literary culture for a century thereafter. 'Moral zeal which he inherited from his father, defensiveness into which the opposition drove him . . . and concern about his society's political unrest, all led Arnold to state the case for literature in tones whose passion and vagueness have characterised much of the argument about the subject' (Mathieson: 44).

The scene was set, the lines learned, even the intonation was prescribed: passion and vagueness, moral zeal and defensiveness. Exorbitant claims were made on behalf of an activity people would only do under compulsion in schools, imposed by a literary minority on a society from which they themselves felt only alienation. But this strange mixture of paranoia and self-aggrandisement was – apparently – the very essence of the literary reader. In *A History of Reading* the Argentinian writer Alberto Manguel discussed the invention of eyeglasses in medieval Europe. In a passage ostensibly devoted to the spread of spectacles (reading glasses) in the fourteenth and fifteenth centuries, he interrupted his historical narrative with an anecdote about his own history:

> Most readers, then and now, have at some time experienced the humiliation of being told that their occupation is reprehensible. I remember being laughed at, during one recess in grade six or seven, for staying indoors and reading, and how the taunting ended with me sprawled face down on the floor, my glasses kicked into one corner, my book into another. (Manguel, 1996: 296)

This personal recollection of childish humiliation was the principal evidence used by Manguel to generalise a notion of an adversarial relationship between 'the' taunted reader and an uncomprehending, bullying world. Apparently, without need for further remark, it applied to 'most readers' over a five-hundred-year period:

> Buried in books, isolated from the world of facts and flesh, feeling superior to those unfamiliar with the words preserved between dusty covers, the bespectacled reader . . . was seen as a fool, and glasses became emblematic of intellectual arrogance. (ibid.)

Within a few pages, the terms Manguel used to oppose reader and world – one side feeling isolated, threatened but superior, an oppressed minority, the other side prone to violence and mocking or ignorant laughter – were applied to something much more significant than lonely four-eyed boys and their tormentors:

> Which came first? The invention of the masses, which Thomas Hardy described as a 'throng of people . . . containing a certain minority who have sensitive souls; these, and the aspects of these, being what is worth observing', or the invention of the bespectacled Book Fool, who thinks himself superior to the rest of the world and whom the rest of the world passes by, laughing? (Manguel, 1996: 302)

'Which came first?' Manguel projected his personal reader's persecution complex, as it were, back into history, then brought it forward to the modern era *as* history. He made Matthew Arnold the modern inheritor of the guise of the bespectacled Book Fool, 'who thinks himself superior to the rest of the world' while 'the rest of the world passes by, laughing'. But Arnold also gave that figure national and even international significance. For Arnold installed the idea that 'superiority' in the matter of literary reading, in a period of industrialisation, democratisation and commercialisation, was a prerequisite for national survival.

According to Manguel, Arnold's 'splendid arrogance' in this matter merely followed classical precedent (he cited Seneca and Socrates), in seeking to distinguish between those who could, and could not, 'read well'.

> Right and wrong readers: for Socrates there appears to be a 'correct' interpretation of a text, available to only a few informed specialists. In Victorian England, Matthew Arnold would echo this splendidly arrogant opinion: 'We . . . are for giving the heritage neither to the Barbarians nor to the Philistines, nor yet to the Populace'. (Manguel: 302)

Manguel thought that ancients and moderns alike were deluded: 'The argument that opposes those with the right to read, because they can read "well" (as the fearful glasses seem to indicate), and those to whom reading must be denied, because "they wouldn't understand", is as ancient as it is specious' (ibid.).

A specious argument, perhaps, but as cultural policy it proved spectacularly successful. For one thing, it organised Manguel's own characterisation of reading as a pretext for persecution. More importantly, 'correct reading' was to be 'denied' to the 'Populace' (the masses), as well as to Arnold's equally undeserving 'Barbarians' (the huntin', shootin' and fishin' landed gentry) and 'Philistines' (the complacent bourgeoisie), because it was required for the purposes of *government*.

One of the implications of industrialisation was that the popular classes, who had for centuries been regarded as little better than the mob when it came to political activity, were now the sovereign power in the land. They were, at least in significant sections, urban, literate, organised and articulate, unlike generations of agricultural labourers before them (Thompson, 1963). But the prospect they presented to the established classes was of Paris 1789 mixed with Captain Swing – revolutionary insurrection and class vengeance. How to make a barely governable mob capable of government (as traditionally understood by the established hierarchy), at least in the exercise of their votes? How to bridle the 'Englishman's right,' as Arnold playfully put it, to 'march where he likes, meet where he likes, enter where he likes, hoot as he likes, threaten as he likes, smash as he likes' (Arnold, 1869, cited in Williams, 1961: 132)? Universal franchise and universal education *required* that the state should pay attention to what the anonymous masses thought and said, since those masses were, despite their feared tendency towards anarchy, sovereign.

Culture and Anarchy would cast a very long shadow over the history of cultural studies, as it did the curriculum subject English too. Arnold argued that the antidote to 'anarchy' was 'culture'. His three classes, the Barbarians, Philistines and the Populace – loosely based on the British upper, middle and lower classes – were *all* 'uncultured' in his sense. Aristocrat, capitalist and worker – all were incapable of 'reading well'. How to ensure the continuation of national greatness? Those who would take on the burden of public service needed above all to be cultured, and the core of culture was the ability to 'read well'.

Literary reading became a qualification for entry into the imperial civil service. And 'reading well' meant not simply reading, but reading 'well'; that meant reading *literary criticism*:

> I dreamt last night that Shakespeare's ghost
> Sat for a Civil Service post;
> The English paper for the year
> Had several questions on *King Lear*
> Which Shakespeare answered very badly
> Because he hadn't read his Bradley. (Cited in Hawkes, 1986: 31)

A.C. Bradley, Professor of Poetry at Oxford, published *Shakespearean Tragedy* in 1904. It is still in print, and will be, presumably for ever. Terence Hawkes assessed the importance of this book not only by quoting the above facetious comic verse of the 1920s, but also by claiming for Bradley the status of:

> one of those books whose influence extends far beyond the confines of its ostensible subject, permeating the attitudes to morality, psychology and politics of hundreds and thousands of English-speaking people . . . [it] almost functions, through a system of universal education which has established the study of Shakespeare as its linchpin, as part of the air we breathe. (Hawkes: 31).

It was Bradley who instated psychological realism and the study of character on the site of Shakespeare's plays, which were to be read (not attended). 'Shakespeare' became a catechism for learning eternal moral verities, not a popular dramatist.

The ability to discern Victorian–Edwardian moral individualism in Elizabethan–Jacobean political allegory became the test of reading 'well' – reading *into* 'Shakespeare' what *literary criticism* said was there. In fact it wasn't there, nor for historical and other reasons could it be there, as Hawkes elegantly and extensively demonstrated over a long polemical career. Therefore generations of groaning children learned simultaneously that 'Shakespeare' was high-value cultural currency, and that they were unable to figure it out for themselves. This quiet, mass-scale exercise in personal humiliation simply demonstrated that 'reading well' was a minority achievement. Youngsters intoned the catechism when required, and then they watched TV or went to the movies, never alerted to the connections. Meanwhile, prominent persons who wanted to reproach the present times became habituated to a genre of rhetoric that lamented the lack of 'Shakespeare' in educational curricula while pouring scorn on any attempt to teach human, dramatic and moral themes via attention to contemporary drama such as *Buffy, Batman, Mr Bean* . . . and the latest news pictures from Beirut, Baghdad, Beijing.

Margaret Mathieson put in a nutshell why *literary* culture loomed so large in culture wars for so long. The Arnoldian view of art, in a secularising century, required literature to take over from religion as the moral centre of civilised education:

> From Coleridge, through Arnold, to F.R. Leavis, the need has been expressed for a class of cultivated men whose concern is with the quality of their society's life. Since 'quality' had come to be identified with or even equated with the ability to respond to and discriminate between great works of art, this élite has been distinguished above all by its degree of literary culture. (Mathieson, 1975: 40–1)

The stage was set for a kind of struggle for 'superiority' between the 'bespectacled Book Fool', on the one hand, and the 'rest of the world passing by and laughing', on the other. In the name of culture, the former could assess and evaluate the latter. The purpose of art was to reprove, reproach and condemn the products and pastimes of commercial and popular culture, and indeed the entire society in which masses were taught *passive* political conformity – and simultaneously incited to *active* violent excess – through their entertainments (their laughter, in fact). Here was a recipe for the 'superiority' of 'culture' – 'the best that has been thought and said in the world', in Arnold's famous phrase (Mathieson: 41–2) – as a weapon with which to belabour the despised masses, not to enlighten but further to dehumanise them.

This for example was what Q.D. Leavis (F.R.'s spouse), in her influential study of *Fiction and the Reading Public*, made of despicable 'reading to prevent boredom', as opposed to favoured (because uncontaminated by massness) pre-industrial crafts and leisure pursuits:

> But these had a real social life, they had a way of living that obeyed the natural rhythm and furnished them with genuine or what might be called, to borrow a word from the copy writer, 'creative' interests – country arts, traditional crafts and games and singing, not substitute or kill-time interests like listening to radio or gramophone, looking through newspapers and magazines, watching films and commercial football, and the activities connected with motor cars and bicycles, the only way of using leisure known to the modern city dweller. (Q.D. Leavis, 1965: 209)

It is hard not to concur with John Carey, who argued that 'the early twentieth century saw a determined effort, on the part of the European intelligentsia, to exclude the masses from culture' (Carey, 1992: 16–17). They did this partly by pouring scorn on popular culture itself – as Queenie Leavis, above; or else 'they could prevent them reading literature by making it too difficult for them to understand' – which was Carey's explanation for literary modernism! (16)

A further twist to this tale was that in due course the democratisation of higher education meant that increasing numbers of those who, because they rode bikes and read (or 'looked through') newspapers, aroused the ire of literary intellectuals, ended up at college trying to understand the criticisms and the literature of the intellectuals (including Tom Wolfe's 'sages of O'Hare'). That attempt necessarily included a lesson in despising their own practices and backgrounds. 'Sweetness and light' remained restricted to what Arnold's 'class of cultured men' said it was. In practice, that new class judged the world adversely, in the name of a literary conversation from which the world for its part was more or less excluded.

Arnoldian cultural ideology was part of a larger movement of educational modernisation. Until the First World War (when it was conscripted into the war effort in opposition to German *Kultur*), both schools and universities were slow and reluctant to introduce the study of literature:

> As long as English was studied only by working-class children, girls, Mechanics' Institute apprentices and audiences for WEA [Workers' Education Association] lectures, it remained a low-status subject, despised by the great public schools and universities. (Mathieson: 43; see also 125–6 for universities)

This was the situation attacked by Arnold and his followers, especially Sir Arthur Quiller-Couch. Leavis took up the struggle, not to improve the status of mechanics, girls, workers and their children, but of English:

> When Leavis . . . evolved what came to be recognisable as 'Cambridge English', he retained these earlier scholars' sense of mission, 'this sense of obligation' to all levels of education and society, as well as to the furtherance of knowledge, and 'faith in the saving effects of literature'. The two main characteristics of the men responsible for shaping the English Tripos, their belief in the critical method and their concern with the responsibility of education, have distinguished Cambridge English from 1913 through Leavis, to the contemporary work of disciples like David Holbrook and Fred Inglis. (Mathieson: 126–7)

The Cambridge approach was designed to reach 'all levels of education and society'. In other words, it was thought capable of opening to the life of the imagination the minds of the children of 'the masses' and 'the philistines'. But equally, it was held to be good for training future leaders and imperial administrators in literary judgement, not to make them into poets or novelists, but to mature their taste and judgement, the better to run the country, and indeed many other countries in a far-flung empire.

Popular culture – Shakespeare to jazz

The appeal to 'critical method' and 'responsibility of education' were also – and strangely enough – the authentic voice of cultural studies. Here's one of its founding statements: 'It is part of the purpose of education to cleanse the language' (Hall and Whannel, 1964: 334):

> Clearly, one of the great – perhaps tragic – characteristics of the modern age has been the progressive alienation of high art from popular art. Few art forms are able to hold

both elements together: and popular art has developed a history and a topography of its own, separate from high and experimental art. Nevertheless, the connection between the two cannot be denied. In some way difficult precisely to define, the vigour of popular art – whether communally or individually made – and the relevance of serious art are bound indissolubly together. So that when we look at the new media – especially those where the fragmentation between popular and serious art is not yet complete (like the cinema) – we are showing a proper concern, not only for the moments of quality in the popular arts, but for the condition and quality of imaginative work of *any* level, and thus for the quality of the culture as a whole. It is this care for the quality of the culture – rather than the manufacture and manipulation of levels of taste – which is the ultimate *educational* responsibility we try to focus here. (Hall and Whannel, 1964: 84–5)

'Concern . . . for the quality of the culture as a whole', seen as an 'ultimate *educational* responsibility', was Arnoldian ideology incarnate. Setting 'imaginative work' and 'the quality of culture' against the 'manufacture and manipulation' of 'taste' was the classic Leavisite gambit. Yet this passage was co-authored by Stuart Hall; it's from his first book, *The Popular Arts*. Indeed the dust-jacket made the connection with cultural studies explicit: 'Stuart Hall, formerly an editor of *New Left Review*, has recently been appointed Senior Research Fellow in the new Birmingham University Centre for Contemporary Cultural Studies under Professor Richard Hoggart.' The passage quoted above was the conclusion to Part I: 'Definitions'. It could certainly be taken as part of the *manifesto* for academic-educational cultural studies.

Hall and Whannel were unusual in seeking to address the importance of 'holding together' popular and high arts. Arnoldian and Leavisite analysts would find it easy to agree that 'one of the great – perhaps tragic – characteristics of the modern age has been the progressive alienation of high art from popular art'. Where Hall and Whannel departed from the script was in their 'concern for the condition and quality of imaginative work of *any* level'. Indeed, they were prepared to invoke Shakespeare, normally used in this context to demonstrate the 'alienation' bit of the argument; i.e. both that Shakespeare's genius was of a different order from that of the popular arts of the day, and that the mob-like populace were incapable of appreciating Shakespeare.

But here was an argument within the Arnoldian tradition about the *value* of popular art and the *quality* of popular entertainments. To make their point Hall and Whannel invoked the great mid-twentieth-century scholar of Shakespeare's audience, Alfred Harbage, who as an American was OK about both Shakespeare and democracy. In fact, Harbage had much more invested in Shakespeare's *popularity* than in his *alienation* from the populace:

Shakespeare and his audience found each other, in a measure they created each other. He was a quality writer for a quality audience. . . . The great Shakespearian discovery was that quality extended vertically through the social scale, not horizontally at the upper genteel, economic and academic levels. ALFRED HARBAGE, *As They Liked It*. (Cited thus in Hall and Whannel, 1964: 66)

Although Hall and Whannel had departed radically from the Arnoldian script, they were very much still in the same overall argument. For what was at stake for them in 1964 was exactly the same as what had motivated Arnold in 1869, almost a century earlier. It was the connection between culture and government, or culture and politics. The gap between literate elites and 'the masses' was seen in adversarial, i.e. political terms, rather than by means of some other relational metaphor (family resemblance, for instance). This was because they thought that the 'vertical' integration of quality that Harbage found in Shakespeare had been severed: that was the 'tragic' characteristic of the 'modern age'. Thus they saw the only connection between contemporary popular and high culture as dissociation or 'alienation'. Understood this way, it was still almost impossible to imagine any relationship between elites and masses that was not seen as a struggle. But the masses could never be self-represented as such, only spoken for by those who desired to improve or lead them or who feared their ungovernability. It followed that the struggle was to maintain the supremacy of high culture, conducted by literary intellectuals who saw their own reading practices as the foundation of government, and culture.

No one seemed to take on the really radical implication of Harbage's statement that Shakespeare 'wrote for a quality audience' and was reciprocally a creation of it. *Shakespeare's* great discovery was that quality extended vertically through the social scale. If it was true for Shakespeare, why could it not be true for 'the modern age'? Would an investigation of mass culture reveal *quality* in both text and audience? This was a question that the (Arnold/Leavis/Hall) struggle branch of cultural studies could not ask, much less answer.

How did cultural studies deal with the contents of popular culture? As might have been expected, what was seen depended on the stance of the observer. What did the various positions have to say about popular music, for instance? Writing of Wyndham Lewis, 'the intellectuals' intellectual', John Carey reported on Lewis's 1929 book *Paleface: The Philosophy of the Melting-Pot*. Ostensibly a critique of 'the cult of the Negro and the primitive among educated whites', it was in fact a double attack on Black and 'mass' culture, each condemned, as Lewis saw it, for displaying the characteristics of the other. Lewis's racist language was intemperate and untrammelled, but the *hatred* was for the mass. As Carey put it:

> The Negro's gift to the white world is jazz, which Lewis interprets as 'the aesthetic medium of a sort of frantic proletarian subconscious'. . . . In fact [the blacks'] sole contribution to culture is 'a barbarous, melancholy, epileptic folk-music, worthy of a Patagonian cannibal'. Jazz, as developed in the West, is for Lewis unmistakably degraded and degrading, expressing the mindless energy of the mass. It is the 'slum peasant' and the 'city serf' that rejoice in its 'gross proletarian nigger bumps'. Its 'idiot mass sound' is ultimately 'marxistic'. (Carey, 1992: 194–5)

Writing in 1964, Stuart Hall and Paddy Whannel took more seriously those 'marxistic' tendencies. Addressing schoolteachers, they used jazz to distinguish among the terms popular, mass and high culture:

The distinction between popular and mass art will be clearer if we take an example of the difference between a popular artist and a mass performer in their attitudes towards their audience and their work. Both are more 'aware' of their audience than the high artist. But whereas the popular artist, feeling his audience in his bones, concentrates everything on making anew and creating, the mass artist seems to be in total subjection to his audience, nervously aware of it, desperately afraid of losing touch. (Hall and Whannel, 1964: 70)

Hall and Whannel went on to contrast the statements of some prominent jazz musicians with those of Liberace, and they found Liberace wanting. The line between jazz players and Liberace, they concluded, 'is the crucial boundary between popular art and mass art' (72). The production of artistic quality from jazz meant that it no longer had to be 'popular' (well-liked) to qualify as 'popular music':

Jazz, of course, is a minority music. But it is popular in the sense of being *of the people*, and while it is no longer the exclusive property of a small, depressed and exploited community the link there has been miraculously preserved. The jazz ethos is still tolerant and non-conformist. Lively, radical and creative groups of young people in quite different cultures have, during the short period of its history, found in it a common, international language. It costs money to go to a jazz club or concert, and art galleries are usually free: but for many young people jazz is more available than the traditional art forms. (73)

Jazz here was indeed 'miraculous': it was praised for being 'available' – the one quality that the despised 'mass art' could really claim as its own. Jazz was minority, but popular; it was 'of the people', although not any more; it cost money, but was a public good. What it meant, and how it fitted into the cultural distinctions of popular, mass and high, was a matter of *critical interpretation* – which was itself the essence of jazz.

Jazz as criticism; Shakespeare as business studies

How could jazz 'be both what it is and another thing'? Terence Hawkes, in his book *That Shakespeherian Rag*, had an answer to that problem that was as sophisticated as it was generous:

We have only to step beyond the shores of Europe to encounter quite a different notion of interpretation that will allow . . . the sense of a text as . . . an arena of conflicting and often contradictory potential interpretations. . . . The abstract model I reach for is of course that of jazz music: that black American challenge to the Eurocentric idea of the author's, or the composer's, authority. . . . Interpretation in that context is not parasitic but symbiotic in its relationship with its object. Its role is not limited to the service, or the revelation, or the celebration of the author's/composer's art. Quite the reverse: interpretation *constitutes* the art of the jazz musician. (Hawkes, 1986: 117–18)

Terry Hawkes – himself a jazz drummer well known around the pubs and clubs of South Wales – did not introduce lightly this figure of jazz *as* criticism. Taking his cue from 'Geoffrey Hartman's conceit that, as a native American confection, with its unsettling commitment to creative re-presentation and re-interpretation, jazz offers a model for a future notion of literary criticism' (Hawkes, 1986: 125), he wrote:

> Criticism is the major, in its largest sense the *only* native American art. Complaints about America's lack of original creativity in the arts miss the point. Responding to, improvising on, 'playing' with, re-creating, synthesizing and interpreting 'given' structures of all kinds, political, social, aesthetic, these have historically constituted the transatlantic mode in our century and before it, to an extent that might now force us to recognize that criticism makes Americans of us all. (Hawkes, 1986: 118)

Hawkes's main business was neither jazz nor America, though he was interested in literary criticism and cultural studies. He too was concerned with the relations between popular and high culture. Unusually, for a Shakespearean scholar, his view of that relation was notably jazzy – he saw the *elevation* of Shakespeare from popular and oral culture to high literary art as diminishing, even a *decline*:

> From a position as a major instance of English-speaking popular culture, they [the plays of Shakespeare] have over 400 years dwindled to become the exemplars of internationally revered high art. From their function as oral externalization of the tensions within their own culture, they have shrunk to be sacred written texts. (Hawkes, 1986: 86)

How right he was. And how topsy-turvy had the world of cultural politics become. For here was a prominent professor of English praising popular culture and using words like 'dwindled' and 'shrunk' to describe its canonisation into high art.

But his suspicion of international reverence for sacralised 'holy writ' was right on the money. The 'Shakespeare effect' eventually reached the *Harvard Business Review* (HBR), normally a focused and sober journal of 'executive education' from the Harvard Graduate School of Business. But in May 2001 it featured an interview with literary critic Harold Bloom, under the title of 'A Reading List for Bill Gates – and You' (*HBR*, 2001). The list contained but four items (though of course one of them included quite a few unnamed sub-items; plays, poems and the like):

- **Shakespeare**: complete works,
- **Cervantes**: *Don Quixote*,
- **Emerson**: *Essays* (six were named),
- **Freud**: *Psychopathology of Everyday Life*.

For Shakespeare, Bloom was in full reverential mode:

Everything we could possibly want to know about ourselves we can find in Shakespeare. He invented himself so brilliantly that he invents all the rest of us. He is at once the best, the most original, the strongest cognitive and aesthetic writer there has ever been, in any language. And yet he's also an entertainer. (*HBR*: 64)

Worried that not all executives would get Shakespeare in quite this way, *HBR* asked Bloom a pertinent question:

HBR: To learn from literature, it seems as if you must be a 'good' reader. Yet not everyone can recognize in Shakespeare or Cervantes what you see. What can you tell our readers about how to read well?
Bloom: There's no single right way to read well. . . . I do, however, believe it is possible to teach people to read better, and that's ultimately by measuring one work against another, though the judgement is probably best left implicit. Nowadays, the best standard for making these judgements is Shakespeare. There is no other standard really available to us in English. (*HBR*, 65)

The logic of that dialogue was: Question: How to 'read Shakespeare well'? Answer: Read Shakespeare. What Bill Gates made of this lazy tautological advice was not recorded, but Bloom had not finished. He had views on popular culture too.

Popular art is certainly an extraordinary achievement. Unfortunately, there are no popular artists in the United States today. That's because the country has no sense of irony. . . . Great literature, by contrast, is nearly always ironic. Shakespeare was the master ironist of all times. (*HBR*: 66)

Apparently without irony, *Harvard Business Review* editor Suzy Wetlaufer ran an editorial in the same issue on this topic ('Open-Book Management, Revised'. *HBR*: 12). While it was generally supportive of Bloom, on the grounds that 'his reading list prompted more than the usual amount of debate among HBR's staff', it closed with this: 'I should add that some editors raised red flags for managers seeking edification through literature. In a word, they said, "Don't."'

'Because literature concerns itself with the ambiguities of the human condition, it stands as a threat to the vitality of the business executive, who must at all times maintain a bias towards action', explains executive editor Nick Carr, who happens to hold a master's in literature from Harvard. 'It is far safer to stick with throwaway thrillers, which at least provide a distraction from the stresses of the day. Forget the deep stuff. Read anything by Tom Clancey, Robert Ludlum, or Jeffrey Archer.' And while you're at it, read *HBR* too. (*HBR*: 12)

It seemed the culture wars were not over: Bloom wanted culture ethnically cleansed, as it were, of all but pure Shakespeare; the executive editor thought literature might affect the 'vitality' of decision-making people of action. Here was a banal form of the 'alienation' of high from popular culture: a literary critic not giving a damn about American business people's cultural specificity (whatever the question, the answer was Shakespeare) vs. an editor too concerned with that specificity (vitality, action, stress), with no faith in the 'deep stuff'.

The idea that there might be anything *in common* between Shakespeare and contemporary authors of popular fiction seemed to occur to neither side. Alfred Harbage's democratising insight of the 1940s had been forgotten. It will be recalled that Harbage wrote that Shakespeare 'was a quality writer for a quality audience. The great Shakespearian discovery was that quality extended vertically through the social scale, not horizontally at the upper genteel, economic and academic levels' (cited in Hall and Whannel, 1964: 66). With Bloom, 'quality' narrowed rather than broadened. Now there was no extension of it even horizontally between the 'economic' and 'academic' levels, never mind vertically between 'masses' and 'classes'. Harbage's heroic imaginative optimism about the national scope of popular Elizabethan theatre as 'a democratic institution in an intensely undemocratic age' (Harbage 1941: 11), had dwindled (using Hawkes's word) to the spectacle of a pissed-off literary critic using the name of Shakespeare to piss in Business's swimming pool.

This loss of faith in the democracy of quality represented the last gasp of the *struggle* school of thought. But Harbage's *democratisation* strand of thinking had nevertheless, and meanwhile, remained influential within cultural studies. As has been noted above, Hall and Whannel were clearly on the side of jazz as a popular but serious art, and they wrote too of new media where 'the fragmentation between popular and serious art is not yet complete (like the cinema)' (1964: 84–5). This strand of thinking, in other words, was still, despite misgivings about commercial or mass culture, willing to look for Shakespearean quality in the works – and the audiences – of popular culture.

'Cardiff School' cultural studies

An early proponent of this way of looking at things was S.L. Bethell, of University College Cardiff (later Cardiff University) during and after the Second World War. Incidentally, here was a direct line of intellectual filiation that has not been recorded in the standard cultural studies genealogies (but see Turner, 1990: 83). Bethell taught Moelwyn Merchant, who taught Terry Hawkes, who taught me. Bethell taught at Cardiff in the 1940s and 1950s, Terry Hawkes for virtually his whole career (mid-1950s to late 1990s), me in the twilight years of the twentieth century (1996–2000). Merchant taught at Exeter, though his connection to Cardiff was heartfelt. As for me, I thought it was a fitting recognition of the intellectual movements described in this chapter that I rejoined an English department where as a student I could not study what I was now appointed to profess.

But in fact the organisational entity didn't really bespeak much intellectual integration. Indeed, Hawkes himself had been horrified when Journalism arrived in the English department during a period of managerial restructuring that had justified amalgamating English, Philosophy, Linguistics, Communication and

Journalism on the grounds that they were all 'about writing'. His fears seemed well founded when an enterprising journalism student wrote a rather unflattering pen portrait of some of the critical luminaries in English (notably Catherine Belsey), which was prominently published by the *Mail on Sunday*, a middle-brow national tabloid newspaper, despite a number of professorial protestations about being interviewed under false pretences. By the time I arrived, the two sections were barely on speaking terms, and soon afterwards the unwieldy English department split. I headed a new School of Journalism, Media and Cultural Studies. Even this proved to be controversial – Kate Belsey and others argued that as a critical practice the name 'Cultural Studies' should not be used as an institutional title, and in any case it belonged in the Critical Theory section of English: the journos were welcome to their own school but would they kindly leave cultural studies where they had found it? In the event, cultural studies went with media and journalism, and some of its genealogy was lost. The new school professed cultural studies, but its official ancestor figure was not Bethell or Hawkes, who retired the same year; it was Tom Hopkinson, wartime Editor of *Picture Post* and first journalism professor at Cardiff, and indeed in the UK, in the 1970s. In this case cultural studies had migrated away from the imaginative textual system of modernity (literature), towards its realist textual system (journalism) (see Hartley, 1996).

In 1944 Bethell published *Shakespeare and the Popular Dramatic Tradition*. In it he propounded a new thesis, designed to counter the supremacy of classicism, rationalism, naturalism and realism in highbrow theatre since the Restoration. He proposed 'that a popular audience, uncontaminated by abstract and tendentious dramatic theory, will attend to several diverse aspects of a situation, simultaneously yet without confusion' (Bethell, 1944: 28). He called this the 'principle of multi-consciousness' (29). He explained the concept by reference to the popular drama of his own time, 'music-hall, pantomime, revue, and musical comedy, together with the average purely commercial Hollywood film' (24–5).

> Where the Victorian critic laughs, he must love; but a popular audience is never under this necessity. . . . The modern cinema-goer has a similar adaptability. . . . A pair of lovers steal away from the company, discover a convenient garden seat, and, after some preliminary conversation, break into a love-duet, to the accompaniment of an unseen orchestra. Even those little conversant with the etiquette of high society must be aware that this is an unusual method of proposing marriage. . . . In this instance, story is accepted as story, and song as song; simultaneously yet without confusion. (Bethell, 1944: 27–8)

The point of Bethell's argument was not simply to insist upon the technical niceties of theatrical performance in an era of Bradleyan psychological and scenic naturalism, nor to remind critics that Shakespeare's own audiences must needs have retained 'dual awareness of play-world and real world' (27). His argument was much more ambitious. He wanted to demonstrate that 'a flourishing drama is the epiphenomenon of a flourishing and organic national culture' (29).

The implication of such a claim, in the unprecedentedly belligerent 1940s, where national survival was not assured for all combatants, and where rationalist calculations were responsible for dehumanising policies including those that led to the Holocaust, not to mention carpet bombing by the Allies of mass civilian targets in Germany, was that nations had better attend to their drama if they valued their nationhood. In particular, the Arnoldian intellectual tradition that hated or despised the masses for their culture and sought to exclude them from national culture (as Carey argued) was courting much more serious disaster than its petty snobbishness seemed to indicate. The cultural exclusion of the popular masses was intrinsically a dehumanising gesture. To argue in the opposite direction from within the overall framework of mid-century intellectual assumptions was unusual, perhaps unique, but this was Bethell's project. He sought to explain what was needed for a national culture to 'flourish', and he found it not in intellectual culture but in the *popular dramatic tradition* itself. His urge was towards inclusiveness, to learn from popular audiences and arts.

Bethell argued that national culture had fractured during the 'cultural revolution' of the seventeenth century. The political Restoration of Charles II in 1660 masked a 'cultural cleavage' between the court and the 'nation' (Bethell, 1951: 100), which was thereby already beginning to take on the characteristic of excluded 'mass'. But as the age of reason took hold among 'court' and governmental circles, something of the 'flourishing national culture' remained in popular drama:

> As Heaven grew inaccessible, man shrank in importance. . . . Neo-classicism next gave way to naturalism; the last citadel of human dignity fell before the march of mind; and man became 'a poor, bare, forked animal' indeed, though with a complicated pre-natal history. Only the popular mind, as revealed in the popular theatre, preserved in crude melodrama something of the ancient wonder, and a sense that man is not himself an adequate cause of his own remarkable history. On this, if on anything, the future of the drama – as of any social decency – must ultimately depend. (Bethell, 1944: 83)

The 'future of the drama' and of 'social decency' alike, from this perspective, would depend on contemporary vehicles for the conveyance of 'multi-consciousness', of 'the ancient wonder', and of a sense of humanity's inadequacy as the cause of its own history. Bethell made much of the connection between contemporary cinema and Elizabethan drama. Movies were explicitly cast in the role of that hope for the future:

> The mixture of comic and tragic in Shakespeare is too obvious to require elucidation by modern instances, but it is interesting to observe that Hollywood preserves this aspect of the popular tradition. Passages of pure farce, stylised and non-naturalistic, still occur in quite serious drama; and devotees of the detective film (or the detective novel) will remember the impossibly comic and ineffective policeman who may

obtrude into scenes of violent death and sudden bereavement. This sort of thing is often censured by the film critics whose correct 'high seriousness' requires unity of tone. Any survival, however, in the slick world of commercial entertainment, at least suggests a hope that beneath the polished coating of *ersatz* art, genuine artistic qualities may lurk, perhaps to emerge in better times. (1944: 112)

This passage was published in 1944, towards the climax of the biggest armed conflict in world history, even though the villain of the piece still seemed to be '*ersatz* art' rather than buzz-bombs and mass destruction (coyly, Reverend Bethell went so far as to give bad art a German adjective). But more seriously Bethell, who was by and large a convinced Leavisite (T.S. Eliot wrote the introduction to his book), was nevertheless obliged by his own analysis to look for hope not in Shakespeare directly, but in his *audience*, and within the lowest forms of contemporary mass art. Hope came from the 'popular dramatic tradition' whose contemporary manifestation wasn't high modernist literature at all but the 'slick world of commercial entertainment'.

There wasn't long to wait – 'better times' were round the corner, and with them emerged, pretty much directly from the 'slick world of commercial entertainment', a new vehicle for popular drama, and thence a new hope for the future of a flourishing national culture. It was television.

Terence Hawkes was the first Shakespearean critic of any stature – perhaps the first of all, period – to claim in a serious way that television was 'a fundamentally dramatic medium and – dare I say it – a fundamentally Shakespearean one' (Hawkes, 1969: 125). In 1967 he wrote two articles, 'Stamp Out Live Theatre' and 'Drama in Camera', which started life as radio talks on the BBC Third Programme and were published to considerable controversy in its weekly magazine the *Listener* (1 June 1967: 711–12; and 8 June 1967: 743–4). They were reprinted with added material in his book *Shakespeare's Talking Animals* (Hawkes, 1973: 215–41). Citing Bethell directly on television and its audience's 'multiconsciousness' (221), Hawkes argued that television was the 'true heir' of Elizabethan theatre:

> [The Elizabethan theatre's] audiences, and its plays, were genuinely 'popular'; the result of an amalgam of the elements of the culture, and an artistically honest 'projection' of it. When that amalgam disintegrated, the 'universality' which can be felt in the plays vanished. . . . Its absence forcefully imposes itself when we place the plays of the Restoration beside those of the Elizabethan and Jacobean theatre. That theatre can never be reproduced, but its true heir in our culture can only be television. Television constitutes the only really 'national' theatre our society is likely to have. (1973: 231).

Hawkes thought that television's 'persistent omission from the realm of scholarly discussion and analysis . . . by now almost occasions embarrassment'. 'That television connects vitally, formatively, and numerically with our own society in ways that the theatre can no longer hope to match is a situation that mockingly devalues the standard academic disdain which the medium encounters' (1973: 4). He concluded that:

> Finally, to take a broader view, television serves, as all communal art does, to confront a society with itself. That may be said to be the ultimate purpose of drama. . . . For our society, in contrast to that of Elizabethan England, is a dispersed and diffracted one, in which unity tends rarely to be a felt actuality. The effect of television on such a society proves at once diagnostic and remedial. . . .Television's most significant quality, then, is also the one for which our society has most need. It manifests itself as the general ability to bring otherwise disparate entities together; to create unity; to impose wholeness on life. (240)

That approach to television concatenated directly into my first book, co-authored with John Fiske: *Reading Television* (Fiske and Hartley, 1978). Our book cited Bethell, Hawkes, and even Shakespeare, within its first few pages (13–16). It was published as one of the first four titles in the New Accents series, of which Terry Hawkes was general editor. It dubbed television 'bardic' (85–100). It was the first book-length treatment of television from a textual and cultural point of view. It was perhaps the only book of its time, in the UK at least (Horace Newcomb was doing similar things in the USA), to take TV as it found it, without seeking to pathologise its supposed effects. The book sought not to chastise TV on behalf of externally applied values, but instead tried to apply analytical techniques, derived from linguistics and semiotics as well as literary and social criticism, which would account for its cultural form and popular reach. It seemed to answer an analytical need: it sold strongly in the UK, USA and around the world, was still in print more than twenty years later, and had also been translated into Chinese, Croatian, Danish, Greek, Japanese, Polish and Romanian.

Liberating culture – liveness or television?

Raymond Williams was known in English departments less for his work in *New Left Review* than for his first book, *Drama from Ibsen to Eliot* (literary modernist theatre), published in 1952, and revised in 1968 to include *Drama from Ibsen to Brecht* (leftist modernist theatre) (Williams, 1968). Williams was appointed as King Edward VII Professor of Drama at Cambridge in 1974. In his inaugural lecture, 'Drama in a Dramatised Society', he made a Hawkesian connection between drama, society and television: 'most dramatic performances are now in film and television studios'. Through TV, 'drama, in quite new ways, is built into the rhythms of everyday life'. Analysing drama proved to be 'effective not only as a way of seeing certain aspects of society but as a way of getting through to some of the fundamental conventions which we group as society itself' (Williams, in O'Connor (ed), 1989: 11). It followed, of course, that to analyse television was to analyse 'society itself'.

Williams had in fact prefigured this move at the very end of *Drama from Ibsen to Brecht*. In 400 pages that book steadfastly held its gaze to the modernist, literary, 'serious drama', written for minority theatre but perhaps more widely *read* than *attended* (certainly reading was Williams's own first encounter with it, on his return from wartime service in 1945; see Williams, 1968: 2). Film and television were never mentioned (nor were popular theatrical forms) until, in the last couple of pages, they emerged, almost as a *deus ex machina*, to resolve the 'difficulties' into which modernist naturalist theatre had got itself:

> In method, film and television offer certain real solutions to many of the recurrent problems of modern dramatic form, though in practice, in ordinary use, they often simply repeat some familiar deadlocks. At the same time, these potentially liberating media, which have already released certain newly mobile forms, are often, by habit, still treated as inferior. They may get audiences, but the important work, it is felt, is still in the culturally warranted form: the theatre, where drama happens, as opposed to film and television, where entertainment happens. I do not know any real country in which this comparison can be seriously made. . . . As a cultural convention, however, the contrast persists. (Williams, 1968: 399–400)

Williams signed off from modernist literary drama with a promise: 'I shall try, in a later essay, to connect the history of modern drama, in its theatrical forms, with the already major achievement of modern film drama, and the already interesting achievement of television drama' (1968: 401). That attempt bore fruit not only in 'Drama in a Dramatised Society', (in O'Connor, 1989), but also in Williams's book *Television: Technology and Cultural Form*, both of which were published in 1974.

But just as Williams was penning the last pages of *Drama from Ibsen to Brecht* in 1968, that year of imagined revolutions, Terence Hawkes was getting what was coming to him. The blast came from Kenneth Tynan, firebrand critic for the *Observer* (9 June 1968), who denounced Hawkes's views on live theatre as published in the *Listener* of the previous year (see above). Apparently Hawkes had neglected the revolutionary potential of the 'living event'; the 'dangerous electricity' of live performance that even dictators feared. Speaking the following month (July 1968) at a conference in Canada, Hawkes allowed himself the luxury of a reply (Hawkes, 1969: 124–5). He noted that the latest theatrical productions – as evidenced by theatre criticism in the *Observer* alongside Tynan's piece – were '*Hedda Gabler* (1890), Galsworthy's *The Foundations* (1917), Clifford Odet's *Golden Boy* (1937, with music added) and Ivor Novello's *The Dancing Years* (1939)'. Commented Hawkes:

> I will accept that these works do in fact constitute the 'living events' that can create a 'dangerous electricity' in the experience of . . . Tynan and others of our well-bred revolutionaries. No doubt such things disturb and astonish them. But perhaps we ought to consider the possibility that large numbers of people find a more adequate and disturbing contact with living events through another kind of electricity. In the week that the London theatres shuddered under the impact of *The Dancing Years*, millions whose fate had denied them contact with such living events saw Robert Kennedy murdered, the latest act in a tragedy of truly Shakespearean proportions, before their eyes, in their 'living' rooms, on television. (Hawkes, 1969: 125)

The intellectual 'habit' of denigrating popular culture and mass media was seriously damaging to intellectual credibility. Kenneth Tynan's defence of live theatre, like Harold Bloom's defence of Shakespeare, looked risible and bathetic when compared with the much larger contemporary culture that they couldn't see right under the noses down which they looked. As John Carey later argued:

> It is evident that for the majority of people television has immensely extended the opportunity for knowledge. It has also given the majority, in Britain at least, unprecedented access to traditional culture, not only through such star ventures as . . . the BBC Shakespeare series, but through countless everyday drama productions and documentaries. It is almost certainly true to say that thanks to television, the proportion of the British population that has actually seen drama performed is greater than in any previous age. Following this trend, 'culture' has made itself more widely available in other respects too. (Carey, 1992: 214)

This was just what lent most emotional force to the intellectual dislike of popular/mass media: they 'created an alternative culture which bypassed the intellectual and made him redundant' (Carey: 6).

However, there was a sting in the tail of this analysis for cultural studies, since it was just as much an heir to intellectual traditions as it was committed to serious exploration of mass or popular media. John Carey – not one to use tact when a well swung sock-full-of-sand to the temple would do – made the point:

> The new availability of culture through television and other popular media has driven intellectuals to evolve an anti-popular cultural mode that can reprocess all existing culture and take it out of the reach of the majority. This mode, variously called 'post-structuralism' or 'deconstruction' or just 'theory', began in the 1960s. . . . Whereas television must ensure that it can be understood by a wide and not necessarily highly educated audience, 'theory' must ensure that it cannot. (215)

In other words, cultural studies was in danger of repeating the same dehumanising, anti-popular manoeuvres that Carey had already castigated in the intelligentsia of the first half of the twentieth century.

But this was the same cultural studies that had learnt its poststructuralist ABC from a little primer called *Structuralism and Semiotics*, by none other than Terence Hawkes in his own New Accents series. Of course Hawkes was forewarned of the possibility that this might not go down well. The opening sentence of the book read: 'To the average speaker of English, terms such as "structure", "structuralist" and "structuralism" seem to have an abstract, complex, new-fangled and possibly French air about them: a condition traditionally offering uncontestable grounds for the profoundest mistrust'. Hawkes tried to sound reassuring: the concepts were 'not entirely alien to our trusted ways of thinking, nor did they spring, fully formed with horns and tail, out of the sulphurous Parisian atmosphere of the last decade' (Hawkes, 1977: 11).

In such a context, where new things needed to be said in new ways, and neither native intelligibility nor its Frenchified opposite was any guarantee of virtue (or its opposite), cultural studies could act as a *mediating* discourse between vernacular and intellectual cultures. Hawkes's book concluded with the view that structuralism was useful for exploring (in Jonathan Culler's words), 'the problems of articulating a world'. Hawkes wrote: 'How we articulate our world determines . . . how we arrive at what we call reality. There could be no more crucial objective for any discipline' (1977: 160). Far from dehumanising and excluding, this vision of intellectual work was 'mediating', like the media themselves.

Carey's enthusiastic denunciation of postmodernist intellectuals on the grounds that they had inherited the prejudices if not the project of their modernist forebears, was not without force. Cultural studies, like its literary and sociological neighbours, was by no means exempt from hatred of the mass. There was real *intellectual* work to do to emancipate intellectual 'articulations of the world' themselves from what had already been dubbed in 1968 by Williams the indefensible 'habit' of treating 'potentially liberating media' as 'inferior'. There was a default setting, as it were, which allowed each new intake of cultural activists to oppose, for no other reason than its popularity, the most popular form or mode of culture. More always meant worse.

But that was no reason to abandon the attempt to 'mediate'. Meaghan Morris, in fact, put this activity at the centre of cultural studies' long term agenda:

> Critics work primarily as mediators – writers, readers, image producers, teachers – in a socially as well as theoretically obscure zone of values, opinion, belief and emotion. If we can and do become involved in broader social and economic struggles, whatever political effectivity we might claim for *critical* work can be registered, most of the time, only by gradual shifts in what people take to be thinkable and do-able in relation to particular circumstances in time, place, and space. (Morris, 1998a: 226)

Perhaps as a result, Morris characterised as 'absurd' a habit inherited from the 'English' traditions examined in this chapter:

> All the same, it does seem hard for cultural studies as, let's say, an ethos, a collectively shaped disposition, to throw off the megalomaniacal idea inherited from 'English' that a training in reading can and does form a caste of total subjects . . . fit to administer a nation or even the world. Few critics would want to avow such an absurd aspiration. (Morris 1998a: 228)

Impossible to avow; hard to throw off. The reduction of 'reading well' from a *governmental* ('megalomaniacal') to a *media* ('mediating') practice was a long term project of cultural studies in its 'democratising' if not its 'struggle' guise. It was no more than a recognition that cultural studies lived in the 'obscure zone' of both teaching and values, both reading and emotion, both writing and belief. But it was also a recognition that the popular, mass media lived in the same zone. It required a 'gradual shift' not only in what people took to be 'thinkable and do-able', but also in what intellectuals thought about the media.

Meaghan Morris, like Bethell and Hawkes, found hope for the future in mass art. She wrote: 'The intellectual fantasy of control historically invested in van-guardist thinking about the future – the manifesto, the utopian programme, that great book to change the course of history – may itself become obsolete'. She went on:

> I quite like that idea. Classical utopian writing depresses me profoundly, and my idea of an empowering vision of the future is the ending of *Terminator 2: Judgment Day*. But I doubt that the future is quite as open as that wonderful film suggests with its affir-mation that freedom and responsibility are possible, not only in the fantasy futures by which we dream our opposition to regimes of grim necessity, but as real practices in the present of an indeterminate and unpredictable historical time. (1998a: 232)

There could hardly be a more 'classic' instance of mass, commercial art than Arnold Schwarzenegger's second *Terminator* movie. So what was 'wonderful' about James Cameron's box-office sensation of 1991? Was it, as the *Oxford History of World Cinema* (especially the chapter by Joseph Sartelle, 1996) surmised, because *Terminator 2: Judgment Day*:

- starred Arnold Schwarzenegger as **idol**: 'throughout most of the world, Hollywood film-makers and stars, such as Steven Spielberg and Arnold Schwarzenegger, have become the cultural idols of a generation' (Nowell-Smith, 1996: 483)?
- was directed by James Cameron as a 'machine-made box-office **blockbuster** star vehicle'?
- had 'extremely fast **pace** and its emphasis on **plot** over character' (516)?
- 'was **dark**, brutally and routinely **violent**, and preoccupied with issues of sheer survival'?
- 'played for both **comic and sentimental** effect the subplot in which the white male killing machine is re-educated to be a responsible, protective caretaker. But just when the Terminator has been reformed enough to under-stand why people cry, he insists that he must be destroyed if the world is to be saved. The film thus suggested that his identity was too closely tied to his origins as a killer; something which even sensitivity training could not over-come. In short, like so many films of its time, *Terminator* was a meditation on the problem of the white man'?
- was an ideological fantasy 'about the relationship of the **American nation** to the realities and implications of its own recent history'; 'on the one hand America's traumatic experience of defeat in Vietnam, and on the other by the emergence of newly militant demands by women and "minorities" (racial, ethnic, and sexual) for greater representation and equality at all levels of American society and culture'?
- starred Arnold Schwarzenegger as **camp mannerist**: 'Like Madonna, Schwarzenegger embodies the fantasy of success. This self-made man has literally crafted his own body to fit the appetites of the culture industry. . . .

Like Madonna, Schwarzenegger's charm derives in part from a self-mocking humour which in no way detracts from the appeal of his exaggerated masquerade of gender'?

- represented a 'more complicated response to **feminism**' as one of 'what might be called "women-with-guns" movies, such as *Aliens . . . Terminator 2, Blue Steel*, and *The Silence of the Lambs*,' which were 'meditations on the unstable nature of gender roles and identification in American culture during this period'?
- a 'festishization of the victim': 'even in movies like . . . the two *Terminator* films, in which the bodies of the male action heroes are fused with hard metal machinery, the narrative emphasizes the hero's capacity for **suffering**: he is shot, stabbed, crushed, dismembered, burned, or otherwise tortured' (Nowell-Smith, 1996: 514–22)?

It could only be concluded that something with so much potential for 'meditating' on the most important issues of personal, national, racial, gender and sexual identity currently in circulation, to which a popular and global audience could respond 'multi-consciously', was working for its society in the very way that Shakespeare's plays did for his.

3

'Beating the Whites with the Red Wedge'
From public service to dinner service (destination Kate Moss)

Cultural studies and art history

Cultural studies was a combination of ingredients. How they were mixed and processed to produce something new was a question of method. But method was itself controversial, since from the start cultural studies was regarded by proponents and critics alike as an avant-garde enterprise, which entailed that it was hard to accept any standardisation or codification of method. And the kind of work done by those with a literary training (see Chapters 1 and 2 above), differed markedly from what was done in social science contexts (see Chapters 4 and 5 below). Social sciences were more interested in methodology, and more likely to propose replicable research routines, often quantitatively based, while people from the arts and humanities were apt to rely on critique, the essay form, and one-off analytical performances.

There was debate about what counted as evidence, how it was collected, and whether it could be generalised. How to analyse spoken and written language, visual images, audio-visual sequences for their cultural meanings? How to produce evidence of 'causal sequence' (in Veblen's phrase) connecting the world of meaning with the world of power? How to bring to bear on those questions new theoretical, philosophical or political ideas, including Marxism, feminism, structuralism, poststructuralism, deconstruction, postmodernism, postcolonialism, globalisation (Lucy, 1997)? These were all significant and disputed issues.

Realism and constructivism

Even more fundamental doubts lurked around cultural studies, inherited not only from literary or social-scientific methodology, but also from *art*. These were questions about the nature of the *real*, and about the status of *knowledge*. What was the real, and how did you know? And who were *you* to ask? Such questions arose in a number of fields throughout the modern period. But as a practical methodological problem, no one had more at stake in the answers, and in the routes taken to seek them, than artists and art historians and critics. Indeed, 'modern' art – impressionism, constructivism, suprematism, futurism, cubism, surrealism, abstraction, Dada, minimalism and the rest – was a sustained methodological experiment (see Wolfe, 1999), dedicated at least in part to the question of how to address the question of the real, and whether it is even possible to 'represent' something in painting other than paint, especially during an era of photo-realism and motion pictures. Art criticism began to flourish as artists grappled with what were first and foremost philosophical and political questions, requiring an informed and sophisticated literacy on the part of viewers.

Thus art criticism was already a fully developed form of what later came to be called cultural studies long before the latter was even named. It had developed social as well as aesthetic criticism, as the important, impressive, and still accessible work of Arnold Hauser amply demonstrated in 1951 (1999: see especially the second volume, *Mannerism* and the fourth, *The 'Film Age'*). But one particular critic brought art and cultural criticism together, and politicised the issues at stake in those questions, for a popular readership. This was John Berger. Berger's *Ways of Seeing* (1972) was a BBC television series, accompanied by a book that went on to achieve wide and continuing prominence. Like other pioneering texts of cultural studies it was published by Penguin (in association with the BBC). Like them it combined attention to a canonical cultural form – fine art – with political passion in a good democratic cause, using enterprising publishing and in this case television itself, to address an ordinary lay readership, the better to teach them what was at stake in different 'ways of seeing', including their own:

> Seeing comes before words. The child looks and recognises before it can speak. But there is also another sense in which seeing comes before words. It is seeing which establishes our place in the surrounding world; we explain that world within words, but words can never undo the fact that we are surrounded by it. The relation between what we see and what we know is never settled (Berger, 1972: 7)

This was a foundational statement of the 'relativist' cause in contemporary cultural theory – the proposition that reality was constructed from the way(s) it was perceived, at both the individual and the epochal scale, rather than remaining fixed or unarguable and independent of its observation. Taken to extremes – almost always by scoffing opponents – this position eventually resulted in what was called 'irrealism', the contention that reality was an Alice in Wonderland affair, capable of being whatever 'we' decided, a postmodern world where 'anything goes' and therefore the rules of evidence were suspended.

None of these positions was in fact proposed by Berger (and rarely by others who argued that reality was constructed), but he did seek to politicise and disrupt perceptions that had become naturalised (e.g. about women's bodies) and reverential (e.g. about genius), to the point where art criticism had more than a whiff of religiosity – appreciation of the old masters had become a kind of secular worship. In fact *Ways of Seeing* was in part a polemical response to the series *Civilisation: A Personal View*, made by Kenneth (later Lord) Clark, that had been broadcast by the BBC a few seasons earlier in 1969. Clark was almost self-parodic in the effortless superiority of his patrician taste and judgement (he was an adviser to the monarchy on art). The religiosity of his vision consisted in his 'way of seeing' the Western canon as the foundation of values that he simply assumed were universal – his was a full-throated reaffirmation of the Arnoldian dictum that culture was 'the best that has been thought or said in the world'. Clark knew what was best, and why. His unruffled confidence certainly impressed his viewers, who even thirty-odd years later were converts to the cause: as a five-star consumer comment from Amazon.com put it:

> **Still the Prince of All Documentaries**. April 27 2002. Reviewer: richiesteinquist (see more about me) from Basking Ridge, NJ USA.
> Although there have been a number of very good documentaries over the last few years, with spectacular venues and budgets, the wonderful series 'Civilisation' still remains the benchmark for erudition and entertainment in documentaries with regard to history, culture and art.
> Make sure your children see this, if you wish them to be 'civilised', since it does not repeat on television anymore these days. This is a necessary framework to help them get the 'big picture' of the Western tradition which the schools are rarely able to accommodate anymore.
> A must see, again and again over the years. It reminds us of who we are, and how we have gotten here. (http://www.amazon.com, 'Civilisation Kenneth Clark', accessed May 2002)

John Berger was opposed to the use of art for 'reminding us of who we are and how we have gotten here', if by that was meant that 'we' were made by the Western values attributed to art by Lord Clark of *Civilisation*. Berger argued that 'who we are' was shaped more by:

- **religiosity**: art as icon, used by high priests (like Lord Clark) to instruct untutored populations (like TV audiences) what they should believe;
- **gender**: Berger was influential in popularising the idea that there was such a thing as the male 'gaze', especially in relation to the Nude in art;
- **possession**: Berger used Marxist analysis to draw attention to the commodity form of art and its economic value to the modern bourgeoisie;
- **publicity**: innovatively for an art critic, Berger included an analysis of the imagery of advertising, media and publicity as an intrinsic part of his study of 'ways of seeing', bringing contemporary popular culture into the purview of art criticism.

Berger's influence on cultural studies was enormous, not least because tapes of his TV series made superb teaching materials for hard-pressed college lecturers searching for audio-visual aids in classes about ideology. He also engaged in on-screen dialogue, promoting perhaps a more dialogic spirit among viewers (and students) about the provisional and arguable status of criticism itself. These were all innovations in method, because they allowed for the widespread extension of the practice of criticism, or critical 'reading' of non-word media, at a time when 'ideology critique' was taking hold in media and cultural studies both within and beyond the academy, in both teaching and activist contexts.

Thus the methodology inherited by cultural studies included a *constructivist* version largely imported from the visual arts, as well as a *realist* version more familiar in the social sciences.

- **Realists** sought to use scientific observation and empirical methods to ascertain objective information that existed independently of the investigator.
- **Constructivists** sought to show the constructed nature of the real – especially its socially constructed nature. For them, the thingyness of things was not an objective or natural fact, but expressive of some inner structure, or it was a highly contingent state achieved historically, and often expressive not of *nature* but of *power*.

Indeed, the deep structure that produced surface phenomena was increasingly thought to *be* power, variously defined, in sociological, Marxist, feminist or Foucauldian terms. Other candidates were also advanced, such as the universal structures of the human mind, as in structuralism derived from Lévi-Straussian anthropology and Saussurean linguistics. But the concept and analysis of power became central to cultural studies, not least because it was the object of study for both realists and constructivists. Realists found power in the ownership and control of modern corporations and government, while constructivists found it in language, ideology and discourse.

Indeed, both realist and constructivist positions were themselves recognisably *modernist*: one derived from scientific theory, the other from high modernist literary and visual art. Both were dedicated to a correct conceptualisation and understanding of the real. Scientific realism had its influence in the sociological and other social-science reaches of cultural studies, plus early semiotics (the 'science of signs') and some versions of Marxism (Althusser), as well as anthropology, both ethnographic and structural. But the constructivist method certainly attracted more attention if not notoriety to the field. Relativism, postmodernism, textualism and theoreticism all seemed to point *away* from engagement with the real, said the critics, towards an anything goes methodology where truth was abandoned.

However, the constructivist method originated in claims to a *superior* realism over mere naturalistic description. These methods were first developed by artists rather than critics, as will be discussed later in this chapter.

Recipes for success

Meanwhile, the notion of method implied also a more homely practice: working out a practical order in which to *do* things. This was the method of the recipe. Its association with domestic rather than political economy, and with practical skills rather than with theorised discourse, not to mention its gendered aspect, where it was feminised outside the world of celebrity chefs, meant for a long time that cooking enjoyed low prestige as a model for method in intellectual work in general. It was understood to be at the same level as artisanship, mechanical skills and craft. In the early modern period when methods of intellectual investigation were being thought through, such callings as that of cook or even chef were deemed to be unworthy of the gentlemen who pursued knowledge; they were servile not liberal arts.

It is only very recently that the humble cook was recognised for what she was: a 'knowledge entrepreneur' who made millions by 'selling her know-how' – not by selling cakes, but the recipes from which cakes could be made (Leadbeater, 1997: 28–36). Charles Leadbeater has argued that 'there is no better metaphor for the products of the knowledge economy than the recipe' (28). The recipe marked the shift from tacit, embedded, local knowledge (learning from Mum) to explicit, portable, global knowledge (learning from recipes); from the manufactured product (food) to the intangible economy (knowledge); from consumption that used up a product (eating) to consumption that transferred, replicated and reproduced knowledge (software). In short, the recipe is the emblem of the new economy – the economy that, as Leadbeater put it, has taken the world 'From Adam Smith to Delia Smith' (Leadbeater, 1997).

Because cultural products never were literally consumed but communicated and reproduced (unlike the products of agriculture and manufacturing), it may be that in the cultural sphere the new economy had a head start of a couple of centuries. Cultural products (plays, books, musical compositions), cultural pursuits (speaking, singing, telling stories), and cultural practices (communication, sense-making, meaningful relations), themselves required a different method to make their 'tacit' knowledge 'explicit'. This was the task of cultural studies; one that it has slowly and painfully developed over a long period. What to do with certain ingredients, in what order, for what practical outcome? These were questions for cultural studies too.

The intangible knowledge-commodity has attracted intense journalistic and policy-making attention recently not because it is new but because economic investment and analysis has caught up with it. Shakespeare was a 'knowledge entrepreneur'. His plays were 'recipes' for reproduction by others. But, as Leadbeater has pointed out:

> Know-how on its own is never enough to make money. What stands out about Delia Smith is not just the quality of her recipes but how well she packages and communicates them. Delia Smith's skill is to combine her know-how with the complementary assets and skills – marketing, branding and publishing – which she needs to make money from her idea. (Leadbeater, 1997: 33–4)

Like her American equivalent, Martha Stewart, Delia Smith made her multimillion pound fortune out of 'thin air', as did those who 'followed in her wake, like Rick Stein, Gary Rhodes, Nigel Slater and so on' (Leadbeater: 30). My own TV favourites included Antonio Carlucci (for his voice), Keith Floyd (for his troubled sense of self), and Rick Stein (for the sea, and Cornwall). Personally, as a consumer, I couldn't stand Delia Smith's series, but this misalliance of personal chemistry merely indicated that the culture of the knowledge entrepreneur was as important as their recipes and marketing. Their utility was more than the pro-vision of useful knowledge designed to assist self-help. They were also entertainers and personalities; the content they sold included themselves.

Perhaps the earliest cook to do all this, certainly in the English sphere, was Mrs Isabella Beeton. Her book of *Household Management*, first published in 1861, transformed tacit into explicit knowledge; her method took cooking from home-craft to a global knowledge-exchange. A recently republished version of the book claimed it as a 'great unread classic', although it was much read and uni-versally known in my childhood, largely in popular editions that filleted out the recipes from the management:

> A founding text of Victorian middle-class identity, *Household Management* is today one of the great unread classics. . . . Written when its author was only 22, it offered highly authoritative advice on subjects as diverse as fashion, child-care, animal hus-bandry, poisons, and the management of servants. To the modern reader expecting stuffy moralizing and watery vegetables, Beeton's book is a revelation: it ranges widely across the foods of Europe and beyond, actively embracing new foodstuffs and techniques, mixing domestic advice with discussions of science, religion, class, indus-trialism and gender roles. [Readership: Undergraduate and postgraduate courses in Victorian Literature, women writers, Cultural Studies, Victorian History, Food Science and Consumer Science.] (http://www.oup.co.uk/isbn/0–19–283345–6)

One example of how Mrs Beeton prefigured Delia Smith and Martha Stewart by more than a century was her exploitation of *globalisation* (often thought to be ultra-contemporary). Leadbeater made the salient point about the globalisation of knowledge:

> As our tastes have become more cosmopolitan so people have wanted to cook a much wider range of food. At bookshops we can buy in cookery know-how from Thailand, Korea, Tuscany and Australia. . . . The global market in cookery know-how provides us with a much wider range of expertise to draw upon. Globalization is good for our palates. (Leadbeater, 1997: 30)

Mrs Beeton and her publishers were certainly of that opinion. A new 1909 *Every-day Cookery* edition of her book included recipes from across Europe and around the Empire, so that 'those living under other skies' could share with household-ers at home the cuisine of India, South Africa, Canada and Australia. Among the recipes offered was this: '**PARROT PIE (Australian Recipe)**': Take '1 dozen paraqueets [*sic*] (a small, long-tailed tropical parrot). . . . Prepare the birds, and truss them like a quail or any other small bird. . .' it began. 'TIME. – 2½ hours. COST, uncertain' (Beeton, 1909: 533).

On *method*, Mrs Beeton advised the 'young housekeeper, cook, or whoever may be engaged in the important task of "getting ready" the dinner or other meal, to follow precisely the order in which the recipes are given. Thus, let them first place on their table all the **ingredients** necessary; then their **method** of preparation will be quickly and easily managed' (Mrs Beeton, 1909: 140).

The title of this chapter – 'Beating the Whites with the Red Wedge' – may then appear to refer to a method of preparing eggs. But in this context 'beating the whites' would be a mistake. *Whole* eggs could be *beaten*, as could the *yolks* – 'when beaten to a froth, they are a means of introducing a good deal of air into a mixture, and thus increase its lightness' (Beeton, 1909: 102). But for their part, *whites* were not beaten; they were *whipped*, or *whisked*. 'Success . . . depends largely upon the whites of the eggs being whisked to a proper degree of stiffness. When the eggs are fresh, all that is necessary to ensure this is careful separation from the yolks, the addition of a pinch of salt, and that the air whipped in is as cold as possible' (86). A couple of recipes from Mrs Beeton showed the difference:

> **EGG NOG (For Invalids).**
> INGREDIENTS. – 1 white of egg, 1 tablespoon of sherry or brandy, 1 tablespoonsful of cream, castor sugar to taste.
> METHOD. – Put the wine or brandy into a tumbler, add the cream and a little sugar, and mix well. *Whisk the white of egg* to a stiff froth, stir it lightly into the contents of the tumbler, and serve.
> TIME. – 5 minutes. COST, 5*d*.

> **EGG NOG, HOT (For Invalids).**
> INGREDIENTS. – The yolk of 1 egg, 1 pint of milk, 1 tablespoon of castor sugar, 1 tablespoonsful of brandy or whisky.
> METHOD. – *Beat the yolk of egg* and sugar well together, then stir in the brandy or whisky. Bring the milk to boiling point, then pour it over the mixed ingredients, stir well, and serve.
> TIME. – 10 minutes. AVERAGE COST, 6*d*.
> (Mrs Beeton, 1909: 346–7)

Method in cultural studies owed no direct debt to Mrs Beeton, although her practical advice was wise (get your ingredients laid out, do things in order, and the method would become clear). And the value of the recipe, of know-how and tacit knowledge, was to become much more important in the study of culture at the turn of the twenty-first century (see Leadbeater, 1997; Leadbeater and Oakley, 1999, and Chapter 5, below). In the meantime, at the turn of the twentieth century, other things were cooking that had a more direct influence on method in cultural studies. The ingredients were art, politics, philosophical modernisation, and theory. The method was revolution.

Constructivist art as politics

It so happened that the edition of Mrs Beeton that I had to hand when I wrote this chapter belonged to my colleague Elaine Harding. Like me, she remembered the book as a staple on everyone's bookshelf when she grew up in Brisbane, Australia, half a world away from where I did, and like many she kept her family copy (I think one of my sisters got ours). It was inscribed to one of Elaine's grandmothers thus:

> To Gertie
>   with love
>   from
>   Ben
> Feby. 19th 1917.

February 19, 1917, the day before my mother Dorothy was born, was witness to some stirring events on the other side of the world that also, briefly and bizarrely, featured cooks. 'Beating the whites' featured prominently too later on, but first, here's how *cooks* and *futurists* were seen as common ingredients that might rise to the top given the right revolutionary *method*:

> There is a story told by Mayakovsky's close friend, the poet Nikolai Aseev, just after the February Revolution of 1917, when they were walking together in the streets of Moscow. 'After February 1917, when all the fences were covered with election lists of the various parties aspiring to participation in the government, the old parties, whose names were well known, came to the fore nevertheless. But apart from them there were the cadets and the renovators, the anarchists and **the association of cooks**, and whoever wanted to play the game. One day Mayakovsky was walking with me in Nyeglinna Street, looking at the placards and lists, when suddenly he proposed that we make up our own list. What list? Well, one with the names of the futurists. . . . To my surprised question as to who would vote for us, Vladimir Mayakovsky replied thoughtfully, "Who knows? Times being what they are, one can even be elected president. . ."' (Woroszylski, 1972: 181, quoted in Railing, 2000: 16)

This story, set at a founding moment of the February Revolution in Russia in 1917 (i.e. not the Bolshevik coup of 7 November in the same year), showed how at times of rapid political change anything seemed possible. It showed how artists thought that their revolutionary spirit qualified them to *rule* ('be elected president. . .'), introducing the theme of artistic vision as a part of *government*. Indeed, the point of the anecdote was that Mayakovsky was prompted to make his proposition by the realisation that revolutionary artists – in this case the futurists – were at least as plausible as 'cadets', 'renovators' and 'associations of cooks'; and much more so than the 'old parties'. Here too were characteristically modernist elements: the city street as site of citizenship; the cityscape of posters, publicity and propaganda as political communication; these media addressing a vast but anonymous, untutored but sovereign crowd.

Who were the futurists? Why did they see artistic vision as part of government? And what was their method?

> The futurist poets and painters were, by their own definition, revolutionaries. They . . . were revolutionaries of language and a new poetry and painting, but that could come

only from a revolutionary spirit. . . . When the revolutionary days began in early 1917, artists of the Left – i.e., the futurists who were looking towards the Future and turning their backs on what they considered the dim and dismal Past of Right-wing reactionaries – were ready to move all their commitment into creating a new, more just, society. (Railing, 2000: 17)

Here were the *ingredients* for progressive social change, as served up by visual and verbal artists oriented to the future. Their method was sometimes called *constructivism*.

Among the best-known constructivist artists were El Lissitzky (who collaborated with Mayakovsky; see Mayakovsky, 2000) and Kasimir Malevich. In 1913, Malevich, who called his own art suprematism, painted the very last picture in the history of art. It was exhibited in 1915. Called *Black Square*, it was a black square painted on a white field. It was intended, Malevich said, to 'free art from the ballast of objectivity' – from the description of things; from figurative representation:

> This was the artistic equivalent of the political revolution which everyone knew was imminent. . . . It consciously marked the end of an epoch in art history. . . Malevich also wanted it to point towards a new kind of art in which representation was of no importance: it was not a painting of a square, it *was* a painted square, which is something quite different. (Whitford, 1987: 49)

In 1917–18, year of *the* Revolution, most influential political event of the twentieth century for good and ill (see also Hawkes, 1986), he did it again, even more radically, although, as Frank Whitford has pointed out, 'the gesture was so radical that it could not be repeatedly made' (51). This painting was *Suprematist Composition: White on White* (later acquired by the Museum of Modern Art, New York; see Figure 3.1 on p. 68). Here was a *white* square painted on a white field.

Painting could hardly get less representational of a superficial or naturalistic real. Malevich's constructivist colleague, the artist El Lissitzky, wrote:

> Malevich believed that with the square he had taken painting to the end of its path, brought it to zero. But when we explored our subsequent works, we said: yes, the path of painterly culture has, narrowing, come to the square, but on the far side a new culture begins to blossom. . . . And we realised that the new painting which grows out of us is no longer a picture. It describes nothing, but it *constructs* extensions . . . for the purpose of creating a system of *new composition* of the real world. To this new edifice we gave a new name: PROUN [*PROekt Utverzhdeniia Novogo*: Project for the Affirmation of the New]. (Lissitzky, quoted in Mansbach, 2000: 181)

Constructivism 'describes nothing', but constructed 'a system of new composition of the real world'. Its claim over 'the real world' was at its most militant in the very moment when that world, as a representational inventory of things that might be described empirically or even scientifically, disappeared.

The 'political theory behind Lissitzky's suprematist-constructivism' was described by the political scientist Barry Seldes thus:

The constructivist wings of the Soviet avant-garde sought to indicate to workers, long habituated to fatalism and to deference to established hierarchies and symbolic orders, that long-established forms and institutions were not given by God but were changeable. The constructivists would make built forms and structures transparent, show how things worked, offer new perspectives, and otherwise crack the physical, visual, and other cultural and aesthetic orthodoxies which sustained the old regime. Painted and printed surface, theatre, social club, apartment building, civic centre and factory design; town and suburban plan: all would become sites upon which to organise a democratic-collectivist sensibility. Workers would thus gain the confidence needed to exercise power within a vastly enlarged public sphere. (Seldes, 2000: 145)

How were the avant-garde to develop 'democratic-collectivist sensibility'? By what method? How could they extend *into* that 'vastly enlarged public sphere' the skills needed for 'public' duties like self-government, material advancement, modernisation of the spirit?

[Lissitzky's] purpose was not so much to charm students and viewers with sublime machine-age constructions as to teach them to experiment with composition, to arrange new elements along various axes, to rotate them to form new relationships, to chart linear and curvilinear movement, and thus to develop confidence in their own tactile and intellectual abilities to convert emptiness and chaos into order and certainty. (Seldes: 146)

Here was *method*: the use of 'visual language' itself to *teach* experimentation with disassembly, analysis, (re)construction. What for? To do the same with society; indeed, with the future: to analyse by dismemberment, getting rid of superfluous detail, to reveal the forces at work. Scientific understanding often required the destruction of the thing studied – the cadaver on the anatomy table, be it mouse or man, had to be destroyed in order for knowledge to advance (and of course the same might be said for cooking).

No more famous visualisation of this method – penetrate; disassemble; reconfigure; in the service of 'revolutionary spirit' – came forward than El Lissitzky's *Beat the Whites with the Red Wedge* ('Klinom krasnym bei belykh'; 1919–20). This was a poster not a painting, designed to exploit modern technologies of mass communication to reach the 'vastly enlarged public sphere' of the revolutionary classes of proletarians, peasants, intellectuals and communists. 'The Whites' were counter-revolutionary forces, backed up by Cossacks and foreign interventionist armies, and payrolled by the imperial governments of the West, who sought by military means to overthrow the Bolsheviks in the period 1919–21. So *Beat the Whites with the Red Wedge* had military as well as political and artistic overtones.

It used abstraction and constructivism as direct visual language. It communicated the relationship between the reds and the whites literally, as the penetration and destruction of the latter by the former. The poster showed the Red Wedge (Bolshevism) as dynamic, mobile and strong, though of smaller dimensions than the white circle. By visual and graphic means alone (plus some masculine psychology of perception, perhaps) it appeared to be irresistible.

Shape (triangle), colour (red), line (dynamic diagonals) and composition all seemed to require the forward movement of the wedge into the broken white circle, adding up to victory ('beat the whites') (see Figure 3.2).

Whatever its effect as propaganda (untested, as far as I know; audience research was nascent in the 1920s), the poster was certainly influential in the histories of art and of cultural studies – which were fused as one history at the outset of cultural studies in the work of John Berger, art historian and cultural critic. The Lissitzky poster was widely copied in commercial designs, and still frequently pops up as part of the clip art (the literate allusion, in other words) of visual literacy in design, advertising and political agit-prop. It bubbled away, its colours and shapes appropriated; here for a fashion spread, there for a poster supporting the workers in an industrial dispute; over there a stage backdrop for a film festival discussion forum. Author, politics, origin, message, all deleted; like light, it went in all directions equally. It became an empty signifier of . . . whatever was wanted (see Figure 3.3).

Figure 3.1 Kasimir Malevich – *Suprematist Composition: White on White* (1917–18)

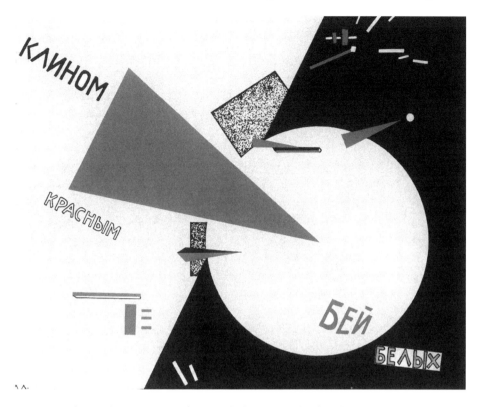

Figure 3.2 El Lissitzky – *Beat the Whites with the Red Wedge* (1919)

And its method – associating abstraction, visual language and avant-garde intellectual militancy with political renewal – was part of the essential baggage of cultural studies. For cultural studies too was engaged in a project of emancipation by 'affirming the new'. Just as the literary forebears of cultural studies were facing up to the difficulties of 'intellectual emancipation' for poor people and women especially so (see Chapter 1, above), in the visual arena too, cultural studies was faced with a disenfranchised population.

Fine art as politics

To understand why the exclusion of ordinary or common people from the domain of art, the republic of taste, might have seemed of sufficient importance to require a *military* solution, it is necessary to track backwards in time, from the Russian Revolution to the period when political modernity was newly established in the West. For the old regime that the constructivists sought to overthrow in art was an integral part of the *ancien régime* that ruled Europe politically until the storming of the Bastille on 14 July 1789 – a symbolic event that signalled the decisive and irrevocable irruption of 'the people' into

Figure 3.3 Advertisement for Esprit, *Hero* magazine Australia, 1986

history. It was a Tuesday, and it took about four hours. Political modernity was the stake, and as it turned out, the outcome – the slow, begrudged, hedged and occasionally defeated transfer of sovereignty from monarch to people. Debate about freedom raged throughout the eighteenth century in Europe; debate that periodically boiled over into rage more directly expressed. It also convulsed Britain's first empire in the Americas, resulting in the events of 1776 and the subsequent revolutionary war that established modernity's first non-hereditary republic. It ventilated the writings of Enlightenment philosophy throughout the century, especially in France; philosophy that was not confined to academic thinkers, but spilled over into journalism, gossip, insurrectionary propaganda and even pornography, all done in the service of exposing the corruption and unfitness to rule of the monarchy and its aristocratic hangers-on (see Darnton, 1997).

In England, a peculiar political compromise had been reached in 1688 that earned for its pragmatic accommodation of the interests of crown, land, commerce and Church the wonderful misnomer of the Glorious Revolution. Glorious it was not, but a revolution, in the long, English way, it may eventually prove to have been. Nevertheless, within the pragmatic English compromise remained ideological elements that barely changed in three hundred years. For instance, an aesthetic theory was developed to justify national and civic governance by a class that was not much wider than the scions of the aristocracy and gentry. It remained intact (though not unchallenged) at least until the latter part of the twentieth century, when it blossomed yet again, this time as popular instruction, in the form of Kenneth Clark's *Civilisation* series on television (discussed above). Clark's notion of civilisation – and the sense of *noblesse oblige* that went with it – was drawn directly from eighteenth-century aesthetic theorists such as the Earl of Shaftesbury.

Taking their cue from Aristotle and Plato, the aristocratic beneficiaries of the Glorious Revolution sought to square political theory with the realities of their own situation. Classical antecedent was helpful here, because although Athens was a republic during the most admired classical period, it was a republic in which only a minority were free citizens – excluded were women, slaves, minors and foreigners (people from other cities, even within Greece). In England after 1688, sovereignty had certainly been wrenched from the sovereign, but it had not devolved upon 'the people'. Instead, it rested with those who could demonstrate 'freedom'. Freedom was the exercise of *civic virtue*, not a human right; by no means could it be extended even to the mercantile or 'mechanical' classes of traders and artisans, never mind the 'labouring' classes or women. The exclusion from citizenship of all but men of independent means, and restriction of 'the public' to those who could govern because heritable land gave them leisure, was important for both politics and culture.

For *politics* it meant that extension of the franchise, even to include the newly powerful bourgeois class of capitalists and merchant venturers, was not regarded as a necessary or desirable step. The enfranchisement of male, middle-class property-owners in Britain had to wait nearly 150 years after glorious 1688, to the Reform Act of 1832 (workers waited until 1867; women and younger men to 1918).

For *culture* the Glorious Revolution cemented into public life, and thereafter into many still-extant institutions, a classical idea of the gulf between 'public service' and 'servility'. For instance, at the prestige public service end of the scale, the Royal Academy (whose summer show in Piccadilly became and has remained a major 'society' event) was founded in 1768. It did for *art* what the Royal Society had already begun to do for *science* since its foundation a century earlier (it was still worth a pay rise to be elected an FRS, in British universities at least, at the turn of the millennium). At the utilitarian, 'mechanical', end of the scale (here be *cooks*), 1754 saw the foundation by William Shipley of 'a Society instituted at London for the Encouragement of Arts, Manufactures & Commerce', later awarded a Royal prefix as the RSA. The division of 'art' into 'arts', and the need for *two* Royal institutions to encompass, but to separate, the 'fine' and the 'useful' arts, was indicative of a continuing hierarchy in which, in the 'republic of taste', some kinds of art remained more equal than others.

By this distinction, *freedom* was converted into 'class' terms, within what John Barrell called the 'republic of the fine arts, in which painters aspired to be citizens', and the 'republic of taste, where the consumers of the arts were imagined to be gathered' (Barrell, 1986: 13). Barrell traced the intellectual history of the idea of the public in these two 'republics'. It was founded (for painters and consumers alike) on a critical and persistent distinction between 'liberal citizens and unenfranchised mechanics'.

Painting was itself a 'mechanical' and technical practice in that artists were 'employed in converting the materials of nature into material artefacts' (Barrell, 1986: 12) – like a cook, turning *raw* materials into culture. This was a 'servile' action (like house-painting), not a 'liberal' art (like philosophy). But it was nevertheless possible to claim 'liberal' or gentlemanly status for painting:

> If it could be established that the materials of nature could be used to represent its ideal forms, and that it could 'address the imagination' . . . then it could be freely acknowledged that, when painting departed from its idealising function, to represent mere appearance and the merely particular, it did indeed become the *merely* imitative art, 'the poor child of poor parents' that Plato had described it as. It became, in short, a manual, not an intellectual activity; not a liberal but a 'servile' art, the art produced by a class of men who, because they perform 'bodily labour', are 'totally devoid of taste', 'incapable of thinking', unable to arrive at ideal conceptions of things, and so who hardly deserve 'to be called men' (Barrell: 14)

There were two consequences to this argument beyond its ostensible object of emancipating the public service branch of fine art painting (i.e. turning it from decoration to philosophy). One concerned method in cultural studies. The other concerned practice in politics.

First, *methodologically*, knowledge of 'mere appearance and the merely particular' was reduced to the status of 'manual activity', promoting instead what can only be described as *abstraction*. It took another two centuries before the visual content of fine-art paintings themselves was pared down to the minimal limits of abstract art – a process that Tom Wolfe has exposed to his usual acerbic but not unarguable wit in *The Painted Word* (1999). But a theory of representation was already in place to drive such a process of abstraction well before the movement of that name became visible:

> Painting's true function was to represent, not the accidental and irrational appearance of objects, but the idea, the substantial forms of things. Painting was thus a liberal art insofar as it was an intellectual activity, disinterested, concerned with objects which, because ideal, could not be possessed. (Barrell, 1986: 14)

Saving art from the taint of commercial or servile corruption simultaneously delivered it to theory. The distinction between an intellectual and a manual mode of practice was an important indicator of the longevity and the ambition of a trend still noticeable within cultural studies; a trend towards abstraction and theory. It was certainly evident in the radical constructivism of revolutionary artists such as El Lissitzky. It was the argument that abstraction, construction and good theory were *more* representative of the real – were a better *method* – than mere description or slavish adherence to the merely particular. Modernist science from the seventeenth century onwards was also engaged in abstraction and reduction, stripping away surface variety to reveal causal sequence in phenomena. In this respect the classical theory of painting was like science. But disdain for imitative or decorative arts – for copying rather than anatomising nature – found its counterpart in an equally jaundiced view of instrumental or descriptive sciences, especially any science dedicated to profit. From these ingredients, cultural studies inherited a methodological recipe of pursuing high modernist abstraction in the form of theory, mixed with an equal portion of suspicion for mere naturalistic empiricism in the quantitative sciences – e.g. sociology and its commercial sibling, audience research, and psychology and its commercial sibling, marketing.

Second, *practically*, the intellectual/manual, liberal/servile distinction provided yet further reasons for maintaining political control over mechanics:

> Because mechanical arts are concerned with *things*, with material objects, they do not offer the opportunity for exercising a generalising rationality. . . . We can sum up these beliefs by saying that, to the mechanic, the 'public' is invisible; and that is why, for Shaftesbury, the 'mere Vulgar of Mankind' cannot act virtuously out of public spirit, but only out of '*servile* Obedience'; and, to ensure that obedience, they 'often stand in need of such a rectifying Object as *the Gallows* before their Eyes'. (Barrell, 1986: 8; the internal quotation is from Lord Shaftesbury. See also Ian Hunter's contribution to Grossberg, et al., 1992: 359–61; and Lisanne Gibson's account of the growth of Mechanics' Institutes in colonial Australia, in Gibson, 2001: 11–27)

Thus in a certain sort of painting (heroic history painting), abstraction, idealisation and theory produced works designed to teach 'public virtue' to rulers, or to gentlemen capable of governing. Barrell pointed out that while the 'mere Vulgar of Mankind' were thought to stand in need of the gallows – and other 'rectifying objects' like penal Australia and the panopticon prison – to 'rectify' their deficiencies of vision, quite the reverse was thought to be true of the gentleman educated by the liberal arts into civic virtue. He quoted John Dennis: 'publick Virtue makes Compensation from all Faults but Crimes, and he who has this publick Virtue is not capable of Crimes' (Barrell: 19). As Tom Wolfe would have said: Beautiful! Well-nigh flawless! (But it remained forceful: this doctrine was the very reason why heads of state like Jacques Chirac could not be prosecuted for corruption while in office.)

Sir Joshua Reynolds sang to the same tune. Barrell argued that Reynolds's theoretical *Discourses on Art*, delivered in 1776 to the Royal Academy, were 'dedicated to an attempt to establish a public painting, whose function will be to confirm the audience for art as the members of a republic, or a community, of taste, and, by that means, to confirm their membership also of a political public' (Barrell: 70). The stakes, then, were high; this was an attempt not merely to associate 'virtue' and 'taste', but to make that association the qualification for government.

Capitalism and democratisation – art as antidote

This aristocratic association of liberal arts with unchallengeable rule was under-mined from within, for eventually the private interests of commercial capitalists and the rational philosophies of political economists like Adam Smith began to attenuate, then appropriate, the idea of public virtue. Barrell argued that although they were mostly polite about it, 'a mercantile class, relatively powerful econom-ically but, politically, relatively weak', came into increasing conflict with a 'ruling class which represented itself – from whatever various sources its wealth was in fact derived – as a landed élite, which had claimed for itself a virtual monopoly of the public spirit and public virtues which alone gave it a title to rule' (Barrell: 45).

The idea that self-interest or private interest might have been an acceptable motivator of public actions took a long time to gain any credence, despite the rise of capitalism. If Adam Smith's *Wealth of Nations* was right, and demand decided value, then citizenship of the 'republic of taste' itself would necessarily extend to consumers. Consumers exercised demand in the market. But con-sumers were not gentlemen schooled in abstract theory:

> [The main] objection to Smith is not that he has allowed self-interest to come out of the closet, and to announce itself as a legitimate component of human nature, but that he encourages the belief that the value of art is to be determined by 'the wants and caprices of the million', and not by those occupying 'the summits of civilization', and that this represents 'a political jacobinism, as unworthy of the liberal merchant as of the loyal citizen'. (Barrell: 50)

In short, any extension of *cultural* enfranchisement was 'jacobinism'. As the eighteenth century gave way to the nineteenth, and political modernity lurched forward once more on the streets of Paris, taste politics lagged behind. The idea of popular enfranchisement in matters of taste continued to be resisted; the more so in countries like Britain that were politically opposed to the French and had lost their first empire to republican America. 'The people' might be clam-ouring for sovereignty, but the idea that 'the mob' could lift its collective head above the level of its own sensual gratification to attend to government and public service on civic principles of educated taste was not understood to be pos-sible. One of the things that made it impossible was that the capricious millions could not do theory; could not (it was held) abstract public ideals from their pri-vate sensations. All they could manage were manual arts – woodwork and metalwork; shelves and fences.

In the end, the impossibility of reconciling public service based on the 'repub-lic of taste' with the industrial-strength public created by ever-widening political franchise and divisions of labour, meant that the 'republic of taste' separated from the political 'republic' (Barrell: 338). Painting shied away from noble por-traiture or classical subjects towards private portraiture or landscapes – depicting private property (Constable) or the visions of individual genius (J.M.W. Turner).

Meanwhile, useful toil prospered. A review of an early volume of the RSA's *Transactions*, published in the gentlemanly *European Magazine and London Review: Containing the Literature, History, Politics, Arts, Manners & Amusements of the Age* (by the Philological Society of London), brought out the tension between theory ('philosophy') and practice ('mechanics'):

> This is the *fifth* volume with which the Public has been favoured of the Transactions of this *respectable*, and, what is more, this *universally respected* body of – so to describe them – mechanico-philosophical patrons of useful industry, of laudable ingenuity.
>
> In the publication now before us . . . we find a variety of papers, fraught with information, novel as well as important, on subjects highly interesting to every nation that wishes to profit by a proficiency in the knowledge of mechanics. . . . While thus interesting to others, not a little honourable as well as interesting are they to ourselves, from the fresh proofs they exhibit of our superior talents as well as superior success in the wide-extended circles of scientific improvement. (*European Magazine*, 13 January 1788: 26–9)

Barrell's work has alerted the reader to the import of such words as 'mechanical', 'useful' and even 'ingenuity' in this period. There was the hint of a slightly raised supercilious eyebrow in a review where it was thought necessary to insist at such length on the 'respectability' and 'honour' of a level of knowledge that nevertheless brought 'profit' and 'success' to the 'nation'.

But at the same time, it was significant that the reviewer struggled to compensate for the almost inevitable sneer associated with 'laudable ingenuity', 'useful industry', the 'knowledge of mechanics', even while the tautology of the term 'mechanico-philosophical' was wittily played upon for the amusement of gentle readers. Whatever affront to gentlemanly sensibilities may have been caused by crashing 'mechanico-' into 'philosophical' knowledge ('base' metal into gold, as it were), it seemed that it could no longer simply be dismissed as 'servile' – it had become 'highly interesting' and 'not a little honourable'.

And so the Philological Society of London allowed itself to be instructed on, among other novelties, the wonders of mangel wurzels, the efficacy of drilling rather than broadcasting seed, the advantages of painting with wax rather than with oils, and the breeding of silkworms in England.

The discursive struggle between 'liberal' and 'useful' understandings of culture persisted. A 'liberal' (as in 'liberal arts') disdain for commerce grew rather than retreated as the market economy flourished through the nineteenth and twentieth centuries. It took the form of an opposition between 'civilisation' and 'capitalism' that characterised the literary tradition associated with Matthew Arnold, F.R. Leavis, T.S. Eliot and others (see Chapter 2). In this tradition, capitalism was considered the 'bad object' as much for its assault on the *ancien régime* of *taste* as for the impact of its astonishing productive/destructive energy on labour, landscape and lives. Cultural-intellectual work *comprised* creating a chalk-and-cheese distinction between 'taste' and commercial consumerism. The purpose of public writing about culture was to persuade the public at large to oppose the very forces that produced them as workers, consumers, subjects. The definitive statement was Leavisite:

> The school training of literary taste does indeed look a forlorn enterprise. Yet if one is to believe in education at all, one must believe that something worth doing can be done. And if one is to believe in anything, one must believe in education. We cannot, as we might in a healthy state of culture, leave the citizen to be formed unconsciously by his environment; if anything like a worthy idea of satisfactory living is to be saved, he must be trained to discriminate and resist. (Leavis and Thompson, 1933: 3–4.)

Here was a strange beast: universal state education was to be used to 'train' the mass population brought into being by commercial capitalism to 'resist' its own culture in the name of 'taste'. So far, perhaps, so good; but the Leavisite vision of 'a worthy idea of satisfactory living' was founded firmly on the principles identified by John Barrell (above) as 'civic humanism'. This same tradition saw the mass as a mob, commerce as servility, and capitalism as a threat to good government. Its aristocratic insistence on the formation of 'taste' by leisured gentlemen *was* the 'worthy idea of satisfactory living' that Leavis and his scrutineers wanted to be 'saved'. Thus, the 'training of literary taste' was, literally, *noblesse oblige*. Sir Arthur Quiller-Couch, addressing the students of English literature at Cambridge University in 1913, exhorted them thus:

> Since of high breeding is begotten (as most of us believe) a disposition to high thoughts, high deeds; since to have it and be modestly conscious of it is to carry within us a faithful monitor persuading us to whatsoever in conduct is gentle, honourable, of good repute, and so silently dissuading us from base thoughts, low ends, ignoble gains; seeing, moreover, that a man will often do more to match his father's virtue than he would to improve himself; I shall endeavour . . . to scour that spur of ancestry and present it to you as so bright and sharp an incentive that you, who read English Literature and practise writing here in Cambridge, shall not pass out from her insensible of the dignity of your studies, or without pride or remorse according as you have interpreted in practice the motto, *Noblesse oblige*. (Quiller-Couch, 1946: 102)

The language of the Glorious Revolution – 'gentle', 'honourable', 'repute', 'base', 'low', 'ignoble gains', 'virtue', 'ancestry', 'dignity' – remained absolutely rock solid in Quiller-Couch's aristocratic prose of 1913. Indeed that was what worried him: how to emancipate the poor into that culture?

Nor did the subsequent modernising fury of the Russian Revolution and two world wars entirely wash away the language of civic humanism. Writing in 1952, F.R. Leavis made the same claim for literature that the civic humanists of the early eighteenth century were making for art; namely, its *abstraction*:

> Without the sensitizing familiarity with the subtleties of language, and the insight into the relations between abstract or generalizing thought and the concrete of human experience, that the trained frequentation of literature alone can bring, the thinking

that attends social and political studies will not have the edge and force it should. (Leavis, 1952: 194)

The formation of taste in commercial democracies, then, was held by the best authorities to be neither a matter for commerce, nor for democracy, but for 'noblesse oblige' applied to reading, as taught to the compulsorily schooled children of artisans, merchants, 'mechanics', servants, agricultural labourers, factory-workers and the rest. For such folk, the ingredients of art and literature were not so much recipe as medicine – an astringent antidote to be applied to all those who'd over-imbibed of commercial, democratic culture. One of the places where they could go to take their medicine was television, where they might receive an eleven-hour inoculation in the form of Kenneth Clark's *Civilisation: A Personal View*.

A real, constructive method

This was where cultural studies came in. Through the work of John Berger and others it inherited the tension between futurist delight in the modern and liberal disdain for the commercial, and added to these an increasingly confident inter-est in the taste of popular culture itself. Something was needed to get beyond the armed stand-off among all these forces, to bring together the culture of cultiva-tion (silkworms and mangel-wurzels), the culture of liberally educated literary-artistic taste (Lord Clark), and the culture of capitalist consumption (mass media and mass entertainment). Bringing different ingredients together for the purpose of taste and consumption . . . sounds like a *recipe*. What better to signal the attempt to accommodate and reconcile opposing tendencies?

In 1990, just as the Soviet Union, whose future had been imagined so furi-ously by the futurists, suprematists and constructivists earlier in the century as the modernist antidote to the *ancien régime* of *noblesse oblige*, was itself collapsing under the weight of 'command bureaucracy' and Cold War arms race (Gorbachev, 1996), all these ingredients did in fact come together. They were 'cooked up' in an unknown and unsung wonder of cultural studies – a book by Marianne Saul with photographs by Johannes Booz, published in Berlin, called *Perestroika: The Dinner Party*.

In 1990 the Union of Soviet Socialist Republics was still the second most pow-erful state on earth. The Cold War was barely over. Mikhail Gorbachev judged it to have ended at the Malta summit, on board the *Maksim Gorky*, 2–4 December 1989. He wrote 'The Malta summit convinced me that we had finally crossed the Rubicon. . . . It took us some time to comprehend fully the significance of what had happened. . . . The Malta summit had drawn the curtain on the Cold War, although we would still have to live with its difficult legacy' (Gorbachev, 1996: 516). Nevertheless, the USSR was still armed to the teeth, and no one knew how elements within its 'command bureaucracy' or military might react to provocation. And political changes were occurring at breakneck speed, not only in the fifteen republics of the Soviet Union itself, but also in those under its sway, especially the Warsaw Pact countries in Eastern Europe.

Meanwhile, after the Berlin Wall was breached in November 1989, the German Democratic Republic (East Germany) had already effectively collapsed. German reunification occurred faster than anyone had predicted, on 3 October 1990. In that year, there was increasing turbulence in the Soviet republics in the Baltic and central Asia, leading to declarations of sovereignty by most of them. Soviet leader Mikhail Gorbachev was elected President of the Soviet Union (i.e. head of state, not just party leader), and he ended the Communist Party's 'leading role', confining the once-mighty Politburo to party officials with no role in governing the country. He also ended party control of the media during that year. Two further summits were held between Presidents Gorbachev and Bush. And Boris Yeltsin was elected President of the Russian parliament. Two weeks after the unification of Germany, Gorbachev was awarded the Nobel Peace Prize (Gorbachev, 1996: 707–9).

Into this atmosphere of risk, danger, hope, opportunity and general amazement, came a cookbook. It was a sort of 'futurist' manifesto for East–West co-operation at the level of ordinary people. Published by Benedikt Taschen, noted for its photography/pornography art list, there was no doubt that *Perestroika: The Dinner Party* was partly an art book (Figure 3.4). And its kitschy, good-humoured presentation of its subject matter was doubtless self-consciously jokey, in a very 'Berlin' kind of way – you know, camp *Cabaret*-style sensual indulgence in the teeth of political turbulence and potential disaster. But there was no question about the quality of the recipes, or the scrupulous, even 'German', precision of the *method*. Mrs Beeton herself would have approved of the meticulous attention to forward planning and timing of preparations, including snap-out cardboard shopping and activity lists for the days counting down to the party (wittily headed the 'Five Day Plan'), and a suggestion for how to make a table on which to serve the feast.

But more to the point, considering the date of publication (i.e. before the collapse of the Soviet Union), there was no reason to doubt the *project* of the book. Author Marianne Saul wrote:

> Friendship between East and West can be fostered in a variety of ways. The one in this book appeals directly to all our senses – especially the palate. Unlike other national cuisines, Russian cooking is almost totally unknown in the West. This is of course quite unjustified, as you will no doubt see for yourself, and it won't be long before the opening of the borders also includes the cultural aspect. (Saul, 1990: 6)

The eye-catching thing about *Perestroika: The Dinner Party* was that it was 'both more and less than an ordinary cookery book. Less because it only gives you nine dishes, more because it is the complete scenario for a long Russian evening for up to eight people' (6). Part of the 'complete scenario' was the provision of press-out stencil shapes, printed in red and black on white card, that 'quoted' El

Lissitzky's *Beat the Whites with the Red Wedge*, which thereby finally arrived at an appropriately culinary destination (Figures 3.5a and 3.5b).

> To provide a suitable atmosphere for the sumptuous eight-course meal described on the preceding pages, we will now give some suggestions how to decorate the room and the table. The best thing to do is to gather a group of friends and start decorating two or three days before the *perestroika* dinner party.
>
> Each wall can be decorated with some painted strips of pages from *Pravda*. With the detachable stencils in the cardboard section, this is quite an easy job. Put together in different sequences and painted with different colours, the stencils enable you to recreate the art of the Soviet avantgarde of the 1920s. (Saul: 57)

The plates too were painted white porcelain, 'inspired by a dinner service by Nicolai Suyetin in 1917'.

Perhaps allowing the slightest of supercilious smirks to play about their lips as they made suggestions for tablecloths, the organisers recommended: 'As paper table cloths are nothing unusual in the Soviet Union, you may like to use the appropriate material for the occasion and serve your *perestroika* dinner party on copies of the Soviet newspaper *Pravda* (which means "truth")' (59) (Figure 3.6 on p. 82). Then there was the 'dynamic table':

Figure 3.4 *Perestroika – The Dinner Party* (cover)

Figure 3.5a

> Our final suggestion is a very smart solution, although it involves rather a lot of work. It is based on Kasimir Malevich's painting *Dynamic Suprematism* of 1916 (Ludwig Museum, Cologne). You start off by cutting a white paper tablecloth so that it fits the table. Then copy the picture onto it, making sure that the geometric shapes are rendered as accurately as possible, using the same colours as on the *Pravda* strips. (63)

Naturally, improvisations were permissible. For instance, on their white paper, latter-day Suprematists were quite free to paint a *white* square, although the book itself was silent on this possibility.

This dinner party marked the emergence, perhaps the emancipation, of 'DIY' ('Do It Yourself') as a *method* in cultural studies:

- It promoted the knowing but good-hearted, literate but friendly, **cordialisation** of relations among parties with a long history of opposition and conflict.
- It was **voluntarist** – buy the book or not; do the party or not; include this or that dish, detail, design, or not.
- It demonstrated the definitive relocation of the **public** sphere into the realm of the **private**.

Figure 3.5b Two designs for table decorations *(Perestroika – The Dinner Party)*

- It elevated to **art** the culinary cultural practices previously thought 'servile' and 'mechanical'.
- It celebrated the **feminisation** of knowledge.
- It brought the militant **avant-garde** of the modernists into the **home** – part kitsch, part homage.
- It substituted **consumer** satisfaction for ideological purity.
- It was an example of the **new economy** of intangible knowledge – creating wealth by marketing recipe, not food.
- It **democratised** the 'republic of taste' with nine tasty dishes: kapusta (red cabbage salad), kvas (bread beer), baklazhannaya ikra (eggplant caviare), piroshki (pasties), solyanka and shchi (soups), kulebyaka (cabbage pie), sharlotka (trifle), bliny (pancakes), plov (rice).
- It **anonymised** democracy, suggesting that ordinary folk might take charge of the Party . . . by partying.

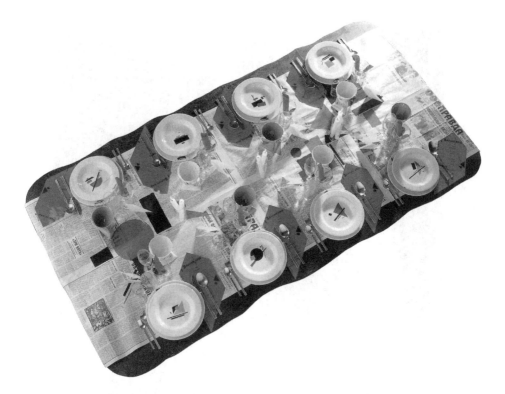

Figure 3.6 The Pravda Table (Perestroika – The Dinner Party)

Redactional society – editing the mix

Mixing existing ingredients to produce something new became such a feature of contemporary culture that it is possible to argue that this characterised the millennial era, in much the same way that 'criticism', from jazz to literature, succeeded nineteenth-century realism as the defining creative practice of the American century, as Hawkes argued (see Chapter 2). Originality now consisted in manipulating a philosophy of plenty – it was inclusive, even plagiarist, partnering users with artists and forms of the past or from elsewhere, rather than claiming modernist uniqueness as the criterion of innovation.

In the domain of recorded music, for instance, 'mixing' became the art form. Sampling, 'mash-ups', rap, tribute bands, Napster and the rise of the star DJ, were all phenomena that relied on bringing together existing materials to make something new, turning the act of choosing, editing, and customising into both art and enterprise.

In the domain of writing, journalism entered a phase when editing became more important for the profession than newsgathering. So much material was available directly to readers and consumers that mere provision of news (newly gathered knowledge) was no longer enough to justify the undertaking. The instantaneous availability of primary information on the Internet meant that the public utility and commercial future of journalism depended more than ever on choosing, editing and customising existing information for different consumers.

This was 'redaction' – the social function of editing. Redaction meant bringing materials together, mixing ingredients to make something new – a creative practice in its own right, and one that came increasingly to define the times. The word 'redactor' is Russian, German and French for 'editor', but the term has a history in the English language too. To 'redact' is:

> To bring (matter of reasoning or discourse) *into* or *to* a certain form; to put *together* in writing. To bring together *into* one body. To reduce (a person or thing) *to, into* a certain state, condition or action. In modern use: to draw up, frame (a statement, decree, etc.) (*OED*).

The term was imported into cultural studies from an obscure branch of theology called 'redaction criticism', which sought to discover the cultural presuppositions of the Gospel writers by examining how they edited their materials. An updated and secularised version of redaction criticism might, therefore, be an examination of how the editorial practices of news media revealed their presuppositions about their culture and various groups within it, enabling conclusions to be drawn about in the treatment of different identities, from business leaders and celebrities to foreigners and Indigenous youth (Hartley, 2000a).

A *'redactional society'* would thus be one in which editorial practices determined what was generally understood to be *true* (and what policies and beliefs should follow from that), and what was understood to be the contemporary equivalent of *beautiful* (e.g. innovative, artistic, entertaining, cool, original or strange). Such a scenario did indeed emerge out of the combination of late twentieth century economic and technical ingredients, including: the convergence and integration of IT, media and telecoms in the context of the new knowledge economy; the globalisation of media and entertainment content; and the beginnings of mass scale in the use of interactive communications technologies. Editorial practices were required to make the potentially overwhelming and chaotic possibilities of such plenitude into coherent packages for users, whether these were individuals, businesses or even nations.

Redactional journalism expanded most noticeably in non-news formats such as magazines. For instance, the democratisation of fashion accelerated in the late 1980s, led by magazines such as *Elle, Vogue, Harper's Bazaar* and *Marie Claire.* They used the device of the supermodel and the appeal of the existing form of couture to expand fashion to the high street and 'fashion literacy' to global readerships. Hard on their heels came the capture of male readers via the 'lad mags' (*Loaded*) and style bibles (*The Face*). The sexualisation of fashion models, not just in *Playboy* and the lad mags but also in the classiest titles from *Dazed & Confused* to *W*, contributed to their cross-over appeal and celebrity status. The success of retail phenomena from Calvin Klein to The Gap could not be explained without the expansion of fashion into everyday life. In turn that could not have occurred without a visually literate population who had become habituated to fashion's recipes and rhythms via redactive communicational media. In short, the commercial and socio-sexual attractiveness of magazine-mediated fashion became a primary location and driver of innovation in popular aesthetics.

The supermodel, and subsequently, celebrity fashion models more generally, were redactional figures. They wore – and they *were* – an 'edited' mix of available meanings. It was Kate Moss, Naomi Campbell, Elle Macpherson, Claudia Schiffer, Helena Christiansen, Christy Turlington, Cindy Crawford and Linda Evangelista (and their successors) whose beauty, bodies, style and A-List lives became the icon of the redactional society. The image of one supermodel, globally circulated via news, catwalk, paparazzi or fashion photography, summed up in an instant the 'mix' of fashion (successive renewals of look and style), personal identity (character and relationships as well as beauty or sexuality), branding (much more valuable than clothes) and celebrity (models became national as well as style icons, and 'modelled' clubs, music and rehab clinics as well as fashion).

The supermodel was commercially exploited as a siren of retail – and object of sexual – desire for men and women alike, attracting the attention and improving the knowledge of people far beyond the circle of those who would buy couture or even designer-label (diffusion) garments. She 'modelled' ensembles of contemporary experience as well as the look of the season.

This being so, and photographers being artists, fashion models were used for explorations of a much edgier kind – dark-side imaginings and fantasy scenarios that sometimes went well beyond the normal limits of the sayable. It wasn't just the perennial worries about heroin chic, 'anorexia' and under-age sexuality, but also the imagined worlds and meanings that top photographers and designers 'modelled' for the viewer. The implied narratives and scenarios in fashion shoots were often light-years away from the supposed sumptuousness of the fashion world, exploring very grown-up themes in sometimes quite testing environments (see Hartley and Lumby, 2002).

Indeed, *commercial* fashion photography was the undisputed avant-garde visual art of the era. Popular and elite aesthetics remained in touch with each other here, as they had not in either literature since Dickens or music since Elgar. The work of the most challenging as well as the most eminent artists was in the hands of millions, every month, for a few dollars or pounds. Ordinary consumers were tutored, tested, treated, troubled, transported and trashed by the very best practitioners in the world: Nick Knight, Corinne Day, Rankin, Craig McDean, Elaine Constantine, Inez van Lamsweerde and Vinoodh Matadin, Stephane Sednaoui, Juergen Teller, Mario Sorrenti, David Sims, Paolo Roversi, Peter Lindbergh, Ellen von Unwerth, Mario Testino, Steven Meisel, Bruce Weber, Sante D'Orazio, Thomas Schenck, Helmut Newton and Alice Springs, Guy Bourdin, Arthur Elgort, Bert Stern, Richard Avedon, Herb Ritts, Gilles Bensimon and others (see also Cotton, 2000).

Naturally, many artists, such as Tracey Emin, Jock Sturges, Nan Goldin, Barbara Kruger, Bettina Rhiems, Chen Yifei, even the Chapman brothers (and others), circulated their work *as* fashion photography, and fashion photographers worked outside fashion, often fuzzying the boundaries between fashion, art, pornography and documentary. Corinne Day's unmistakeable look turned up in English *Penthouse* (September 1997), while Bruce Weber documented a Welsh mining valley ('Never Alone: the Story of a Town, a Girl, a Factory and a Rugby Team') and the aristocratic Welsh-castle life of Lady Amanda Harlech ('Lady be Good!') *as* fashion spreads in successive issues of *Vogue Italia* (565 and 566, September and October 1997). By the turn of the twenty-first century Jock Sturges's and Bettina Rhiems's equally distinctive photographs of young girls began to surface *as* fashion photographs (*Rebel*). In another continent Chen Yifei transmogrified from hyper-realist oil painter to fashion entrepreneur with his imaginative and retail fusion of 'space, fashion, art, beauty, culture, technology', including *Vision* magazine, a model agency, interior design stores in Shanghai and New York, and a website (http://www.yifei.com/cn).

When the Tate Modern opened in London, British *Vogue* replaced its usual 'Point of View' fashion set with a feature on English model Kate Moss *as art*:

FASHION MEETS ART IN VOGUE THIS MONTH:
We celebrate these two powerful forces in twenty-first century culture.
(British *Vogue*, May 2000, 157)

Vogue invited British artists Gary Hume, Sarah Morris, Tracey Emin, Sam Taylor-Wood, Jake and Dinos Chapman and Marc Quinn to 'represent Moss in any way they choose', and added a new portrait of her by Nick Knight for good measure. The project turned out to be an exercise in cultural studies:

> If their work is, among other things, an exploration of how to present 'reality' in a different way, then Kate Moss is the perfect subject: the dream girl-next-door who became the emblem of 'real' beauty – through the extreme artifice of high-gloss fashion and air-brushed advertising photography (Picardie, 2000: 162).

The project explored 'hell', in the form of the Chapman brothers' latest work in a 'grim industrial estate off the Old Kent Road'; but, as journalist Justine Picardie reported from the scene, it 'ended with a reach towards heaven':

> Kate Moss is standing on the portico of St George's Church in Mayfair, a stone's throw away from Vogue House and Bond Street and just across the road from Sotheby's, thus neatly positioned right in the middle of the common ground between fashion and art. Kate, in a new-season Boudicca leather jacket, looks like she could be dressed for a fashion shoot; yet she's weeping for the sake of art – as directed by Sam Taylor-Wood, who is photographing Kate as a modern Madonna, eyes toward heaven and a perfect tear rolling down her porcelain cheek. (Picardie, 2000: 162)

It seemed that fashion could achieve transcendence where religion itself had faltered. It was just a matter of putting the right ingredients together. Despite the jacket, the main thing being promoted was the Britishness of the assembled artists, the model herself and the Tate Modern; extending even to the church where Kate Moss posed, named for England's patron Saint George, and the designer label she wore, named after the British warrior Boudicca (Boadicea), Queen of the Iceni. The sampling or mix of fashion, art, Englishness and the Virgin Mother was 'a compelling sight, and one that draws a small crowd within minutes':

> Southeby's staff gather on the pavement across the road alongside office clerks and wideboys, tourists and shop assistants. One man rushes over and presents Kate with a single pink rose, blushing as he does so, but most persistent of her admirers is a tramp. 'Look at my hands', he says, waving his grimy, bandaged fists at her. 'I need our beautiful lady to kiss them better . . .'.
>
> It's not clear whether he recognises Kate Moss as one of the most famous models in the world, or if he sees her as a miraculous Madonna, whether our girl is in fact Our Lady, this afternoon at least. But for Sam Taylor-Wood . . . 'Kate Moss is the cultural icon of our age, being represented as the ultimate icon'. (Picardie, 2000: 162)

These reflections on the iconicity of the age were a self-conscious attempt at sanctification through fashion. The scene was simultaneously 'democratised' by the characterisation of the onlookers as a Chaucerian group of latter-day pilgrims, marked by class distinction, lovelorn yearning, a pauper seeking a healing miracle, and a general devotion to 'our lady' among Southeby's staff, office clerks, wideboys, tourists, shop assistants and a tramp.

In the domain of art (even without a commission from *Vogue*), redaction and the fashion/art interface became the *subject* as well as the *method* of new artworks. A charismatic example is shown on the front cover of the present book, and once again the cover-girl is fashion model Kate Moss. But this is an artwork, called *Sacred Figures 1 – Kate Moss*, by Russian neo-Academist artist Olga Tobreluts (b. 1970). Her 'Sacred Figures' series also included re-workings of actor Leonardo di Caprio as Saint Sebastian, model Linda Evangelista as Elizabeth of Austria, and Naomi Campbell transported to imperial Venice.

Tobreluts posed Kate Moss as the suffering Madonna's erstwhile self, the Virgin Mary, on the brink of modernity: the portrait was based on a 1476 painting of the *Virgin Annunciate*, by Antonello da Messina. Messina was a Renaissance pioneer of the then new communications technology of oil painting (as opposed to the egg-emulsion or fresco media of the medieval era). In Tobreluts's picture, Moss's face artfully replaced the Virgin's. Her mouth was slightly open. She was discovered at her book of devotions, but on the page could be glimpsed only the word 'Calvin' (i.e. Klein, not the Reformation protestant John Calvin), and her eyes, unlike those of Messina's Virgin or Sam Taylor-Woods's weeping Madonna, were not demurely or spiritually averted but fixed on the viewer. Messina pioneered perspective and foreshortening, and Maria Annunziata's expressively posed hands were a marvel of realism in their time. Tobreluts drew attention back to them by adding a bee to the tip of one of the fingers. The bee was itself a medieval symbol of the Virgin, because bees were thought (following Aristotle, and like Mary) to be able to produce posterity without losing their virginity. Tobreluts used a redactional technique to bring together existing elements – portraits of Kate Moss and of the Annunciate Mary, the chaste bee and the 'Calvin' graphic – but she made of these something altogether new and strange, fusing contemporary iconography with the iconicity of religion (see Hartley and Lumby, 2002).

Her picture was also a form of cultural studies. It performed historical analysis in its own right – it employed the then new technology of computer art to fuse 'old master' oil painting techniques with modem art criticism, the medieval illuminated manuscript book of devotions with the fashion advertisement. The result was not a 'high culture' effect where the art of the past was used to reproach the media culture of the present, but almost the reverse – it was vision of the beauty and desirability of the icon of the Virgin in a secular era: an effect produced by the *art of redaction*.

Sacred Figures 1 – Kate Moss appeared in an exhibition called *Heaven* at the Liverpool Tate Gallery in 1999, popularising the theme of the fusion of fashion and the sublime, celebrity and the sacred, icons of fame and faith. When the exhibition opened, the *Observer* newspaper's *Life* magazine featured the Moss picture on its cover. In other words, redactional journalism did the publicity for redactional art. Tobreluts was quoted as saying that when art embraced abstraction at the beginning of the twentieth century, 'fashion and cinematography took over the theme of beauty, together with the hearts of many fans'. Journalist Gaby Wood commented: 'If art has lost us, then the icons we have now can bring us back to it' ('Idol worship'. *Observer (Life)*, 28 November 1999: 30–3). On a website presenting some of Tobreluts's other work, a commentator (possibly the artist) described how the fashion/art interface revived and energised both domains:

> Both initial images [of the model, and of the painting] reveal their natural peculiarities and get amplified as they acquire additional artistic energy that allows them to live another life and another series of adventures. This very possibility to activate classical art appropriated by museums and dissociated from the present and by the same act to endow contemporary existence silently soaring over TV screens with the energy of history – this possibility makes electronic art the main discovery of the 1990s. (http://www.digbody.spb.ru/to/mixeng.htm: accessed 18 June 2002)

In fact, art had escaped artists and art historians alike. Its heart had been won by popular and commercial culture, its beauty was in celebrity, fashion and the supermodel, its medium of choice was electronic – cinema, TV and the computer. The popular traditions continued the themes upon which Antonello da Messina had meditated at the birth of the modern era, and they used techniques that, like his, and like those of Russian constructivism, perestroika and neo-academism alike, were designed to force recognition of the real via what Australian art critic Robert Hughes (1991) had once called 'the shock of the new'. The philosophy of plenty was the theory; redaction the practice. Kate Moss was the inspiration; cultural studies the method. And the recipe? – The democratisation of the sublime.

'Priyatnovo appetita!'

4
Waiting for the Kettle to Boil
Culture and Consciousness (destination Celebration)

Cultural studies and political economy

Cultural studies was the study of the nexus linking consciousness and economy. It inherited this persistent preoccupation from Marxism, although it was always perhaps somewhat lopsided in its treatment of the two elements linked by that nexus. While devoted to the proposition that consciousness and economic forces were linked, cultural studies was evidently more comfortable with consciousness as a theoretical construct and as an object of study than it was with economics. Indeed, writing on consciousness, subjectivity, identity and personal experience became the speciality of early cultural studies. For its rather uneven attention to the economy it was (and continued to be) frequently chided by social scientists and socialist writers who saw the study of culture as subordinate to the analysis of economic forces (see Storey, 1999: 150–6, for a discussion of some of these criticisms).

In his essay 'Political Modes of Writing', Roland Barthes pointed out that Marxist writing operated with 'a lexicon as specialized and as functional as a technical vocabulary; even metaphors are here severely codified' (Barthes, 1967: 28–9)). One metaphor favoured by Marxists from Karl Marx onwards was drawn from simple physical chemistry to explain their idea of social change: the metaphor of the boiling kettle. As a kettle boils, the water in it changes slowly, literally by degrees, while the temperature rises. But at a certain point, quite suddenly, water changes into steam; the *quantitative* change in temperature results in a *qualitative* change in state. For Marxists, this notion applied directly to human society; qualitative societal change on the model of water changing to steam was 'revolution'.

The metaphor was used for instance by the Scottish Communist leader Willie Gallacher, one of two Communist Party MPs elected to the post-war British House of Commons, in his 1949 Penguin Special *The Case for Communism*:

> When this principle [water to steam] is applied to human society, it suggests that development takes place not only by a series of slow gradual changes, but that there are points in these slow, gradual changes where there is a jump, a 'revolutionary break', when there is a rapid change and a fundamental alteration in the character of society. Finally, dialectics shows us that development is the result of the

conflict of opposing tendencies, and that the 'revolutionary break' is the point at which the progressive tendency overcomes the old declining tendency. (Gallacher, 1949: 15–16)

In other words, for Marxists, revolution was a matter of physics – it was the 'inevitable' (i.e. in the end merely technical) outcome of social and historical 'laws' (Gallacher: 27, 31–2). But this qualitative change was determined in the economic sphere alone – it resulted not from people's ideas but from 'the opposing tendencies between social production of wealth and the individual ownership of the wealth' (Gallacher: 17, 30). The contradiction in capitalism expressed itself in class conflict between the capitalist and working classes. Therefore it followed that the 'revolutionary break' would result from class struggle, organised in the economic sphere itself – at the factory gate – by working-class organisations such as trade unions, co-operatives, socialist parties and workers' associations of various kinds. Only then could political and cultural transformation occur.

Why was the *economy* thought to take priority over *culture*?

Determination

Culture was seen as a *product* of the economy. This was the classic Marxist doctrine of causation, stating that productive economic activity in large-scale, complex, industrialised societies *determined* what people thought, not the other way round. In opposition to liberal or idealist philosophies which instated individual consciousness as the driving force of any society, Marxism stressed the importance of the economic base over the cultural superstructure in *determining* the 'ruling ideas' or ideology of any era. 'It is not the consciousness of men that determines their being, but, on the contrary, their social being that determines their consciousness' (Marx). Understanding culture required attention neither to the *subjective* ideas of the age, nor to creative works whether individual ('art') or mass ('entertainment'), but to the *objective* ('material') economic forces that were said (in the last instance) to *cause* such works.

This was in direct opposition to the culturalist position of Matthew Arnold (1869 – see Chapter 2), who wrote during roughly the same period as Engels (if not Marx). He launched English literary criticism on its own long university career by proclaiming that 'culture' was supreme over 'coal'. In other words, during the period when British imperial supremacy was sustained by the world's most advanced industrialisation and the world's most powerful navy, themselves both sustained by steam-coal, he attributed 'England's greatness' to the literary tradition of Shakespeare. Marxists refuted such idealism entirely. 'Culture', such as it was for most folk from miners and railway-workers to seamen and imperial armed forces, was determined by coal.

The culture industries

Culture itself was thought to be undergoing a process of commodification, becoming more highly capitalised. Meanings, experience, cultural pursuits and products were being transformed from the realm of human activities operating outside or independently of the economy, into highly capitalised commodities. This critique of modern life originated with the Frankfurt School (especially Theodor Adorno and Max Horkheimer) in the years after the First World War, and continued via successors such as Hannah Arendt and Hans Magnus Enzensberger (who called them the 'consciousness industries'). It became a staple of mainstream sociology. Meanings were thought to be generated not by common custom (via myriad anonymous interactions), nor by shaping artistic visions (via individual creative imagination), but by the intentions of profit-seeking corporations and associated power-seeking populists in the political sphere. What any given cultural product meant to any individual consumer mattered less than the overall organisation and power of the cultural industries themselves.

The original idea of the culture industries was developed during the ascendancy of Fascism in mid-twentieth-century Europe and the ensuing wars. Early writers saw the culture industries as vital components of mass manipulation and propaganda. They were held responsible for stopping dead in its tracks the historic process of epochal social transformation from capitalist to socialist society. This was because they rendered the supposedly vanguard masses into docile dopes or dupes; they distracted workers from their historic task (class struggle) with mindless entertainment – Hollywood being the main culprit and model. This was the 'dope' theory of the cultural industries, closely associated with Adorno, who held that popular music rendered its listeners passive.

Or, worse, the culture industries were said to be used directly for political manipulation, spreading both generalised pro-capitalist ideologies and more specific (and pernicious) propaganda messages. The main culprit and model here was the Minister for Propaganda in Nazi Germany, Josef Goebbels. This was the 'dupe' theory of the cultural industries. The theorist most concerned with the idea that the cultural industries were intrinsically Fascist because they could be used for demagogic purposes was Hannah Arendt.

Walter Benjamin also warned against the 'aestheticisation of politics'. Turning political action into a mass aesthetic/sporting media spectacle, a cross between the Nazi rallies at Nuremberg and the Olympic Games at Berlin in the 1930s, simply played into the hands of Fascism, and rendered 'mass' media for ever suspect. Later in the twentieth century the work of Hans Magnus Enzensberger (1976) updated the Frankfurt critique of the cultural industries in the light of the third world liberation struggles and the counter-cultural politics of the 1960s and 1970s, and in relation to expanding international media. Later still the Frankfurt position remained evident in both mainstream sociology and in the anti-globalisation movement, which held the media, entertainment, leisure and

sporting industries, by now integrated with fast food, fashion and consumer corporations, responsible for global inequalities.

Culture as a site of struggle

Even though economic determinism was rejected by many writers, it remained
as a kind of background assumption, especially for those working in the Marxist
tradition of the Frankfurt School, as well as in the political economy approach to
culture. For such writers, culture was interesting not in itself, but for its role in
social change. Did it impede the class struggle, as Adorno thought? Or could it
be the key to a new cultural struggle? Especially in Britain, where neither industrial agit-prop (agitation and propaganda) nor elective politics had delivered the
mass revolutionary consciousness that was necessary for qualitative change,
culture came to represent the best hope for a politics of radical rupture, most
notably in the work of Stuart Hall and his followers.

Culture came into increasingly central focus as a sphere of both analysis and
action in progressive politics. In other words, led by cultural studies (associated
with but by no means confined to the Birmingham Centre for Contemporary
Cultural Studies under Stuart Hall's directorship) the nexus between culture and
the economy was radically re-theorised.

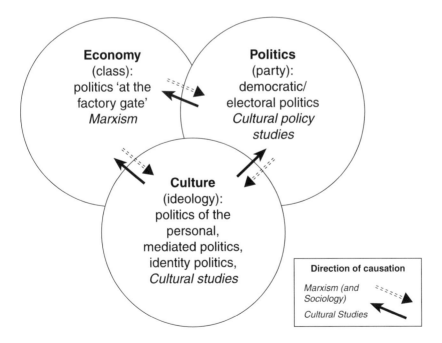

Figure 4.1 'Relative autonomy' among the economic, political and cultural spheres:
coexistence and dialogue, not causal sequence

Classic Marxist-derived models presumed that the causal flow was pretty well all one-way: the economic base caused superstructural phenomena, including ideas, consciousness and culture (see Figure 4.1). In such circumstances, it made sense to concentrate political activism at the factory gate – to mobilise the masses *as* economic agents, as the organised productive class. So convinced by this analysis were socialists from Marx onwards that they turned their backs on the elective political sphere altogether, seeing parliaments and the apparatus of normal government (the state) as just another weapon in the armoury of their class adversaries. But eventually reformist (keep heating the water) as opposed to revolutionary (hasten the change into steam) progressive parties were formed, and Marxist-derived politics moved into the elective–administrative sphere itself, either directly through communist parties, or conceptually via their contribution to the theoretical tool-kit of Labour and other socialist parties.

When neither mass organisation nor legitimate political action had delivered the decisive and qualitative social changes expected, attention turned eventually to culture. It was investigated both by those who maintained the classic Marxist analysis and simply wanted to know how culture was being used to deceive the masses, and by those who thought there might be more to it than that.

The idea of culture itself as a determinant of social change grew, and became especially associated with the events of 1968, where counter-cultural alternative lifestyles and insurrectionary politics coincided in Paris (May 1968), Chicago (the Democratic Party Convention) and London (the anti-Vietnam demonstration outside the American Embassy in Grosvenor Square). It seemed that culture might have relative autonomy from the economic and political spheres, and might itself have some determining effect on consciousness and therefore politics. Very gradually, the theoretical tide began to turn. The causal flow between consciousness and the economy was looked for as something that might move in the other direction as well – culture might be investigated as a *cause* rather than an *effect* of economic circumstances and political outcomes (Figure 4.1). It was therefore a suitable place for class struggle to occur.

This was where early British cultural studies came in. The Communist Party of Great Britain at this time (the late 1960s and the 1970s) was a political minnow. Socially its influence was negligible outside some important enclaves in London, Scotland and Wales (and some comrades among the grad students at the Birmingham Centre for Contemporary Cultural Studies). Politically the CPGB was a tough, no-nonsense workerist party with a Stalinist organisation, an unsophisticated theoretical apparatus – and a passionate love of the music and charisma of Paul Robeson (an African-American hero who did for his time what Muhammad Ali would do for a later generation, that is, combine popular appeal with radical political views). But the 1960s was an era of counter-cultural politics, mind expansion by drugs, music, media, the pill, social mobility and mass education, high levels of social unrest and industrial adversarialism, the strong state and the Vietnam War. Communism itself and Marxism more generally needed a theoretical make-over. Hall and his colleagues, and interlocutors outside the Birmingham Centre, were up for that.

They began to focus on the modernisation and revitalisation of Marxist analysis in their own publications (various books, the periodical *Working Papers in Cultural Studies* (*WPCS*) and their Occasional Papers series), in leftist periodicals (*Universities and Left Review* and *New Left Review*), and also in dialogue with other journals, such as *Screen* (semiotics and psychoanalysis) and *Media, Culture & Society* (political economy and sociology). The main theoretical achievement of the Centre and its intellectual allies was to produce sustained re-readings of Marx, especially via new interpretations of continental Marxist philosophy. In particular, they promoted the work of Antonio Gramsci (Italian Communist leader of the 1920s and 1930s, imprisoned by Mussolini's Fascists) and Louis Althusser (French communist philosopher) (see Gramsci, 1971; Althusser, 1969, 1971). These they used to reposition Marxist theory in Britain (although it should be noted that the writer who claimed to be the first to introduce Gramsci's concept of hegemony into English, in 1959, was the Welsh communist historian Gwyn Alf Williams). From Althusser came a reconceptualisation of ideology and subjectivity, and the concepts of interpellation and the 'ISAs' or Ideological State Apparatuses (one of which, for Althusser, was culture). From Gramsci came the concepts of hegemony and the national–popular, and new ideas on the state and the political role of intellectuals. This body of work was not only used to do basic theory, but also to introduce the study of culture, consciousness, media, entertainment, sport, style, fashion and music into the analysis of class antagonisms.

It became possible to ask (in a 'serious intellectual way', as Hall would put it) whether consumerism and personal consciousness might have political effectiveness. Lurking in the stylish but anti-social antics of subcultural tearaway youth were glimpsed new possibilities for political avant-gardism. This was an important part of early cultural studies, associated especially with the work of Dick Hebdige (Hebdige 1979, 1988), but actually commenced by Phil Cohen, a radical social worker whose study of working-class delinquency introduced the basic theme of subculture as the 'magical resolution' of class inequalities (Cohen, 1972: 23), in the same issue of *WPCS* where Paul Willis published a study of motorcycle subculture. Hall himself wrote a critique of the hippies ('The Hippies – an American "Moment"', issued by the Centre as Stencilled Occasional Paper no. 16). Bourgeois and white they may have been, but were they evidence for entirely new forms of politics based on lifestyle? Meanwhile, feminist writers, including those working at Birmingham, continued to show how the classic Marxist model of causation left women at the effect side of the nexus (see Women's Study Group, 1978). Feminism demonstrated strongly not only that the personal (consciousness) was political but also that women's experience challenged the very basis of political action organised around the factory gate.

False consciousness

Marx's famous observation that religion was merely a popular mind-numbing and pain-assuaging narcotic ('the opium of the people') had been anticipated by many decades in the writings of Thomas Paine. Tom Paine was herald of the American Revolution (with his pamphlet *Common Sense*) and harbinger of the long English one (with his *Rights of Man*), as well as being an elected Deputy of the National Assembly in France during its Revolution. *The Age of Reason* was in fact written while Paine was incarcerated in Paris during the Terror in 1793. In it the great practical political moderniser challenged the principal belief system underlying the *ancien régime*, the doctrine of Christian redemption itself.

Paine argued that the idea of Christ redeeming other people's sins by his crucifixion was a *pecuniary* idea – it derived from economic, not from moral criteria. It was like a benefactor paying off someone else's debt (still called 'redeeming' a debt) to release them from debtors' prison. It 'has for its basis an idea of pecuniary justice, and not that of moral justice'. For Paine, *moral* justice could not allow (Christ's) innocence to stand in for (humanity's) guilt 'even if the innocent would offer itself', because sacrificing an innocent person in place of guilty ones is the *negation* of moral justice. It amounted to double injustice, in that an innocent person was punished, and the guilty ones were not brought to justice at all (Paine, 1938: 22). 'Redemption' seemed to Paine to be explained not by divine but by strictly historical factors: it was nothing more than a 'theory' concocted by the early Church to insert itself as an intermediary between people and the divine, in order to produce not salvation but *income* (Paine, 1938: 21–3):

> The invention of purgatory, and of the releasing of souls therefrom by prayers bought of the Church with money; the selling of pardons, dispensations, and indulgences are revenue laws, without bearing that name or carrying that appearance. (Paine: 21)

It may be added that the Roman Catholic rule of priestly celibacy was also based on 'pecuniary' not moral or theological origins: it originated in a decree of the early medieval Church that was designed to stop the children of priests inheriting church property. It was therefore a fundamental plank in the long-term accrual of the Vatican's wealth. It came back to haunt that Church among others in the early twenty-first century, with revelations of widespread child sexual abuse by priests who couldn't cope with celibacy. It was noteworthy that so naturalised had the 'false consciousness' about the original purpose of celibacy become by then that public discussion never mentioned it, although it remained a 'pecuniary' matter to the last, as the Church manoeuvred uncomfortably between its own contrition for the sins of its fathers, and compensation lawyers for the victims of those fathers' crimes. In short, *institutionalised* religion had always to face 'pecuniary' as well as theological issues, for its own institutional survival. Tom Paine was among the first in the Christian West to argue – and to argue with a popular readership in mind – that in the end the religion itself was compromised by institutional imperatives.

All the elements of what was later to become Marxist 'historical materialism' were present in Paine (who by the way was a 'deist', not an atheist, seeing divinity in creation, not in religions). Challenging the 'ruling ideas of the age' – the legitimacy of the Christian religion – was achieved by showing the *economic* or 'pecuniary' advantages accruing to those who benefited from widespread belief in the ideas. Paine saw causation running not from what people believed but from what was in the economic interests of the socially predominant force: from the economy to consciousness. This insight was taken up and 'codified' (in Barthes's terms) in Marxist theorising.

Paine's (and Marx's) scepticism about the sources of consciousness was ambitious and daring in the early modern period. His scepticism, though not the legal jeopardy he put himself in for expressing it in published form, survived unscathed into early cultural studies. Raymond Williams was not the only writer to advise cultural analysts to ask of any cultural institution, practice or activity not only what it meant, but also 'who benefits?' This 'historical materialist' approach to culture sought to demonstrate how the most traditional, widespread and cherished beliefs could be explained in economic, not cultural terms. The implication was that culture was but an 'epiphenomenon' – a product of the interests of the 'ruling class' of the time. The 'ideologies' of Christianity and of divinely ordained monarchy suited the class system of the *ancien régime*. They were its 'consciousness'.

But modernity itself produced new class structures and antagonisms. Economic ascendancy shifted from land to capital. The economic interests of those who owned and controlled capital were thought therefore to determine the ideas of the new modern epoch of capitalism. It followed that the 'ruling ideas' of societies that had evolved to the capitalist mode of production were ideas that benefited the capitalist class.

Such ideas achieved their fullest and purest expression in the USA. Here the (capitalist) 'belief system' of individual freedom in the pursuit of private prosperity was most fully 'socialised'. And this was the origin of anti-Americanism in radical writing, including cultural studies. America became shorthand for corporate monopolistic capitalism. Belief in such 'American' values as *freedom, democracy, progress, technology, science, modernity* and *prosperity* came to seem like so much more 'false consciousness':

- **Freedom**: compromised by its negation in third world tinpot dictatorships supported by the USA;
- **Democracy**: negated by military and 'strong-state' force, and by international monopolistic corporate power;
- **Progress:** progress for some was poverty and prostitution for others;
- **Technology:** became a 'fix' rather than an agent of social transformation in favour of human values, and was as likely to be used for 'state terrorism' (e.g. in the Vietnam War) as for civic advancement;

- **Science:** militarised (Hiroshima) and commercialised (pharmaceuticals and agribusiness), more recently given over to ghoulish manipulations of nature (biosciences);
- **Modernity:** rendered horrific in death camps, and hollow in its promises to women (see Felski, 1995), racial and ethnic groups;
- **Prosperity:** the gap between rich and poor widened in the USA itself, while middle-of-the-road affluence in Seattle relied on sweatshops in Indonesia.

Such bleak diagnoses routinely 'forgot' the positive side of the ledger (for an antidote, see Evans, 1998); just as the triumphant rhetoric of 'free enterprise' neglected the 'human cost' side of economic expansion.

Waiting for the kettle to boil

Despite the organisation of industrial workers into unions and political parties, the 'inevitable' changes predicted by the Marxist model of class antagonism did not eventuate in the form of a 'revolutionary break', least of all in the USA. Following the Second World War, right up until the fall of the Berlin Wall in 1989, elective communist parties were strong in countries such as France and Italy. Industrial organisation did produce many advances for working people, often in the face of bitter opposition from employers, the state and law-enforcement agencies. But there was no general spontaneous 'qualitative' change of the kind predicted by the boiling kettle metaphor.

Indeed, in the countries where they most prominently held sway, communist parties had largely gained power by military force ('out of the barrel of a gun', in Mao Zedong's famous phrase). Where they achieved *electoral* success (e.g. Allende's Chile, Nicaragua, Angola, Mozambique), Marxist political parties tended to be attacked (and overthrown) by reactionary (military) forces, frequently assisted by American foreign policy. Communist governments, especially in Europe, quickly fell under the hegemonic sway of the USSR. In the context of both Stalinist command bureaucracies and the politico-military tensions of the Cold War, workers in the workers' states were clearly not in full control of their own destinies. The 'workers of the world' did not emancipate *themselves* in the way specified in the *Communist Manifesto*, which, as Engels had explained, insisted that 'the emancipation of the working class must be the act of the working class itself' (cited in Gallacher, 1949: 58).

However, the failure of the workers to step up to the historic destiny proposed for them and to impose the dictatorship of the proletariat was not merely a matter of otherwise revolutionary masses being prevented by coercion (see Hartley, 2000b: 3–4). Even in the very heartlands of modern capitalist industry – Britain, Scandinavia, Germany, France, Italy and pre-eminently the USA – communism did not take root universally as a popular philosophy. Nor was it a practical political alternative to the principal mass political parties that were dedicated to economic development and social reform.

In the context of critical intellectual work, however, Marxism's legacy remained profound; nowhere more so than in those branches of social inquiry that sought to link culture and the economy. Many concepts that came to seem taken for granted were directly borrowed from it. For instance:

- the persistence of the **base/superstructure** model of economic determinations (a model that didn't fit the new economy of interactive media at all snugly);
- continuing insistence on analysing **ownership and control** rather than *content* (reading off the ideology of media from knowledge of the identity of the CEO, for instance);
- the idea of the **primacy of production** over consumption; and almost total neglect of distribution (which in cultural industries and media systems, not to mention agribusiness, is primary);
- the idea that there were historically '**progressive**' and '**declining**' tendencies (e.g. Raymond Williams's notion of 'emergent' and 'residual' cultures);
- the widespread intellectual **suspicion of private enterprise** as opposed to state-owned businesses, often identified as 'public service' media for instance;
- the presumption that **corporations** and **consumers** were in an **adversarial relation** to each other;
- the idea that **revolutionary** breaks (between historical 'epochs') are either inevitable or necessary (resulting in suspicion of reformism within existing structures);
- the idea that **class antagonism** and struggle was the **motor of history**.

Culture as epiphenomenon (and utopia)

Classic Marxist analysis simply couldn't deal with culture as *determinant*. Its idea of culture was as a product, an *effect* of material causes located elsewhere in the industrial and political spheres:

> Socialism does not bring only an industrial and political transformation; it also brings a revolution in culture, ending the class and caste divisions and creating versatile individuals using their creative energies for the benefit of society. Only by transforming the material conditions of life, can man's spirit be free to rise above the daily scramble for existence. (Gallacher, 1949: 114)

But that 'free spirit' was nevertheless to be socially organised, along industrial lines. Gallacher predicted that:

> From being a nation of spectators we shall become a nation of participants in everything concerning life. . . . The Press, the cinema, and broadcasting will all be taken over

by the State, the newspapers will be controlled and run by the Trade Unions, Co-operatives and other socially useful organisations, films by workers, technicians and acting personnel, and broadcasting by the Government through a Board representing in the fullest sense the people of the country. Materials and equipment will be provided for local trade union, co-operative or other organisations set up by the people in the factories, armed forces or residential areas, so that they can organise the production of their own newspapers, film groups, drama societies, sports clubs, music, painting, or any other form of cultural activity. (Gallacher: 114)

This workers' utopia (surely it didn't persuade even party members? – so joyless and bereft of beauty was its idea of 'useful' culture, turning the world of symbol into glum amateurism) was contrasted with the status quo:

For [workers], culture is limited in the main to what big business has to offer at the cinema, or the capitalist Government in its broadcasting monopoly. They can be spectators at various forms of sporting events, such as football, cricket, and . . . at greyhounds or horse racing. Excellent public libraries exist, it is true, but guidance in the best use of books is sadly missing for literally millions of people. . . . Not human beings, but fragments of human beings are chiefly what our educational and cultural institutions aim to produce. (Gallacher: 112)

There was a certain flavour of Monty Python's 'What have the Romans ever done for us?' (*The Life of Brian*) about this rhetoric. Present-day advantages were always somehow flawed. The fact that broadcasting was already a state monopoly in the UK was dismissed because the government was 'capitalist' (it was a Labour government at the time); or 'excellent' libraries existed ('it is true'), but readers lacked guidance; or education occurred but produced only specialists – 'fragments of human beings'. As for the media and sport, they reduced workers to spectators and gamblers.

Nothing could be right till *everything* was – in the socialist state of the future, after the kettle boiled.

The 'D'-oh' theory of citizenship: dopes, dupes and dumbing-down?

It was believed that once working people understood the scientific basis of the Marxist analysis of historical and economic forces, political reforms would inevitably follow. The important thing for folk to understand was that socially organised economic forces created value and thence wealth, and the working or productive classes played a fundamental role in creating that value, but got to share little or none of the wealth. There was a division of labour between those who toiled, and those who enjoyed the fruits of that toil. In other words, Marxist theory thought that all of the surplus value generated by industrial methods of production was 'appropriated' – stolen – by the class of capitalists, and that once the more advanced and organised sections of the industrial workforce understood this they would do something about it. They would overcome this fundamental contradiction of capitalism (socialised production but individual ownership of its product) by 'socialising' capital, and if they cracked a few heads while they were about it, well so be it.

The failure in the UK of industrial and political activism to provoke or hasten mass social change under the leadership of communist parties eventually led to questions about what working people actually thought and believed. One of the first systematic inquiries into this question was the 'foundational' text of British cultural studies: Richard Hoggart's *The Uses of Literacy*. Stuart Hall was also preoccupied with the consciousness of young people. This was an interest he developed directly out of his political work as a Marxist activist. It became clear to him out on the stump that even straightforward political messages like 'Vote Labour!' – never mind Marxist theory and the forms of politics following from it – were hopelessly out of touch in the context of 1950s youth and suburban culture (Hall, 1959; see also Chapter 2 above; and see Hartley, 1992: 18–20).

War-generation Marxist theorists and communists like Willie Gallacher went little further than the doctrine of false consciousness to explain why people believed in ideas, supported parties, and engaged in activities that were at odds with their supposed objective interests. Marx himself for instance thought the doctrine of the divine right of monarchs to rule was merely the false consciousness of landed aristocrats whose *real* interests were in the maintenance of control over *ground rent* (Marx, *18th Brumaire*). In other words, their economic interests as landlords determined their ideological beliefs: in this case a theory of state legitimacy and succession protected their property rights and income.

As for the general population, including the working class, they were, it was thought, deceived by fables and doctrines that had grown up over millennia to account for blatant inequalities. Again, Willie Gallacher put the by now traditional Marxist view – non-revolutionary consciousness among the masses was the outcome of an unholy combination of *capitalist* propaganda and *labour leaders'* treachery:

> Consider what we are up against. There is the national press, with circulations going into many millions, with innumerable local papers, carrying the propaganda of the press Barons into almost every home. There is the B.B.C., the films and the Churches, all of which, in greater or less degree, put the case for present social relations and eagerly join in the clamour against the Communists. (Gallacher, 1949: 196)

In other words, the entire sphere of consciousness was for activists an explicitly *anti-communist* obstacle; culture was almost completely equated with propaganda and thence false consciousness. The 'case for present social relations' was being put by BBC radio – presumably 'clamouring against the Communists' in *It's That Man Again* and *The Goon Show*.

Meanwhile, the industrial and political spheres were lost to the cause by treachery:

> In Britain, the working class, deceived by the right-wing leaders of the Labour Party, are now awakening to the treachery of which they are the victims and are going into action to beat back the attack on their living standards and to put an end to the Government's policy of war. (Gallacher: 150)

Brave hope! This was the 'awakening' that resulted within another couple of years in the election of a Tory government. The Tories then held power in the UK for 35 of the ensuing 45 years, until their political hegemony was finally broken by the election of the Blair government in 1997, almost two generations later. Even this event was greeted with dismay on the intellectual Left, because Blair's can-do social democratic reformism was based on moral not ideological precepts.

It had become pretty obvious that by itself a reasoned, scientific and modern understanding of the economic basis of consciousness would not reform consciousness itself. The swift overthrow of religious, political and mythological superstitions would not occur by organising trade unions. So eventually it became clear that the realms of ideas and belief, information and knowledge, culture and custom, were not tied *directly* to the spheres of economics and politics. People didn't behave quite as their supposed class or historical interests said they should. Why not? Were they dupes? Dopes? Dumbed-down? Or was there something specific about the cultural field that needed to be understood before the desired political reform and social modernisation could successfully occur? Marxism's early modernist notion of false consciousness began to be revised, especially via the work of Gramsci, to take account of culture, language, the role of intellectuals, the nation, education – all previously neglected in Marxist theory as epiphenomena.

The decisive step was taken by Stuart Hall, writing in the *Universities and Left Review* (*ULR*) in 1959. This was a decade after Gallacher's book was published, and well into the first stint of that long period of Tory supremacy – but it was also a decade prior to Hall's assumption of the directorship of the Birmingham Centre. In answer to dogmatic sectarian socialists who had criticised his interest in style, culture, and even *advertising*, he commented:

> I do not anywhere suppose that we can read straight from advertising copy to the attitudes of working class people. . . . But the result *could* be, not a break-up of the class-system, . . . but a sense of confusion about what class *is* and how much it matters, and where 'class' allegiances lie. . . . In other words (this was my ideological point), the superstructure of ideas (in this case, false ideas, false consciousness) *is* going to affect directly the course of events. And if admission of this fact makes us reconsider some of the more primitive notions – still current – of *how* to interpret Marx's dictum that 'It is not the consciousness of men that determines their being, but, on the contrary, their social being that determines their consciousness', I, for one, can only say, 'Long Live the Revisionists'. (Hall, 1959: 51)

Hall was still quite willing to call what young people thought 'false consciousness', but he wanted to show how consciousness, false or otherwise, '*is* going to affect directly the course of events'. That became the project of the Birmingham Centre, and of important strands of cultural studies both elsewhere in the UK and in other countries, especially the USA, Canada and Australia.

Marxism moved from the political to the intellectual field. As Roland Barthes put it:

> The spreading influence of political and social facts into the field of literary consciousness has produced a new type of scriptor, halfway between the party member and the writer, deriving from the former an ideal image of committed man, and from the latter the notion that a written work is an act. (Barthes, 1967: 32)

Communism remained a potent force mostly in intellectual circles, as a theoretical narrative *about* modernity; a mode of writing that signified the writer's choice of commitment. Increasingly Western Marxism became associated with a critical rhetoric that saw itself as an *antidote* to modernity (just like its own early adversary, Arnoldian–Leavisite literary leftism, see Chapter 2), not its *completion*.

On 'not giving a damn' about popular culture

The materialist, if not Marxist, conceptualisation of history, together with a 'committed' mode of writing, persisted in many branches of social inquiry from sociology and anthropology to literary studies and even some versions of psychology. It persisted also in cultural studies, often in the form of dialogue or engagement with these other disciplines. No one working within the tradition of cultural studies thought that culture could be understood without recourse to some analysis of political economy, although intellectual and disciplinary specialism did make some writers – myself among them – leave the economic heavy lifting to others with more expertise.

Many important social, cultural and media analysts in the USA sought to show how commercial organisations and media did set the ideological agenda for modernising America. They ranged from C. Wright Mills and Edward Shils to Herbert Schiller (1989). Without espousing Marxism, either as a theoretical or a political template, they applied Marxist-derived critique, combined with an Enlightenment belief in political economy as a science of government, to the analysis of mass mediated meanings in mass societies. The interests perceived to be benefiting were corporations rather than a class, but the analysis nevertheless mirrored Marxism because it prioritised the interests and intentions of corporations over the meanings circulated within cultural systems (from advertising to entertainment), or the uses to which such products were popularly put. That is to say, they explained cultural products and practices by following the flow of revenue, and thus determining causality, back to the corporation, not the flow of communication or sense forward to the consumer.

In the USA this strand of (unmarked Marxist) critical thinking was branded as social science, although elements of history, psychology, literary criticism and a good dose of journalism were also prominent in the analysis. It remained a force within media analysis for many years, being part of the basic conceptual training kit for PhDs. It influenced writers as diverse as Vance Packard (a journalist), Marshall Sahlins (anthropologist), Herbert Gans, George Gerbner, James Carey, Elihu Katz, Todd Gitlin, Carolyn Marvin, Margaret Morse and Marjorie Ferguson. Few of these writers would have identified themselves as practitioners of cultural studies; indeed several were well-publicised opponents of certain tendencies within it (e.g. Gitlin, Carey, Ferguson – see especially Ferguson and Golding, 1997). Nevertheless, not only did cultural studies share many of its own disciplinary and theoretical antecedents with them, but the very dialogue of engagement, criticism and adjustment eventually became part of the warp and woof of cultural studies itself.

In the UK, the same concern with structural determinants of cultural phenomena became associated with an approach that went under the name of 'political economy'. It was made up largely of academics trained in social sciences and active in socialist politics, both party-political (e.g. James Curran's or Nicholas Garnham's work for the Labour Party and the Greater London Council), and theoretical (e.g. Murdock and Golding's successive contributions to *Socialist Register*).

Leading proponents of this approach included members of the Leicester University Centre for Media Research that was influential in and after the 1970s under the leadership of James Halloran. Graham Murdock, Peter Golding (see Golding and Murdock, 1997), Philip Elliott and Halloran himself were prominent in politicised critique of media, concentrating on issues of ownership and control (Murdock and Golding later decamped to Loughborough University where they continued the Leicester line). Other groups with similar agendas formed around James Curran at Goldsmiths College in London (see especially Curran and Seaton, 1987), and Nicholas Garnham at the Polytechnic of Central London (later Westminster University) (see especially Garnham, 1987). The Glasgow University Media Group under John Eldridge and later Greg Philo also favoured an economically determined model of society, while Jay Blumler led a group concentrating on political communication (election coverage) at the University of Leeds. Again, few of these writers would identify directly or simply with cultural studies – they were mostly media sociologists or experts in politics and journalism. But over the years, not least through the influential journal *Media, Culture & Society*, on whose board several were long-serving editors, their overall political economy approach to media power permeated the atmosphere breathed by anyone else working in the area, including those in cultural studies.

What they contributed to cultural studies *dialogically* was an insistence that the analysis of meaning must be interdisciplinary. It was no good spouting on about the content of mass media, especially television and the press, from an 'ahistorical' perspective, as some literary critics were wont to do when they analysed literary texts in isolation from the circumstances of their production. In particular, the question of who benefits from culturally ubiquitous media, and thence from the ubiquitous if not ruling ideas of the epoch, was reduced to a much simpler question – who owns and controls the media? Marxist-derived presumptions required that the answer to that question also revealed the location of the nexus linking economy and consciousness. The interests of the private companies and state bureaucracies that owned and controlled mass media in commercial democracies (to say nothing of undemocratic regimes with centralised power elites) were thought to explain the content of those media, and indeed popular culture in general.

This was however a *reduction* of the question about 'who benefits', since it allowed for no benefit at the 'consciousness' end of the nexus. The equation of 'ownership and control' with 'power', 'power' with 'economics', 'economics' with 'capitalists', and 'capitalists' with media moguls, meant that the requirement to analyse all the links in the cultural value chain from producer/distributor to consumer/user could all too easily be reduced to a fixation with individual corporations and their frequently demonised chief executives. Understanding the *Sun* meant investigating neither its content nor its readers, much less the cultural and historical context of popular politics to which it was a rude but exuberant heir, but Rupert Murdoch.

Ownership and *control* by these individuals, or in other instances by state bureaucracies (e.g. public broadcasting), was understood in the political economy approach to account for the *content* of popular media. Tracing the stream of revenue back from consumer to the ultimate pecuniary beneficiary was excellent sport, if nothing else, for media capitalists were often extremely colourful characters, frequently with political views wildly at odds with the supposed interests of the majority of their readers (rather like the medieval cardinals criticised by Tom Paine, perhaps). But it took the political economy approach further and further away from practical engagement with the consciousness side of the nexus between economy and consciousness. If everything within the cultural sphere was explained by something outside of it (everything in a newspaper explained by the identity of its owner), then the sphere of the cultural was of no interest.

As John Storey has pointed out, the political economy approach to culture shared with others a species of what he dubbed 'pessimistic elitism'.

> Cultural studies has always rejected the 'pessimistic elitism' which haunts so much work in cultural theory and analysis (I have in mind Leavisism, the Frankfurt School, most versions of structuralism, economistic versions of Marxism, political economy) which always seem to want to suggest that 'agency' is always overwhelmed by 'structure'; that cultural consumption is a mere shadow of production; that audience negotiations are fictions, merely illusory moves in a game of economic power. Moreover, 'pessimistic elitism' is a way of thinking which seeks to pass itself off as a form of radical cultural politics. But too often this is a politics in which attacks on power end up being little more than self-serving revelations about how *other* people are always 'cultural dupes'. (Storey, 1999: 168)

The tone adopted by Storey bespoke more than mere difference of disciplinary training between this kind of political economy and cultural studies. It may have resulted to some extent from differences in institutional location – cultural studies was often practised much closer to the teaching coalface than political economy was (the latter was a research method). But there was also a suspicion of bad faith by the political economists. Storey thought they were deluding themselves by claiming radical credentials when their method was no more intrinsically radical than cultural studies, despite its Marxist heritage. Furthermore it seemed the proponents of hard political economy felt free to criticise soft cultural studies without any pretence at a dialogue of equals – they refused to take its agenda on board while insisting that it took theirs. It seemed they thought that they didn't have to, since they were at the *cause* end of the chain of determination, and cultural studies was at the *effect* end.

However, although Storey didn't make the connection, what was most trenchant about his criticism of the political economy approach was that it applied directly to Stuart Hall. The idea of the inconsequentiality of popular culture *as such* (its textuality and experiential components), compared with its importance for something else (class struggle), was explicitly propounded by Hall himself. Writing in *People's History and Socialist Theory* in 1981, Hall made two telling points – one theoretical and the other personal:

> [Popular culture] is one of the sites where this struggle for and against a culture of the powerful is engaged: it is also the stake to be won or lost in the struggle. It is the arena of consent and resistance. It is partly where hegemony arises, and where it is secured. It is not a sphere where socialism, a socialist culture – already fully formed – might be simply 'expressed'. But it is one of the places where socialism might be constituted. That is why 'popular culture' matters. Otherwise, to tell you the truth, I don't give a damn about it. (Hall, 1981: 239)

Hall's theoretical point was still the one he'd been expressing since the late 1950s: culture was a worthy object of study not for anything intrinsic to it, but because it was the place where 'socialism might be constituted'; it was a 'site of struggle' against 'the culture of the powerful'. But for himself, after more than twenty years of analysing popular culture and media, he was willing, at just about the time he left Birmingham to take up a new post as Professor of Sociology at the Open University, to concede *precisely nothing* to that culture itself: 'I don't give a damn about it'. Popular culture was important as a battlefield, not for its local ecology. Also, this site of struggle was valuable to the victor. It was 'the stake to be won or lost . . . where hegemony is secured'. It was a class warrior's trophy.

That this rather brutal disavowal of popular culture was no temporary aberration was demonstrated later, around the time of his retirement. Hall expressed regret not at the passing of economic determinism but at the direction of cultural studies thereafter:

> What has resulted from the abandonment of deterministic economism has been, not alternative ways of thinking questions about the economic relations and their effects, as the 'conditions of existence' of other practices [. . .] but instead a massive, gigantic, and eloquent *disavowal*. As if, since the economic in the broadest sense definitely does not, as it was once supposed to do, 'determine' the real movement of history 'in the last instance', it does not exist at all! (in Hall et al., 1996: 258)

Hall called this a 'profound' and 'disabling' 'failure of theorisation', thereby dismissing much of the cultural studies done in his name.

For Hall and the radical political economists, attacking cultural studies came to seem a sort of expression of referred pain after the collapse of the Soviet Union and its satellites. The vehemence of the critique was out of all proportion to the seriousness of cultural studies' crimes, which were that:

- **textual analysis** continued to flourish (this was the crime of 'not doing empirical research');
- **postmodernism** was widely discussed in cultural studies (the crime of 'depoliticisation');
- some people **liked** what they studied (the crime of 'celebration' or 'populism') .

In fact denouncing cultural studies became something of an international academic sport in the few years following those events, egged on by publishers (especially Sage) who saw sales in squabbles: e.g. McGuigan, 1992; Stevenson 1995: 89–101; Ferguson and Golding, 1997; even McRobbie, 1997, at least in the title; Morrison, 1998; Philo and Miller, 1999. This was getting out of hand. Lawrence Grossberg wrote an article about it that caught the right mood: 'Cultural Studies vs. Political Economy: Is Anybody Else Bored with This Debate?' (Grossberg, 1995). Yes, yes!

But it wasn't only that the debate had elements of posturing. More importantly it was a *punitive* discourse against cultural studies. As a 'political mode of writing' in Roland Barthes's terms, it was *Stalinist*:

> Marxist writing has rapidly become, in fact, a language expressing value judgements. This character . . . has come to pervade writing completely in the era of triumphant Stalinism. . . . [Stalinist writing] no longer aims at founding a Marxist version of the facts, or a revolutionary rationale of actions, but at presenting reality in a pre-judged form, thus imposing a reading which involves immediate condemnation: the objective content of the word 'deviationist' puts it into a penological category. If two deviationists band together, they become 'fractionists', which does not involve an objectively different crime, but an increase in the sentence imposed. (Barthes, 1967: 29–30)

Cultural studies had become, even as it left the control of its 'founding parent', a 'massive, gigantic, and eloquent' *deviationist*.

Foucault, citizenship and cultural policy studies

There were, waiting in the wings as it were, some developments that provided cultural studies with alternative ways of both thinking about and dealing with the nexus between consciousness and the economy. The first of these was 'cultural policy studies'. Later on came 'creative industries'. Each was a practical rethinking of this nexus, and both located the nexus itself in the concept of citizenship.

Cultural policy studies was a development within cultural studies in the later 1980s and 1990s, following from Michel Foucault's work on 'governmentality', and associated internationally with the name of Tony Bennett. Bennett began his career as a sociologist at the Open University in the UK, from where he published a book on Marxist literary theory (Bennett, 1979). But he became much better known after moving to Australia, where he founded the Centre for Cultural and Media Policy at Griffith University, before eventually returning to the OU to take up the professorship of Sociology vacated by Stuart Hall on his retirement. Bennett himself was interested in cultural policy not only as a theoretical matter, but also because he saw it as part of the process of governmentality and citizen-formation (Bennett, 1998). Bennett was theoretically ambitious. He wanted to rethink cultural studies from the ground up, to do in the 1990s what Raymond Williams had done in the 1950s, i.e. to retrieve the concept of culture from what had become reactionary positions. And he thought the type of cultural policy studies he proposed ought to make a 'considerable difference' to cultural studies in general, not just take its place as an addition to the field (Bennett, 1992). He was scornful of oppositional cultural critics, for whom 'the mere mention of terms like "government" and "policy" in connection with cultural studies sparks off a yearning for a moment of pure politics – a return to 1968 – in whose name any traffic with the domain of government can be written off as a sell-out'. Bennett wanted to replace Arnold/Williams-derived cultural studies with the study of 'the wider domain of "the cultural" as a field of social management' (Bennett, 1992: 395–397). In practice he was most interested in state institutions of culture, especially museums and their role in forming citizens in and after the nineteenth century (Bennett, 1995: 219–28). Other prominent writers in the cultural policy area were Toby Miller, Stuart Cunningham, Tom O'Regan, Richard Collins and Colin Mercer.

Writing in 1992, Stuart Cunningham argued that the concept of *citizenship* was in fact the 'missing link' between cultural critique and cultural policy. He wanted to close the gap between the 'critical outsider' model of cultural studies, based on 'command metaphors of resistance and opposition', and the 'policy process in modern capitalist states'. He asked:

> What is cultural studies' understanding of its political vocation? What is its vision? . . . What measures are cultural analysts taking to have this vision widely and publicly articulated? What alliances are we forming with cultural activists and producers and policy agents . . . ? (Cunningham, 1992: 10)

His answer was simple:

> The missing link is a social democratic view of citizenship and the trainings necessary to activate and motivate it. A renewed concept of citizenship should become increasingly central to cultural studies as it moves into the 1990s. . . . Replacing revolutionary rhetoric with the new command metaphor of citizenship commits cultural studies to a reformist vocation within the terms of a social democratic politics. This can connect it more organically with the wellsprings of engagement with policy. (Cunningham: 11)

Citizenship was already a concept deeply embedded in various forms of cultural critique, but what was meant by citizenship differed along the lines of intellectual genealogy. That is, the type of cultural studies derived from *literary* origins saw citizenship as an *educational* matter. But cultural studies derived from *social theory* modelled citizenship on the mutual obligations, however enforced, between a *state* and the legal subject.

The former mode was really interested in the citizen for the purposes of consciousness raising. The idea was to use cultural studies to *teach* forms of engagement with public life and culture during an era of mass emancipation and the increasing democratisation of public life. This kind of cultural studies needed a certain iron optimism, because what it was attempting to do was nothing less than to educate the masses for citizenship in a period when popular culture and private life were the grounds to which participation and politics had shifted.

Cultural studies as a pedagogical enterprise began to pose itself *as* a mass medium, as it were. It sought to get into the heads of the hundreds of thousands of young people who streamed through newly democratised higher education without either clear class vocations (ruler, worker, etc.) or much in the way of training in civics. Indeed, the traditional civic disciplines (politics, government, history) weren't especially responsive to the actual circumstances of ordinary suburban experience and mediated public communication (often their academic watchdogs were hostile to all that).

So teacherly cultural studies pitched its tent on the site of ordinary experience – the experience of mediated popular culture, trans-national entertainment, and everyday life, in order to make systematic sense of it with and for the people whose experience it was. Taking the long view, cultural studies of this sort saw itself as a leavening process, introducing the oxygen of analysis to the lumpen-dough of classless and petit bourgeois existence. Like feminism alongside and Leavisism before it, but without so explicit or focused an agenda, it was a mode of consciousness raising. Its greatest champion was also its first exponent: Richard Hoggart.

This was the mode of cultural studies that flourished in the new institutions of higher education in Britain and elsewhere, and it explains why textual analysis became so central. Working through texts of various kinds – newspapers, movies, television, events, places, you name it – the idea was to capture in students a sense of their own involvement and identification with these things, and then to use that self-awareness (consciousness) to explain various issues relating to the public life of nations and societies (economy). It was sensitive to *differences* in such contexts – much more than its forebears in literary studies and art history. So issues of gender, ethnicity, sexual orientation, class, region, age, educational level and so on became part of its own everyday life, because the classroom context required it. Cultural studies in its textual form was a project of cultural emancipation for persons whose citizenship was formed as much by engagement with media as in formal interaction with a state.

Richard Hoggart himself engaged in reformist cultural policy in a big way. Notable instances were his membership of the major inquiry into broadcasting in the UK (the Pilkington Committee and Report, 1960), his famous appearance as witness for Penguin Books in the *Lady Chatterley's Lover* trial, his period as Deputy Director of UNESCO in Paris, and his stint as Warden (president) of Goldsmiths College. But despite this impressive role model, and also its own identification with the project of *forming* the citizen, the textual-teacherly mode of cultural studies proved reluctant to engage directly in the governmental practices of the state itself. It preferred an Althusserian arm's-length relationship with the 'ideological state apparatuses', talking directly to those whose subjectivity was being 'hailed' by dominant ideology, and seeking to develop in them directly some sort of counter-hegemonic consciousness, whether based on class, gender or ethnic resistances. Its practitioners recognised that as university and college teachers they were themselves 'agents of the state'. But there was also widespread confidence that they were 'relatively autonomous' and could therefore intervene in the cultural process of citizenship formation *against* the interest of the state that ultimately, in the last instance, paid their wages.

The other genealogical branch of cultural studies derived its concept of citizenship from more formal social theory, including philosophical writings on the subject, the state and the citizen in Rousseau (social contract), Kant (universal subject of reason), Marx (class subject), and other classical authorities. Sociological theorisations of citizenship were derived from German and American theorists, including Weber, Durkheim, Parks, Parsons, etc., and culminating in the work of T.H. Marshall. But most influential in the formation of a distinctively cultural studies version of citizenship was the work done by the exponents of cultural policy studies in response to the theoretical *oeuvre* of Michel Foucault.

Foucault had become widely influential owing to his studies of *madness, incarceration* and *sexuality*, which had raised profound questions about the historical functionality of *truth* (knowledge), *power* (how 'we constitute ourselves as subjects acting on others'), and *the self* (ethics) (see Foucault, 1984: 351–2). Tony Bennett indicated how the turn to Foucault (and to 'governmentality') was in fact a radical conceptual break with Marxism:

> The main burden of Foucault's critique, it will be recalled, is that Western political thought, up to and including Marxist theories of the state, has proved incapable of

recognizing the capillary network of power relations associated with the development of modern forms of government because it still envisages power, on the model of its monarchical form, as emanating from a single source. The primary concern of political theory has accordingly been to specify how limits might be placed on the exercise of such power or to identify sources external to it from which it might be opposed. To cut off the king's head in political theory, Foucault argues, means 'that we should direct our researches on the nature of power not towards the juridical edifice of sovereignty, the state apparatuses and the ideologies which accompany them, but towards domination and the material operators of power, towards forms of subjection and the inflections and utilizations of their localized systems, and towards strategic apparatuses'. It also means, he argues, that we should forsake looking for a source outside power from which it might be opposed and seek instead to identify the differentiated forms of resistance which the exercise of power . . . itself generates. (Bennett, 1992: 398–9; the internal quotation is from Foucault, 1980: 102)

In particular, cultural policy studies took from Foucault's later work, on the ethics of the self, new 'command metaphors' that they then moulded to the exigencies of public policy formation in social democratic polities. The main concept was 'governmentality' (Foucault, 1991), in the context of 'techniques of the self' associated with Foucault's thee-volume *History of Sexuality*. 'Governmentality' was preferred over 'government' because it went beyond the adversarial notion of state or class power *over* more or less repressed subjects. Instead of seeing power as repression, Foucault saw it as a productive force. And he added what he dubbed 'bio-power' to traditional notions of economic and political power, bio-power being 'numerous and diverse techniques for achieving the subjugation of bodies and the control of populations' (Foucault, 1984: 262).

This was a godsend for method in cultural studies, if nothing else. For it authorised both micro and macro levels of analysis. It required analysis at the 'capillary' micro-scale of the individual *body* and the techniques used to discipline it. In fact, it permitted textual analysis, and the extension of 'text' to include bodies as well as images and words. But simultaneously it encouraged attention to the macro scale of whole *populations* and how they were administered and managed. That is, it permitted social analysis. Foucault's work, in short, simply didn't recognise the methodological divide between particularism (textual criticism and semiotics) and the generalising ambitions (sociology) that had troubled cultural studies since its very inception (see Shuttleworth, 1966: 22–4).

In the development of capitalism, bio-power was indispensable. Foucault's argument involved a profound rethinking of the nexus between economy and consciousness. He acknowledged that capitalism 'would not have been possible without the controlled insertion of bodies into the machinery of production and the adjustment of the phenomena of population to economic processes'. But, he added, this was not all that capitalism required – it also needed these factors to *grow*; it needed their reinforcement and optimisation:

> If the development of the great instruments of the state, as *institutions* of power, ensured the maintenance of production relations, the rudiments of anatomo- and bio-power politics, created in the eighteenth century as *techniques* of power present at every level of the social body and utilized by very diverse institutions (the family and the army, schools and the police, individual medicine and the administration of collective bodies), operated on the sphere of economic processes, their development, and the forces working to sustain them. (Foucault, 1984: 263)

Foucault argued, in fact, that these techniques of bio-power were active in the creation of social hierarchy and segregation – 'guaranteeing relations of domination and effects of hegemony'.

> The adjustment of the accumulation of men to that of capital, the joining of the growth of human groups to the expansion of the productive forces and the differential allocation of profit, was made possible in part by the exercise of bio-power in its many forms and modes of application. The investment of the body, its valorization, and the distributive management of its forces were at the time indispensable. (ibid.)

This wasn't exactly a call of 'If you can't beat them, join them!' (as suspected by curmudgeonly oppositionalists within cultural studies) – but it was a recognition that power was *productive* not repressive, and that it was a feature of 'every level of the social body'. Here was a conceptualisation that enabled analysts of culture to recognise the historical function of private conduct and bodily practices in the development of large-scale economic forces (and for an exemplary study by one of Foucault's pupils, see Jacques Donzelot's *The Policing of Families*, 1980).

Foucault argued that the very increase in productivity attendant on early capitalist expansion reduced the threat of famine and pestilence to such an extent that politics turned from the threat of death (always the ultimate power of sovereign powers) to 'taking charge of life':

> Power would no longer be dealing simply with legal subjects over whom the ultimate dominion was death, but with living beings, and the mastery it would be able to exercise over them would have to be applied at the level of life itself; it was the taking charge of life, more than the threat of death, that gave power its access even to the body. (Foucault, 1984: 265)

The organisation and administration of life required a *knowledge*-power, as opposed to the pre-modern 'murderous splendour' of sovereign power (be that law or monarch) based on threat of death. The sign of power was no longer the fasces – that bundle of rods (instruments of punishment) and an axe (instrument of execution) that had symbolised the legitimacy of the Roman Republic (and its modernist reincarnation, Fascism). Nor was it the scimitar or sword, symbol of aristocratic power from the Knights Templar to janissaries and samurai (and its alter ego, the sword of blind Justice). Its symbol was, in essence, the *calculator*. What was required was a power that would 'qualify, measure, appraise, and hierarchize' (1984: 266). Foucault understood that a 'technology of power centred on life' was one that *normalised* society. This was 'governmentality'. It was the use of Enlightenment sciences like political economy to analyse and administer populations. Eventually, for Foucault, law, justice, politics, sovereignty itself as traditionally understood (pain of death) were all 'governmentalised' – rendered bureaucratic, regulated, administrative, and thence normal – and productive (Foucault, 1991: 102–3).

Furthermore, he argued that modernity was not opposed in this aspect even by those who wished to overthrow capitalist and 'bio' power. 'The forces that resisted relied for support on the very thing [this power] invested, that is, on life and man as a living being' (1984: 266). In other words, apart from cultural and religious fundamentalists (e.g. Hare Krishna and the Taliban, who wanted to abandon modernity entirely, in favour of an eighteenth-century Indian village, and seventh- or fourteenth-century Arab one respectively) there was no significant movement to reinstate pre-modern powers after the French Revolution. Marxist, feminist and other opponents of capitalism wanted for their adherents *more* of the good life unleashed by the productive forces of economic and 'bio' power. They wanted to take control of those regulatory and corrective levers themselves: 'What was demanded and what served as an objective was life, understood as the basic needs, man's concrete essence, the realization of his potential, a plenitude of the possible' (1984: 266–7).

This admission that their own critical and oppositional practices were implicated in the overall process of governance at a given period was the spur that pricked the cultural policy wallahs into engagement with existing arrangements. Cunningham recommended it to cultural studies:

> Governmentality, for Foucault, is an enabling category asserting that 'government' does not stand over and against the individual and civil society. 'Governmental' processes and mechanisms are equally foundational to, for instance, the self-reflective ethical competences of individuals, the organisations of social movements, and the machinery of government in its institutionalised forms. Cultural studies should seek to clarify and articulate the relation between public policy processes and the constituencies they are supporting, assessing, or regulating. (Cunningham, 1992: 170)

It followed that: 'the perspective afforded by the concept of governmentality allows us to plot the *strategic* nature of policy discourse more extensively than hitherto', and that this would, 'of necessity', bring the activism of cultural critique within the 'lineaments' of government policy processes (ibid.). Or, as Tony Bennett once famously remarked about the 'turn' towards policy – it involved critical theorists in 'talking to the ISAs' (ideological state apparatuses).

Meanwhile, the idea of cultural citizenship was also developed out of Foucault's work on how humans turned themselves into subjects. Toby Miller for instance, in two Foucauldian books on selves, media and citizenship (*The Well-Tempered Self*, 1993, and *Technologies of Truth*, 1998), attempted to show how many of the discourses circulating in media constructed for their subjects (the audience) various senses of 'ethical incompleteness' which they would attempt to fill, so to achieve full citizenship. This was the 'government of the self'. Here too the concept of the citizen was used as a bridge between cultural criticism and cultural policy; though in this manifestation it was done as part of critique, not 'governmentality' as interpreted by Bennett and Cunningham.

Interestingly the cultural policy moment – which lasted a decade in Australia – didn't export all that well. This may be because the local political terrain in Australia was more fertile during the years of the Bennett ascendancy – the centrist Hawke–Keating Labor government in power federally throughout the period. That meant that the Centre for Cultural and Media Policy *had* an ISA to talk to. Not long after that government's collapse in 1996, Bennett returned to the UK.

A more substantial weakness was that there was no compelling *content* to policy work. In fact Bennett and Cunningham, following the bureaucratic ethics of Ian Hunter (1988), both saw this as a strength. Although it was a very persuasive concept in historical analysis, there was nothing about 'governmentality' that could specify *what* policies might be appropriate, apart in Cunningham's case from 'social democratic reformism' (whose agenda was largely determined by other agents than cultural analysts).

Furthermore, and perhaps most disabling, the concept of 'governmentality' was – despite its theoretical sophistication – frequently reduced in practice to 'working for the government'. For Tony Bennett, the very definition of culture pointed in this direction:

> The relations of culture and power which most typically characterize modern societies are best understood in the light of the respects in which the field of culture is now increasingly governmentally organized and constructed. (Bennett, 1998: 61)

Point taken, but such a position drove cultural policy studies towards the *government* – as regulator, subsidiser, policy-former. It drew their attention away from the *market*, which was arguably the key locus of culture for most modernised populations, an argument that had in fact been persuasively made back in the 1980s by Nick Garnham (Garnham, 1987). Obviously markets had to be regulated and administered and these were governmental procedures, but the concept of governmentality was cashed-in in practice by *restricting* the life of symbol to those procedures (which Foucault himself had stressed were never totally successful). In other words, there was little room in cultural policy for the energetic, expansive, productive forces that made markets so compelling for producers and consumers alike. To some extent that reflected research funding patterns – government agencies were more prepared to support academic cultural policy studies than were private media and entertainment corporations, entrepreneurs or users. Cultural policy studies settled in as a primarily university-based expert dialogue with public servants – a familiar intellectual set-up that turned its attention away from direct dialogue with either producers working in commercial contexts for the media industries, or users, who were addressed as students by teacherly or democratising cultural studies.

In Britain, as in Australia, broadcasting and the press, as well as leisure and sports, were regarded as part of the overall cultural sphere. Garnham had already argued that broadcasting was the 'heartland' of cultural policy and practice. This was because, despite decades of government subsidy for the traditional arts, broadcasting remained the culture industry that consumed more of most people's time and money than any other cultural pursuit (Garnham, 1987: 35; and see Garnham, 1990).

In fact, policy discourses in countries like Australia and the UK focused almost exclusively on publicly funded institutions (see for instance Bennett and Carter, 2001). But the experience of culture was, for the vast majority of people, most of the time, neither public nor institutional in that sense – it was involvement in a commercial marketplace. Bennett's cultural policy proved useful in areas where governments were already competent, which mostly meant subsidised public institutions like museums and galleries, publicly funded broadcasters and national film industries (i.e. movies not advertisements), and the like. It was far less successful in attracting the attention of commercial media, and failed entirely to make an impression on the development of cultural practices themselves, from the growth of theme parks to creative applications of new media technologies.

Cultural studies in Celebration

In the USA, there was no such thing as *federal* government cultural policy, although states and cities might have their own. Federal cultural policy was handled at arm's length by the philanthropic and endowment sector, and only referred to traditional arts and crafts. Media and entertainment were not regarded as connected with culture in the US governmental set-up – they were seen as subject to market forces (within a framework of legislative regulation guided by the Federal Communications Commission), and therefore no place for the feds. Cultural policy studies found only a precarious hold in the USA, despite Bennett's own good reputation there, and the fact that Foucauldian analysis of culture as a governmentalised administrative/regulatory/ normalising zone would find rich pickings in academic analysis.

Within American culture itself, much that would have been public or national policy in other countries was done commercially – the promotion of national image via Hollywood (known in some quarters as cultural imperialism), or the expression of patriotism via consumption (very noticeable after 11 September 2001, but far from novel then), or the sponsorship of medical and educational institutions by private individuals and corporations. Even opposition was commercialised, in for instance music and leisure cultures from blues to surfing, and in alternative lifestyles from the Rajneeshis to fearsome backwoods individualists for whom 'freedom' meant 'no government at all – on pain of death'.

Such culture was certainly susceptible to analysis, and certainly riddled with policy amounting to a governmentality worthy of Foucault's own talents. But it was completely opaque to cultural policy studies of the Bennett variety, which was dedicated to what Cunningham called the 'handmaiden' role – interacting with governmental bureaucracies in order to find out 'what it could do for them' (Cunningham, 1992: 9ff.; Bennett, 1998).

Instead, the governmentality of American commercial culture found an analyst worthy of its own peculiarities in Andrew Ross, who was not only yet another expatriate scholar from the UK (he was Scottish), but also a well-known exponent of radical cultural critique of the kind challenged by Bennett and his colleagues. Ross's *Celebration Chronicles: Life, Liberty and the Pursuit of Property Value in Disney's New Town* (1999) was an account of a year that he spent in Celebration, a new town of 20,000 homes in Florida, developed by Walt Disney Enterprises, right next to Walt Disney World. Here was a chance to watch a commercially catered community invent itself, in the self-conscious glow of media interest. Ross observed at first hand the (Foucauldian) 'taking charge of life' by means of various 'strategic apparatuses', 'material operators of power', and 'forms of subjection and the inflections and utilizations of their localized systems'.

Ross's book was itself a commercial venture – it had been 'cooked up' over a 'portentous lunch' with his agent and publisher (Ross, 1999: xi), and its method was 'cultural' (it was directly Hoggartian, although Ross himself did not make that connection) rather than social-scientific or policy oriented:

> This book, like the hybrid nature of this community, is supposed to be a cocktail of personal and public observations, laced with those ingredients of analysis that seemed most true to my experience of the town's residents and employees. So, too, I had elected not to be a mute, recording witness. (320)

Ross investigated Celebration's publicity, housing, schooling, retail, urban planning, and the role of the Walt Disney Company, showing how a private entertainment corporation pursued public policy goals as well as shareholder benefit, and the involvement of residents, neighbours and observers in that process. For Ross, it wasn't governmentality as such that intrigued him, but certainly it was an aspect of what confronted him: the fault lines between, and hybridisation of, the interface between public and private:

> This blurring of lines between private and public eventually permeated everything that had come to interest me about this town. Celebration was a living, breathing embodiment of something called the private-public realm. This was a strange beast that had been slouching toward the millennium for much of the latter part of the century. (Ross: 311)

Unsurprisingly, Ross found two opposing but equally plausible scenarios. On the one hand, 'Celebration promised visible proof that corporations could be entrusted with the charge of restoring public space', but on the other, 'skeptics abounded'. Equally unsurprisingly, 'on the ground, I had found that things were a good deal more complex' (312–13). But still, 'in my time there, I watched as some kind of provisional public sphere, built on blunt opinion, common sentiment, and the stoic pursuit of civic needs, pushed its snout into the moist Florida air' (314). Nevertheless, 'the lessons of Celebration, drawn out in scale, suggest that any restoration of trust in these institutions, both corporate and government, requires a sea change in their character' (315–16), or a kettle to boil, perhaps. Any 'policy' conclusions had to arise from a context in which neither 'public' nor 'private' agencies could be trusted, and any sense of community that Celebration's residents achieved seems to come from their resistance to the corporate and government policies planned for them:

> Rudely dispossessed of any lingering illusions that they moved to an instant utopia, Celebrationites encountered obstacles to happiness that compelled them to forge community bonds for which there was no planning blueprint. . . . The sense of community that was most authentic and resourceful emerged in response to perceived threats, challenges, and barriers to people's well-being, and, above all, to their property values. . . . Interests beyond their control, whether commercial (the developer), philosophical (the school), or cultural (the media and outsider opinion), had imperiled Celebrationites' sense of security. It had taken the bitter taste of jeopardy to arouse the appetite for strong society. (318)

Ross's observations of Celebration's mode of citizenship, in a place that was 'governed by a corporation rather than a government', were coloured by his own political predilections. He was especially 'troubled' by the idea that 'efficiency, civic order, and exacting management' were the goal, and argued instead that 'some forms of civic disorder are crucial to the political life of the republic'. He even quoted with approval a resident who had remarked that 'what we need are a few drunks around this town' (309–10).

So the idea of a 'resistive' citizenship was appealing to him: 'Citizens . . . often discover how to be active only when they feel their own rights are threatened or when they see others befouled by injustice, as in the civil rights struggle. Active citizenship has to be learned.' Perhaps this was why Ross spent so much time thinking about the school at Celebration, and about the role of public education. He was curious to know what suburban affluent 'villa people' of Celebration would 'do with their citizenship once it has been activated' – would they 'use it to protect their own resources and privileges or to help remedy the neglect of the city block dwellers?' (221–222). Time would tell.

Cultural studies with funding – the creative industries

Back in Britain, once there was a Labour government in power nationally after 1997, cultural policy not only came into view once again, but this time policy meant addressing the *commercial* aspect of culture directly. Instead of developing a policy (and therefore funding) around cultural institutions and public subsidy, the Blair government set about moving culture from the spending to the wealth-creating portfolios. It became an emergent industry sector, under the brand name of the 'creative industries'. And far from being a drain on public resources, it turned out that cultural production, circulation and consumption – not to mention export – was a major contributor to the British economy, worth about £60 billion annually at 1997 prices, or 4 per cent of gross domestic product, and growing fast. It was bigger than *Ben Hur*. Here was another, quite novel model of the nexus between consciousness and the economy. The creative industries were not only a moral or an aesthetic domain, but an economic one directly (Caves, 2000). British Prime Minister Tony Blair himself made the connection quite explicit in his introduction to a Green Paper on *Culture and Creativity: The Next Ten Years*, published by the Department of Culture, Media and Sport in 2001 (before the 2001 election):

> The Government knows that culture and creativity matter.
> They matter because they can enrich all our lives, and everyone deserves the opportunity to develop their own creative talents and to benefit from those of others. They matter because our rich and diverse culture helps bring us together – it's part of our great success as a nation.
> They also matter because creative talent will be crucial to our individual and national economic success in the economy of the future.
> Above all, at their best, the arts and creativity set us free. (Blair, 2001: 3)

Simultaneously, new interactive media technologies were promising completely new possibilities in the relationships among producers, consumers, clients and the public. Instead of a *broadcast* model of communication, where pre-made commodities were sent to mass audiences, a *telecommunications* model became thinkable, where many-to-many, or even one-to-one messages (as in telephony) were normal. The whole metaphorical and ideological baggage of the broadcast era was undermined. No longer could public policy be based on the power of mass broadcasters or the passivity of consumers, and their concomitant need to be protected or corrected from excesses and deviations in their own and broadcasters' behaviour. No longer could vulnerable people catch ideological diseases from their media consumption. If media were interactive, or becoming so, then users (not 'consumers') could affect and even participate in production, as they began to do with computer-games software. 'The Sims' game (spin-off from Sim-City), for instance, was reported by its makers to be about 40 per cent created by its own users in 2001 (information from Henry Jenkins, MIT). Declining costs for still and video digital cameras meant that media such as television took on new possibilities as a kind of personal *literacy*. Instead of being confined to perpetual *readership* of others' words, individuals could now *write* television much more readily, and because of their decades-long tuition in TV forms and genres, could write TV for public as well as private communication, screening it by VCR or web-streaming.

So there was an immediate context of technological change with profound implications just at the moment when economic commentators were demonstrating how different the new economy was from the model of industrial capitalism it was growing out of. Again, instead of an industrial model of mass production and mass consumption, the new economy was based on quite different relations of production. It was based on knowledge rather than goods – recipes rather than cakes – and required neither creative artists nor cultural critics but 'cultural entrepreneurs' (Leadbeater and Oakley, 1999).

Interestingly, the new economy required very little intellectual support from publicly subsidised institutions of knowledge (i.e. universities). It bypassed traditional sources of analysis altogether, relying instead on a phenomenon that was an *enactment* of its own 'thin-air' ideology – the freelance, entrepreneurial, knowledge-broking journalist-intellectual. Prominent, perhaps exemplary, among these was Charlie Leadbeater. He had downshifted from a formal career with the *Financial Times*, including a period as their prestigious Tokyo correspondent (where the representative of the *FT* was accorded almost diplomatic status). Instead of working for a large industrial knowledge organisation, he chose instead to 'live on thin air' – to work as an independent cultural entrepreneur in the production and circulation of ideas. He published numerous policy reports for the New Labour think-tank, Demos, and his book about the theory and practice of this approach to the new economy, *Living on Thin Air* (1997), was not only an international best-seller, but was taken up directly by the incoming Blair government. Leadbeater himself became a chief adviser to Downing Street on IT and the new economy, but more to the point his ideas began to affect cultural policy and practice.

In 1998 the Department of Culture, Media and Sport produced the first attempt to measure the economic contribution of the creative industries in the UK. These industries were identified on a pragmatic basis – they were deemed to comprise those creative enterprises that were significant to the British economy. They included:

- advertising,
- architecture,
- the art and antiques market,
- crafts,
- design,
- designer fashion,
- film and video,
- interactive leisure software,
- music,
- the performing arts,
- publishing,
- software and computer services,
- television and radio. (Culture, Media & Sport, 2001: 5)

The creative industries were also said to enjoy 'close economic relationships' with:

- tourism,
- hospitality,
- museums and galleries,
- heritage,
- sport. (ibid.)

As Chris Smith, the minister of the day, put it: 'the creative industries have moved from the fringes to the mainstream'. The report estimated that, by 2001:

> The creative industries in the UK generate revenues of around £112.5 billion and employ 1.3 million people. Exports contribute around £10.3 billion to the balance of trade, and the industries account for over 5% of GDP. In 1997–98, output grew by 16% compared to under 6% for the economy as a whole. (Culture, Media & Sport, 2001: 10)

The relationship between this kind of economics and consciousness was direct. It put culture at the centre of the economy, and the policy imperatives that flowed from this were themselves an attempt to strengthen that nexus. Strategies identified as necessary to grow the created industries included:

- stimulating creativity and innovation in young people to ensure we have a long-term supply of creative talent;
- ensuring that at primary, secondary and tertiary education levels, it is possible to identify and develop new talent;
- ensuring that people have both the creative and business skills necessary to succeed;
- ensuring wider public awareness of the importance of intellectual property rights to longer term creativity;
- ensuring that creative businesses have access to appropriate financial support, and that the financial sector is aware of the opportunities and benefits of investing in creative industries;
- responding to global opportunities, promoting UK creativity and innovation throughout the world, removing obstacles to free trade, and opposing the introduction of measures which would harm the competitiveness of UK companies;
- exploiting the opportunities presented by e-commerce and the Internet;
- ensuring the regulatory burden does not fall disproportionately on creative businesses;
- recognising the interlocking relationship and synergies between subsidised and commercial creative sectors, between the creative industries and broader cultural sectors, and promoting the UK's diverse vibrant cultural life;
- continuing to improve the collection of robust and timely data on the creative industries, based on a common understanding of coverage. (Culture, Media and Sport, 2001: 13–14)

That amounted to nothing less than a new manifesto for cultural studies.

Culture-jamming – cultural studies as consciousness resisting economy

The one thing it left out, as usual (although there were hints in its 'promotion' of diversity in 'Britain's vibrant cultural life'), was opposition. This was the other side of the coin in the rise to 'mainstream' economic prominence of creative and cultural activity, and its insertion into governmental strategies of growth, business development and geopolitics. An unequal but opposite reaction was observable in the 'culture-jamming' and 'DIY culture' movements.

'DiY culture, a youth-centred and -directed cluster of interests and practices around green radicalism, direct action politics, new musical sounds and experiences, is a kind of 1990s counterculture', wrote its first academic chronicler, George McKay. Like its 1960s counter-cultural forebear, DIY culture was:

> a combination of inspiring action, narcissism, youthful arrogance, principle, ahistoricism, idealism, indulgence, creativity, plagiarism, as well as the rejection and embracing alike of technological innovation. (McKay, 1998: 2)

If DIY was the activist branch of opposition to commercialised culture, then the culture-jamming movement, a phenomenon associated with the Canadian magazine *Adbusters* and the Canadian writer Naomi Klein (2000), was its theoretical counterpart. Pretty soon this too was available from commercial outlets: Amazon.co.uk for instance posted a culture-jamming booklist on its website:

> Nobody said that changing the world would be easy. But the battlefields are changing, allowing interventions by individuals and movements who turn consumer-power into grassroots activism. You may not be able to live outside the system, but you can find what to read on your travels within it with Amazon.co.uk's selection. (http://www.amazon.co.uk/exec/obidos/tg/feature/–/24290/ref=ed_ra_sp_1_2/qi d=1011256276/sr=6–2/202–0631593–7390252; accessed 17 January 2002)

Amazon offered the following aids to 'culture-jamming':

- *No Logo* – Naomi Klein: We live in an era where image is nearly everything, where the proliferation of brand-name culture has created, to take one hyperbolic example from Naomi Klein's *No Logo*, 'walking, talking, life-sized Tommy [Hilfiger] dolls, mummified in fully branded . . . Read more
- *Why We Buy* – Paco Underhill:
- *Media Virus! : Hidden Agendas in Popular Culture* – Douglas Rushkoff
- *Just Do It : The Nike Spirit in the Corporate World* – Donald R. Katz
- *Reclaiming America : Nike, Clean Air, and the New National Activism* – Randy Shaw: Have activists taken the bumper-sticker adage 'Think Globally, Act Locally' too literally? The author of this text, Randy Shaw, argues that they have, with destructive consequences for America. Since the 1970s, activist participation in national . . . Read more
- *Coercion : Why We Listen to What 'They' Say* – Douglas Rushkoff: Argues that bosses, so-called experts, and authorities real and imaginary have taken over much of the

decision-making power in our lives, and explains how the new technologies and media innovations are being co-opted to shape our world and to damage . . . Read more

● *Adcult USA: The Triumph of Advertising in American Culture* – James B. Twitchell: We see them in flashing kaleidoscopes of colour and sound on television, splashes of neon on billboards, on glossy spreads in newspapers and magazines. We hear the peppy jingles on the radio. We even find them being sneaked past us as 'underwriting' . . . Read more

● *Nike Culture* – Robert Goldman, Stephen Papson: A study of how an advertising image works, using the Nike swoosh logo as the example. The authors investigate the themes and structures of Nike adverts and the logic of sign economy. For students of sociology, cultural and media studies. Read more

● *Lead Us into Temptation* – James B. Twitchell: In exploring the nature and importance of advertising lingo, packaging and fashion, the author argues that the purchase and possession of things are the ultimate self-identifying acts of modern life. He discovers what Americans buy, why they buy it, . . . Read more

(http://www.amazon.co.uk/exec/obidos/tg/feature/–/24290/ref=ed_ra_sp_1_2/qid=1011256276/sr=6–2/202–0631593–7390252)

No sooner was it firmly connected, than the new commercial–governmental nexus between consciousness and new economy creative culture was being systematically pathologised by a new generation of intellectual activists. Whether theirs was the authentic voice of the new cultural studies, or whether that voice was in fact located in the Department of Culture, Media and Sport (which immediately after the 2001 election, under incoming Culture Secretary Tessa Jowett, announced a new inquiry into media ownership . . .), or whether these were but the weekday and weekend identities of the same folk, was a question only history could decide.

Meanwhile, the outgoing Culture, Media and Sports Minister Chris Smith was toppled – presumably because although he succeeded in delivering a whole new economic sector, he had failed to deliver a replacement for Wembley Stadium, home of English football. This was politically much more important, and not only because Wembley was the latter-day fasces or calculator of national identity and pride. It was also the crucible of the very *content* that the creative industries were designed to monetise.

5
The Ordinary as a Sign of Itself
Culture and Everyday Life (travelling, shopping, walking, eating)

Cultural studies and feminism, anthropology, sociology

Cultural studies was the study of everyday life in modern, urban and suburban societies. Everyday life as an object of study differed considerably from everyday life as it may have been lived by individuals and populations. What was studied partly depended on the disciplinary perspective and ideological outlook of the analyst. In this respect everyday life was a bit like speech – everyone knew what it was, and to study something with so much variety, so many individual examples, and so many possible disciplinary approaches or questions, meant that it was not a thing that formal knowledge could recognise as coherent. So what counted as everyday life depended on who was looking, and what they were looking at.

Many if not most studies of everyday life originated from outside of the academy, for instance in journalism, magazines, photography, trade publishing, television, cinema, and among the multifarious specialisms (amateur, commercial and public) that were interested in the activities, pleasures and peculiarities of everyday life itself.

Cultural studies attempted to make sense of everyday life within the terms of its own ongoing inquiry into meaning, power, ideology and subjectivity in contemporary societies. It undertook an anthropology of modern, mediated, managed, multicultural life. But it was also the inheritor of disciplinary and intellectual preoccupations, approaching everyday life less with wide-eyed interrogative naivety than with preconceived or received ideas. Because of cultural studies' own history as a political as well as an academic discourse, these included a strong sense that the purpose of any study of everyday life was *critical* – the point was not simply to understand that world, but to change it. This was a kind of intervention analysis, dedicated neither to the improvement of everyday activities themselves, nor to appreciation of cultural pursuits, but to critique of the society of which these activities were both symptom and stage, with a view to reform, revolution or replacement.

So cultural studies brought its own baggage to everyday life. It was on the lookout for the workings of power, curious about the everyday as a symptom of something else – struggles, ideologies, oppressions, power structures. It was interested in representations and ideologies, and much better at analysing the textuality of everyday life than were traditional social sciences. Indeed, analysts frequently ignored the boundary between everyday life and mediations of it. For instance, sitcoms and soap operas were studied as evidence of the social life of which they were fictional dramatisations, even though characters in sitcoms and soap opera never did the three things that filled so much time and mind in everyday life itself: work; watching TV; having (or trying to have) sex. Nevertheless, everyday *drama* (mediation) was scrutinised for symptomatic signs of whatever pathogen analysts thought was troubling the body *politic* (life). But this was itself hardly a failing; it was more a symptom of the interpenetration of mediation and society (see Abercrombie and Longhurst, 1998).

Despite its interest in how economic forces worked their way through into culture, cultural studies drifted, seemingly inexorably, away from the world of production as an aspect of everyday life in industrial societies, and towards consumption, leisure and domestic contexts. In other words it gave up almost completely on *work* as part of everyday life, although there was interest in the fact that the domestic domain of leisure and refuge was only such for men (and children), whereas it was routinely a workplace for women. Any investigation of waged workplaces that did occur was likely to be looking for experience and ideologies, not formal organisation and practices, for instance Paul Willis's book about mass schooling as a preparation for work, *Learning to Labour: How Working Class Kids Get Working Class Jobs* (1978).

Similarly, like anthropology, cultural studies was interested in ritual, ceremony and custom, but only as these applied to modern secular pursuits – outside of existing theological programmes there was not a cultural studies approach to formal religions. The rituals beloved of cultural studies were more likely to be those performed within sight of the TV set, in entertainment and music venues, amusement parks and the like.

The positive contribution of cultural studies to the study of everyday life came from those distinctive features that differentiated it somewhat from its disciplinary, intellectual and political neighbours. It was characterised by:

- respect for **ordinary** life (cf. Raymond Williams's essay 'Culture is Ordinary', 1958; reprinted in Gray and McGuigan, 1997);
- a willingness to pursue culture into intermediate and otherwise despised or disregarded zones, the paradigm example of which was **suburbia**;
- an openness to the **textuality** of everyday life, and the role of media, symbol and audiencehood within it;
- an interest in **entertainment** and **pop culture** – the modern (not to mention postmodern) aspects of everyday life;
- a propensity (following from the above) to focus analysis on **consumption**, a neglected field in other intellectual paradigms;
- an interest in how people **negotiated** the **management** of their everyday lives and bodies by corporate and state agencies;

- A very strong devotion to notions of **difference** (sex, class, ethnicity, region, age, nation, lifestyle, etc.). Cultural diversity, ethnic diasporas and multi-culturalism were seen as fundamental both to cultural studies itself and to the communities in which it was interested, whether these were geograph-ically located (by city or nation) or identified by some other marker ('the gay community'; 'the Chinese community'; 'the housing estate', etc.).

The everyday life brought into view by cultural studies was suffused with media, power, difference and modern administrative strategies, and was char-acterised by mixture, ambiguity, hybridity, commerce and democratisation.

Kissing cousins

Cultural studies shared the task of analysing everyday life with other intellectual traditions, notably sociology (see Carrington, 2001: 287–91) and anthropology (see Marcus, 2001). It was influenced, not to say overshadowed, by some impor-tant writers within these disciplines:

- from **sociology**: Thorstein Veblen, Georg Simmel, Henri Lefebvre, Pierre Bourdieu;
- from **anthropology**: Claude Lévi-Strauss, Marshall Sahlins, Mary Douglas, Edmund Leach, Arjun Appadurai, James Clifford.

The cross-fertilisation among anthropology, sociology and cultural studies was thoroughgoing, although important differences remained. Raymond Williams incorporated an anthropological definition into cultural studies (culture as 'whole way of life'), and both sociology and anthropology, despite their greater commitment to replicable method and generalisable findings, borrowed ideas, topics and even theorists (especially Raymond Williams and Stuart Hall) from cultural studies. But anthropology's investment in the study of kinship was never cashed in by cultural studies; sociology's interest in social order and social action remained a separate conversation. It was however notable that the Centre for Contemporary Cultural Studies migrated from its original home in the English Department at Birmingham to the Sociology Department. Stuart Hall ended his full-time academic career as the Professor of Sociology at the Open University (without conceding that he was a sociologist), and took up an emer-itus post at the School of Oriental and African Studies, one of Britain's leading departments of anthropology.

In terms of method, unlike sociology and anthropology, cultural studies was relatively indifferent to the *scale* of those parts of everyday life that caught its analytical eye. For instance Australian cultural studies was more interested in the beach as an object of study than could be justified by the proportion of the Australian public who visited beaches. Most Australians, most of the time, were not on the beach nor likely to be heading that way. But for cultural studies the beach was a symbol of culture and national identity, and that needed investigation. It did not seek to produce a proportionate account of what most people did in their everyday lives.

Thus, where sociology and anthropology were generalising, classifying and theorising disciplines, cultural studies retained some of its literary-critical mindset, with a devotion to detailed and passionate engagement with the particular. It also persisted with another not entirely positive habit of literary studies, being prone to universalising from that particular – after a close reading, *this* beach might become *the* beach. For instance, after John Fiske had forayed onto the local sands, which at the time were at Cottesloe (the Western Australian equivalent of Bondi Beach), this became the pre-text for a lengthy meditation on the opposition and ambiguation of Nature and Culture (Fiske, 1983). What made this sort of approach frustrating to the established disciplines was not that it was spurious or inconsequential. On the contrary, enthusiastic engagement with the particulars of everyday pursuits in terms of their overall significance could produce fascinating and thought-provoking results. As with literary analysis, much depended on the excellence of the analyst, since the method was not standardised and replicable. So this was dangerous terrain for trainees, and both sociologists and anthropologists were trained to avoid it (until their apprenticeship was over).

The engagement with theory was also different in cultural studies from the kind of theorising that went hand in hand with empirical research into organised practices and beliefs. Cultural studies was more concerned with theory as a translation – it sought to translate high continental theories into English (Althusser, Gramsci, structuralism, semiotics), and also to re-theorise Marxism itself, translating it into an idiom more suited to the times (thus, one of Stuart Hall's more substantial occasional papers during his time at Birmingham was a re-reading of Marx's *Grundrisse*).

The particularism, passion and theoretical translations of cultural studies all made their dialogic mark on its older-cousin disciplines. Where their concerns could overlap, for instance in some forms of participant observation or ethnography, innovations occurred that were of interest across all three. Equally, there were periods of tension and squabbling, especially over method.

Feminism was also an important influence on studies of everyday life, and it remained an interlocutor with cultural studies from the latter's earliest days (see Lovell, 1995 and Thornham, 2000). As Meaghan Morris demonstrated in her feminist genealogy in *The Pirate's Fiancée* (1988), there were lines of descent that could be traced entirely through women writers, a fact neglected in many accounts of the history of ideas. The influence of feminism and women writers was capillary (in Foucault's sense) rather than being restricted to a few big names. Many prominent feminists were interested in other matters than the culture of everyday life, but their general frameworks were used in that context by others, resulting in some strange but possibly illuminating mixtures, such as a simultaneous interest in psychoanalysis, suburbia and serial TV drama. Within any given topic feminism would inform cultural studies, drawing on specific theorists appropriate to the analysis at hand. Intellectually, the two shared (and borrowed) much common ground, from their interest in private life and the power relations established therein, to questions of identity and sexuality – and the power relations associated with those.

By the time cultural studies was an organised academic field, feminism was well into its stride (Thornham, 2000: 15). One pivotal moment of Birmingham cultural studies was when the Women's Study Group at the Centre put a counter-hegemonic feminist agenda on the table (Women's Studies Group, 1978; see also Hall, 1992: 282; Brunsdon, 1996). As far as the *anthropology of the everyday* was concerned, feminist cultural studies made its mark very strongly in studies of the domestic reception of contemporary media (e.g. work by Dorothy Hobson, Charlotte Brunsdon, Jan Radway, Ien Ang, Ann Gray, Joke Hermes); and in studies of women's articulation with public life (Rita Felski, Linda Nicholson, Catharine Lumby). Feminist writers were interested in ordinary sub-urban life, the home, family and consumerism, from a position that was more than critical, but wasn't characterised by the snobbery and disdain that disabled some classic disciplinary approaches to these areas of life. Feminist initiatives, e.g. the Console-ing Passions series of conferences and books about media, and journals, including *Camera Obscura* and *Signs*, were integral to the overall cultural studies endeavour (see especially Brunsdon et al., 1997).

For some time feminist writers had been working with corporeality as a site of investigation in cultural studies. As the public was increasingly vast and anonymous, made up of the behaviours and choices of myriad sovereign but mutually unacquainted citizens, *the body* had become progressively abstracted from the public sphere. Its reinscription was largely as a result of feminist and also gay/lesbian work, during an era when the politics of the body – whether that body belonged to a cyborg, Monica Lewinsky, or a person living with HIV/AIDS – was unprecedentedly intense.

Fortified by these influences, cultural studies was an anthropology of the everyday life of Western, contemporary, commercial-democratic society. But any ethnographer who sallied forth into this Dark Continent would be confronted not with jungle but jingles. The mode of subsistence they would encounter might be 'hunting and collecting' – but in its modern, profane form of 'working and shopping'. Some superficial aspects of the ethnographic study of culture retained that classic anthropological form of 'Western white folk sitting down among non-Western, non Anglophone folk of colour'; for instance, Daniel Miller in Trinidad or Jamaica, Marie Gillespie among the Punjabi communities in the London suburb of Southall, Eric Michaels among the Walpiri in central desert Australia. But this new ethnography was very much an exploration of the analyst's own home culture. Thus, Miller was investigating the uptake of the Internet in Jamaican popular music culture; Gillespie was observing the British Asian community's use of television; Michaels's interest in the Aboriginal 'invention' of television was because he 'wanted to understand our, not their, media revolution' (Michaels, 1994: 22).

Agents and audiences

This kind of cultural studies was interested in people as **agents** – people *doing* stuff (purposefully and reflexively), not just sitting *watching* stuff. However, these agents were not exempt from modernity – they were tourists, fashion-istas, Visa-card wielding, conscious of brand names and full of desire. Their struggles weren't directly with nature or the elements, nor with landlords and coal owners. They struggled with ideas and images produced for them (e.g. national, sexual and other stereotypes); with amenities designed for them (e.g. environmental ravages perpetrated in the name of road-building); and with cor-porations whose success depended on their own – or their children's – active collusion (e.g. McDonald's).

It was noticeable that the concept of agency was the very thing that brought both sociologically and anthropologically trained investigators into the cultural domain. Media studies had more or less colonised popular culture; most critical attention was devoted to questions of meaning (language, representation, ide-ology, images) in broadcasting, cinema, music and similar entertainment. Studies of popular culture that focused on community (Hoggart) rather than ide-ology (Hall) had declined somewhat. In the 'ideology' version of cultural studies, media were the ground upon which the search for sense-making prac-tices was conducted: 'practices' were thought to be *discursive*, producing *subjectivities*. They were not thought to be *active*, producing *events* (or at least, this was not of primary interest).

For its part, sociology, even sociology of culture, was not well equipped con-ceptually or methodologically to deal with the spoken, written, visual, aural, sung, narrated and photographed content of media, since it was committed to generalisability of findings, and therefore to quantitative data, rather than in-close engagement with individual textual complexity. The exploration of individual meanings was the speciality of those trained in literary, linguistic and screen studies. Combining the production and circulation of meaning with certain classic sociological preoccupations (for instance time, space, institution) and with classic anthropological concerns (practices, customs, ceremonies) became possible with the addition of the agent.

Agents were people doing something. Conversely – or rather, *perversely* – audiences were routinely understood as 'people *not doing* anything at all'. In other words the actual practice and custom of *doing* 'audiencing' (a word to describe this activity doesn't seem to exist) was reduced to an *abstraction*, not investigated as an integral activity of everyday life. It was abstracted from that context to serve as evidence for other issues – class or gender relations, for instance, or more straightforwardly popular taste, belief and opinion.

Sociological studies of 'audiencing' were abstract because a methodological bias in favour of generalisable findings pushed the social sciences towards what became known as empirical audience research. This favoured large-scale sampling using surveys, focus groups, diary-keeping and other methods that might yield quantifiable results (see Morrison, 1998). In effect audiences were regarded as consequential only as the end point in the chain of media consumption. They were the proof of the pudding because they were the ones consuming it, in the form of shows, campaigns, crazes and commodities. But that was about the extent of their interest to empirical research. Their actions and opinions as individuals didn't matter, since audiences, taken as aggregates, were merely a convenient device for measuring the success or otherwise of initiatives taken by agencies and organisations located somehow in opposition to them, since audiences were always located at the 'effect' end of causal chains. And even more strangely, audiences were measured to gauge the effects of media on them, but these data were then said to indicate *demand* – which is a cause, not an effect.

The idea of active audiences gained ground when cultural studies challenged the prevailing assumption that watching TV was passive, but in this instance active too was an abstract idea. It meant 'actively making sense of the communicative content of media', and 'able to make up their own minds', rather than 'doing something'. The actual practice of doing audiencing was rarely investigated in any depth – it was regarded as a relatively straightforward quasi-linguistic transaction. Audiences had a bit of work to do, such as decoding, but what that practice comprised, how long it took, using what internal and contextual resources, and how it fitted into their own purposes and reflexions, was harder to study. Indeed, questions of what exactly *happened* in encounters with texts, and how the moment of sense-making (if it was a moment) could be captured for analysis, were never fully resolved, and still aren't.

The idea of audience passivity was partly required by scientific method. People in a definite context, seeking out and making sense of audio-visual media as part of other activities, were irrecoverable for analysis – too many variables; not an obvious causal sequence. This complexity was reduced to observable behaviour, on the pragmatic grounds that behaviour could be observed more or less scientifically, while the act of sense-making itself was much more fugitive. What happened individually, never mind socially, when people were reading, watching or listening, was not directly observable. And in any case behavioural analysts weren't usually interested in how people *made* sense (people as cause), but in the *impact on* people of what were thought to be ready-made meanings (people as effect).

Psychology in particular persisted with a method that completely evacuated both meaning and agency from audiencing. Audience members themselves were reduced to 'subjects' (often recruited from the student pool at large universities). The text was reduced to 'exposure' (as in 'subjects were exposed to TV segments'). Response was reduced to 'behaviour', assessed either directly (via galvanometers, etc.) or indirectly via reports by the subjects themselves on how they felt after exposure to stimulus.

Cultural studies was generally hostile to psychological and behavioural approaches to audiences. Its qualitative and critical methods favoured ethnographic audience studies, which for a while in the 1980s and 1990s dominated approaches to the media. But these were not the means by which sociologists and anthropologists themselves began to contribute directly to cultural studies, not least because many such studies would not pass muster as replicable or generalisable as required by their disciplinary methodology. Further, cultural studies' long engagement with mediated meanings, with the linguistic, visual and fictional or symbolic components of contemporary entertainments, made it much more sensitive than were the social sciences to the content of the media that audiences consumed. Indeed, it could be said that cultural studies wasn't interested in audiences for functional or instrumental reasons. How many people watched, what the ratings were, and what the effects of media were on individuals' subsequent behaviour, purchases or opinions, were all interesting but secondary questions.

Cultural studies was therefore, in turn, not much taken up by industry organisations devoted to audience research, although some agencies made a name for themselves for doing their own qualitative commentary, which was often indistinguishable from cultural studies, except that it was applied to the business of winning customers, and achieved by methods that Miller et al. identify as 'surveillance' (2001: 210). For instance, Cheskin in the USA produced a report on *Media Content: The Place Where We Live*:

> At the heart of reality is 'experience'. Our moment-to-moment experience of content constitutes a significant, and growing, part of our overall experience of life. The businesses that produce content and distribute it through media increasingly seek to understand what *kinds* of experiences their customers seek. This idea of experience, slowly overtaking an earlier concept that focused on type of programme, story or topic, focuses on the emotional benefits that resonate most deeply with customers. Understand the kinds of experience people want, and business understands the future of content.
>
> This new focus on 'content experience' matters as much in print as it does in film or video. As digital media increasingly come to the fore, be it in print (the current dominant use of the web), or video (the next wave of interactive TV), understanding the desired experiences customers seek will make the difference between success and failure. (Cheskin, 2002: 3)

The focus on the experience of everyday life, on media content as part of experience, and the shift from textual formats and genres to contextual emotion and experience, led Cheskin to assert that 'content is reality'.

This was where cultural studies came in. But cultural studies itself was devoted not to business consultancies but to the attempt to understand subjectivity-formation in modern commercial cultures, and in a non-capitalised 'cultural commons'. This was a theoretical quest as much as an empirical one, so each audience ethnography tended to start from a theoretical interest in, say, class, gender, ethnicity or sexual orientation, not in the everyday practice of 'audiencing' as such.

Studies of audiences ought to have attracted anthropology, since there were more ethnographies of audiences done within cultural studies than you could poke a stick at. The usual line of descent was traced from David Morley in particular and Dorothy Hobson (Birminghamites), via Ien Ang and David Buckingham, to such as Marie Gillespie, Ellen Seiter and Joke Hermes. But these served if anything to drive cultural studies and anthropology further apart, accentuating rather than blurring their disciplinary differences.

Despite its own intra-disciplinary ferment, anthropology was more confident in obliging its PhDs to imbibe a coherent version of its method, canon and purpose than was cultural studies. This was especially the case in the USA (see Marcus, 2001: 179–80), but it also operated in prestige anthropological training camps in London, for instance at SOAS and UCL (the School of Oriental and African Studies and University College London). There was still some (residual) force in the idea that cultural studies looked at the *West* while anthropology studied the *Rest* (Marcus, 2001: 169), and that anthropology was biased towards the study of cultures without commerce (Berry, 2001: 459). While no one would have argued for such distinctions as *necessary*, anthropology still wasn't comfortable with contemporary Western, commercial, Anglophone culture – the very place where media ethnographies abounded – as its training ground. A suspicion remained that the version of ethnography done in cultural studies was methodologically flawed (indeed that cultural studies in general was a methodological wasteland), and that forays into the here and now were better left to more senior anthropologists (Marcus: 179–80).

As a result of these circumstances, where both methods and theoretical orientations differed, the move into cultural studies by sociology and anthropology did not occur in ethnography, the area where most overlap might have been expected. Instead, sociological and anthropological approaches to culture began to thrive when questions of meaning could be associated not so much with *media* as with *agents*.

Travel agents

The agent came into its own via studies of large-scale, modern leisure activities that necessarily involved individuals in doing things, but equally clearly involved mass entertainment techniques familiar from media. Perhaps the paradigm example of this was *tourism*, which attracted considerable sociological attention (John Urry, Chris Rojek, Jennifer Craik).

An early (but hard to come by) treatment of tourism from a cultural studies perspective, called 'The Spectacle of Travel', was published by Paulo Prato and Gianluca Trivero (Prato and Trivero, 1985). Following the French theorist of speed, Paul Virilio, they argued that, if it had one, the essence of modernity was mobility:

> In recent decades, mobility has exploded to the point of characterising everyday life much more than the traditional image of the 'home and family'. Transport ceases to function as a metaphor of progress or at least of 'modern' life, and becomes instead the primary activity of existence. (Prato and Trivero, 1985: 40)

Their approach to the 'spectacle' of travel was in interesting contrast to the way that John Urry combined a sociological perspective with some concerns of cultural studies, in arguing for such a thing as the tourist 'gaze' (Urry, 1990).

How Urry came to tourism as a sociologist was instructive. It was a rather fastidious, paw-shaking approach, to say the least, almost amounting to disciplinary self-loathing. He prefaced his book *The Tourist Gaze* with an acknowledgement that he was only 'prompted to take holiday-making "seriously"' as a result of an initiative by the ESRC, one of the research funding councils in the UK (Urry, 1990: ix). That is, it wasn't tourism itself that attracted his curiosity, but funded public policy. As if to establish his critical distance from the object of study, he presented a series of pejorative quotations about tourism, headed by this, purportedly from Henry James: 'Tourists are "vulgar, vulgar, vulgar"'. And his opening gambit was 'On the face of it there could not be a more trivial subject for a book' (2). Almost ruefully, he conceded that 'making theoretical sense of "fun, pleasure and entertainment" has proved a difficult task for social scientists' (7).

To justify studying something that was too trivial and vulgar to be taken seriously (but that for other writers comprised the 'primary activity of existence' in modernity), Urry introduced two sociological manoeuvres. First, he had a theory: that of the 'tourist gaze'. He took this idea not from psychoanalytic-feminist media work in the tradition of Laura Mulvey (work that was enormously influential in cinema studies, and thence cultural studies) but – more tenuously for understanding tourism – from Foucault's work on the birth of the clinic. Foucault's account of the *disciplinary* gaze of institutional medical practitioners was applied to a much less coherent 'institution' – the retail travel industry. Second, he declared that 'rather than being trivial tourism is significant in its ability to reveal aspects of normal practices which might otherwise remain opaque'. On the model of deviancy studies, the investigation of tourism could 'reveal interesting and significant aspects of "normal" societies' (2). In other words, tourism was interesting because if properly theorised by the sociologist's gaze it could tell the investigator about something else, namely the 'normal'. This 'normal' was in fact 'everyday life' rendered into sociology.

Once the first step was taken, progress could be made. What Urry did find, then, was that tourism conformed to a shift from Fordist to post-Fordist consumption, 'organised' to 'disorganised' capitalism. It was an instance of broader changes towards market differentiation and segmentation, customisation and consumer choice. Urry's attention to 'the gaze' inverted a familiar socio-anthropological presumption that action preceded mediation – i.e. that first there was authentic practice, then there were media representations thereof. The tourist was clear evidence that people were actively travelling all over the world, in industrial quantities, mainly to *experience* what had *already* been mediated – the message of great cities and landscapes as *signs of themselves* (see Frow, 1997: 69–74; esp. 73).

Indeed, as Elizabeth Wilson observed, the 'tourist gaze' turned cities like London and Paris almost inside out. The inner parts, most valued for their metropolitan allure, were the most likely to be 'cleansed, sanitised and rearranged for the delectation of the tourist' (Wilson, 2001: 146). And so any authentic (non-mediated) experience of the same cities would have to travel ever further out to the despised suburbs, beyond the postcards, as it were. Restoration and marketing produced tourist sites that were 'a monument to – rather than a survival of – a lost way of life' (147). Authenticity was a sign, not an experience.

But still, tourism required extremely energetic agents to match reality to their pre-imagined textualisation of it. As the literary theorist and semiotician Jonathan Culler observed, 'the tourist is interested in everything as a sign of itself. . . . All over the world, the unsung armies of semioticians, the tourists, are fanning out in search of the signs' (Culler, 1981: 127).

It was clear that tourism as an activity, not just as an industry, shared important features with media consumption – people could consume places, as well as media. But this was unlike traditional consumption (it didn't use up the thing consumed), and had definite effects on the places consumed themselves. Furthermore, it brought consumption out into the open, into the very space of the public sphere (the agora, forum, town square, pulpit) – the locus of public life. The old idea of consumption as something passive, private, domestic and determined, whereas the public sphere was purposeful and rational, simply didn't work any more. Nor did the idea of cultural customs and practices being somehow prior to or outside of the world of media and mass entertainment. People loitered in public as consumers. Public places were steeped in mediated meanings – all the world was already a stage.

Studies of tourism were very helpful in bringing sociology close to cultural studies. Indeed, John Urry's work itself was taken up by cultural theorist John Frow in his account of 'Tourism and the Semiotics of Nostalgia'. Frow analysed why much critical writing about tourism was itself 'nostalgic': a 'nostalgic narrative of a decline from use value to commodity, from immanence to instrumentality, from the observing traveller to the possessive tourist, and from the world as being to the world as simulacrum' (1997: 87). But he followed Urry (1990: 138–40) in suggesting that whatever the rights and wrongs of such a narrative, the gap between the two poles (authentic origin and postmodern commodification) was bridged by *photography*. Frow wrote:

> The most Platonic of art forms, it [photography] describes what Urry calls 'a kind of hermeneutic circle' between a set of culturally authoritative representations (brochures, advertisements, guidebooks, coffee-table books), then the experiential

capture of those images for oneself, and finally the display of a further set of representations which confirm the original set and its relation to the real. It is a process of
authentication, the establishment of a verified reality between origin and trace. (Frow,
1997: 93)

This was a far cry from those understandings of media representations that kept
them literally *framed* – two-dimensional and out of time. Frow made photography a *'process* of authentication', part of the unfolding practice of tourism, which
was itself dissolving, as Urry had noted, into 'all sorts of other social and cultural
practices':

'Culture' has come to occupy a more central position in the organisation of present-
day societies, whose contemporary culture can be at least in part characterised as
'postmodern'. Postmodernism involves a dissolving of the boundaries, not only
between high and low cultures, but also between different cultural forms, such as
tourism, art, education, photography, television, music, sport, shopping and architecture. What I have termed the tourist gaze is increasingly bound up with and is partly
indistinguishable from all sorts of other social and cultural practices. This has the
effect, as 'tourism' *per se* declines in specificity, of universalising the tourist gaze –
people are much of the time 'tourists' whether they like it or not. (Urry, 1990: 82; see
also Frow, 1997: 92)

Shopping for desire

Another mode of consumption done by active agents encouraged anthropology
to engage more fruitfully with cultural studies. This was shopping. It was a
topic not unknown within cultural studies. Meaghan Morris for instance had
published her celebrated reflection on 'things to do with shopping centres',
which brought suburbia, the mall, feminism and cultural theory into almost
magical-realist focus. This feat was surpassed, perhaps, only by her equally
admirable go at cultural-studies-does-tourism, 'At Henry Parkes Motel' – a
paper that among other things challenged the prevailing rhetoric of women as
place-bound and men as travellers (these essays are collected in Morris, 1998a).
Rachel Bowlby too had published a study of shopping, focusing on Parisian
department stores and their legacy as part of the European literary imaginary
(Bowlby, 1985). That theme was taken up by Mica Nava and extended to orientalism and cosmopolitanism, and to the giant London store Selfridge's,
connecting the worlds of shopping and mobility in the imperial consumers'
imaginary:

My argument has been that the interest of occidental women in a metaphorical orient
[partly promoted at Selfridge's], their fascination with imagined other people and
places – whether geographically located in Persia, Russia, Africa or Argentina – must
also be understood as a form of reaction against the politics and emotional customs of
the moment, as a half-conscious identification with other subalterns, and, moreover, as
a sign of the precariousness of Englishness and English masculinity. (Nava, 1998: 188)

In short, shopping was brought into the purview of major theoretical concerns – imperialism, orientalism, masculinity, subaltern studies, and resistive politics, not to mention the allure of cosmopolitan mobility itself (see also Wilson, 1999).

But it wasn't the *metaphorical* orient that attracted anthropology towards shopping. Like sociology, anthropology was interested in *agents*. When they turned their attention to contemporary culture it was not to the 'imagined other' that they turned, but to the shoppers. Daniel Miller was an important figure here, for he was a bona fide anthropologist, working in a high-prestige institutional setting at UCL. From such a position, and following from the work of Mary Douglas and Baron Isherwood who introduced the study of consumerism as 'material culture' into anthropology in the late 1970s (Berry, 2001: 458), Miller developed an anthropological theory of shopping (Daniel Miller, 1998). He analysed it as an activity akin to sacrificial ritual. He argued that the act of purchasing goods was strongly linked to social relations of love and care, and that in both shopping and sacrifice the ultimate intention was to constitute others as 'desiring subjects'. Here, intriguingly, Miller arrived at the same end point as Foucault had done in the history of sexuality, when he discussed how desire, pleasure and action (respectively) had changed in relative prominence over time. For the ancients, most prominent was action; while for the moderns:

> I could say that the modern 'formula' is desire, which is theoretically underlined and practically accepted, since you have to liberate your own desire. Acts are not very important, and pleasure – nobody knows what it is! (Foucault, 1984: 359)

Desiring subjects, sexuality and shopping: cultural studies had, it seemed, caught up with the pulp fiction of desire, the genre known as 'shopping and fucking' novels.

Miller's analysis was part of a much larger project on 'material culture' within anthropology (which included an excellent journal of that name), and it was but one of many individual studies undertaken by Miller and various colleagues, ranging from Internet use in Trinidad to the material culture of cars, homes and Christmas. Miller remained an anthropologist, but his willingness both to theorise consumption, and to conduct ethnographic fieldwork in postmodern London and postcolonial Trinidad alike, offered new ways for cultural studies to take everyday life seriously. No longer was it blighted by prejudices about the primacy of the mode of production, nor literary-intellectual prejudices about the quality of experience in modern consumer culture. Instead, what consumption was *for*, and what it *meant*, could be explored, via the *agency* of those who did it (see Storey, 1999: 159–63).

Very slowly, then, perhaps over twenty years or more, the interactions among cultural studies, sociology, anthropology and feminism began to focus on the *mode* of consumption – seeing it not in the abstract, as the end product of economic production (i.e. from a Marxist perspective), but as a *practice*. Whether they were tourists or shoppers, people were *doing something*. They were not dumbed-down dupes or dopes, but purposeful and reflexive, sometimes dreaming, but even that had political overtones, as Nava had argued. Their activities were both mediated and commercial, as had been understood by observers as varied as Vance Packard and Roland Barthes. Everyday life itself included 'audiencing' and reading as well as more energetic pursuits; audiencehood like tourism was dissolved into everyday life (Abercrombie and Longhurst, 1998). These activities could no longer be seen simply as the enactment of intentions originating in the boardrooms of media and capitalist corporations. Indeed, as Hermes astutely observed, the *act* of reading was just that, since for some consumers, some of the time, leafing through magazines was a means of passing the time, not of purposefully hoovering up meanings from the page (Hermes, 1995: 12–28). Everyday life in commercial democracies, in short, could be studied as the active making of (material) culture, not as epiphenomenon (see Chapter 4).

Walking the talk

According to the political philosopher Thomas Hobbes (writing in 1651), two things followed when cities waxed fat upon the riches gained from empire – first, *leisure*; and thence, *philosophy*. And for Hobbes, the medium that connected leisure and philosophy was the walk.

> *Leasure* is the mother of *Philosophy*. . . . After the *Athenians* by the overthrow of the *Persian* Armies, had gotten Dominion of the Sea . . . and were grown wealthy; they that had no employment, neither at home, nor abroad, had little else to employ themselves in, but either in *telling or hearing news*, or in discoursing of *Philosophy* publiquely to the youth of the City. Every Master took some place for that Purpose. *Plato* in certain publique Walks called *Academia*, from one *Academus*: *Aristotle* in the Walk of the Temple of *Pan*, called *Lycæum*: others in the *Stoa*, or covered Walk, wherein the Merchants Goods were brought to land: others in other places; where they spent the time of their Leasure, in teaching or in disputing of their Opinions: and some in any place, where they could get the youth of the City together to hear them talk.
>
> From this it was, that the place where any of them taught, and disputed, was called *Schola*, which in their Tongue signifieth Leasure; and their Disputations, *Diatribæ*, that is to say, *Passing of the time*. Also the Philosophers themselves had the name of their Sects, some of them from these their Schools; For they that followed *Plato*'s Doctrine, were called *Academiques*; the followers of *Aristotle*, *Peripatetiques*, from the Walk hee taught in; and those that *Zeno* taught, *Stoiques*, from the *Stoa*: as if we should denominate men from *More-fields*, from *Pauls-Church*, and from the *Exchange*, because they meet there often, to prate and loyter. (Hobbes, 1968: 683–5)

Leisure, youth, the city, walks, loitering, gathering to talk, exchanging the news, passing the time, disputing, 'prating' – this was the very ground upon which Western philosophy, and thence 'academics', 'scholars', 'lyceums', 'peripatetics', 'stoics' and 'diatribes', had been fostered. Hobbes was clear that the 'mother' of all this was affluent under-employment, resulting from wealth won by war – and sustained by slavery, though Hobbes didn't mention that. In Marxist terms, philosophy was therefore the material form taken by surplus value; in Thorstein Veblen's terms it was a form of conspicuous leisure or waste, bringing repute in direct proportion to its disutility or wastefulness (Veblen, 1953: 238ff.).

If leisure was its mother, philosophy's cradle was the city. Leisured youth roamed and strolled in the city, passing the time with purposeless pleasures like hanging around and gossiping about the affairs of the day, gathering in public places to 'prate' and dispute. And via these very activities, they managed to invent Western philosophy!

Hobbes applied this scenario directly to his own early modern city of London. In fact the same aimless drifts of under-employed youth and leisured 'masters' characterised the rapidly expanding cities of modernity, the more so as industrialisation took hold. These 'loiterers' and walkers were not credited with inventing anything so noble as philosophy. Indeed from the apprentices who frequented Shakespeare's theatres onwards, the urban 'youth of today', whenever 'today' happened to be, were a bit of a worry. The city fathers of Shakespearean London complained bitterly about the theatres, precisely because of their attractiveness to under-employed and socially mixed crowds:

> They are the ordinary places for vagrant persons, Maisterless men, thieves, horse stealers, whoremongers, Coozeners, Coneycatchers, contrivers of treason and other idele and daungerous persons to meet together. . . . They maintaine idlenes in such persons as haue no vocation & draw apprentices and other seruants from their ordinary workes and all sortes of people from the resort unto sermons and other Christian exercises to the great hindrance of traides and pphantion of religion. (Cited in Harbage, 1941: 84–5)

However, aimless strollers did eventually attract more positive attention via the concept of the 'flâneur'. This character's walks through the nineteenth-century city were brought to the attention of the critical intellectual imagination by a number of important writers who were, in the main, thinking about Paris. They included the poet and essayist Charles Baudelaire, as well as critics Siegfried Kracauer and Walter Benjamin, writing in the 1930s. There was a flurry of renewed critical interest in the flâneur in the 1980s and 1990s, in cinema studies, social criticism, feminism and cultural studies (see Tester, 1994; and Wilson, 2001 for an excellent discussion of the issues). This set of concerns was given further texture through the work of Michel de Certeau, for whom walking and mapping the city were resistive or 'poaching' practices for otherwise disenfranchised citizens (de Certeau, 1984). It was fascinating that walking – that most basic of everyday actions – could attract so much interest.

As Elizabeth Wilson summarised it, the flâneur's renewed popularity in *fin de siècle* academic writing bespoke both anxiety and disagreement:

> Academic writers seem unsure, or disagree, whether the *flâneur* belongs to the past or still exists today. Some writers have celebrated the *flâneur*, others have seen this figure as merely a narcissist, a privileged bourgeois who functions to endorse and even celebrate the commodification of urban existence. To the first group, to observe the

passing crowd, to loiter in shops and cafés, to explore forgotten corners of cities, is to uncover the secret of urban modernity, but to the second it merely reveals its meaningless banality. (Wilson, 2001: 90)

There wasn't much doubt that Wilson favoured the first of these positions, but had to duck and weave through some debates within feminism, which she chose to conduct in dialogue with Janet Wolff and Griselda Pollock, to sustain this position. Wolff had argued that women were excluded from the public sphere; Pollock that the flâneur was no more than the bearer of the possessive male gaze (see Wilson, 2001: 79–83; 92–3). Wilson, a noted urbanite herself, was reluctant to concede these restrictions, and indeed extended the discussion of flânerie not only across gender, but across time and space:

Some writers suggest that there can still be *flâneurs* in contemporary cities. For them shopping malls and theme parks, especially but not exclusively Disneyland and Disney World, become locations for the new *flânerie*. . . . Susan Buck-Morss goes further, suggesting that the activities of the zapping radio listener, the television watcher, the Internet surfer and the package tour tourist are those of the latter day *flâneur*. She finds 'traces of *flânerie*' in many of the activities of mass society, particularly the 'merely imaginary gratification provided by advertising, illustrated journals, fashion and sex magazines, all of which go by the *flâneur*'s principle of "look but don't touch".' (Wilson, 2001: 90–1; the internal quotation is to Buck-Morss, 1986: 105)

Wilson went on to point out a further ambiguity in the flâneur. 'It is still uncertain whether she or he is simply strolling, loitering and looking (window shopping) or whether these activities must be transformed into a representation – journalism, film novel – in order to qualify as *flânerie*' (2001: 91). In other words, were such activities as strolling, looking, people-watching, window shopping and tourism sufficient unto themselves, or did they only count as flânerie if they were part of a creative enterprise that would eventually make them 'signs of themselves'?

Certainly, people watching in the city was part of the creative process for a number of modes of writing, from dark-side ficto-journalism such as Will Self's *Quantity Theory of Insanity* – where suburbanites were observably *normal*, but *dead* (Self, 1991), right through to Mills & Boon romance writers who sat in cafés, watching the passing crowd, to gain inspiration for their next same-but-different story. An example of the latter was itself deemed worthy of journalistic reporting. Romance writer Helen Bianchin, author of twenty-three books, was presented to local readers as a flâneuse, bringing chance encounters in coffee shops to her readers around the world, and taking inspiration directly from the way people *walked*:

I love people watching. I might be sitting in a café and I'll see an attractive girl who has something that makes her stand out – the way she walks or wears her clothes – and your imagination wanders. You think: 'I wonder what she does for a living. I wonder if she has a boyfriend'. Then I might see an attractive man and my creative juices flow.

I might put them together and build a life for them, a reason for meeting and some sort of conflict. (Helen Bianchin, quoted in 'Heroine Addicts', *West Australian* magazine, 21 March 1991: 19–22)

But the interpenetrations of creativity and the everyday actions of walking and looking among the flux of modern associated life (Velben's phrase) were much more thoroughgoing than such occasional accidents of individual inspiration. A number of modern characters have been licensed in fiction to cross the boundaries that otherwise prevented most people from experiencing at first hand other parts of the society with whose denizens they mixed on the streets. Chief among those fictional agents who walked into dangerous places, on behalf of readers' and audiences' will to know, were:

- the **detective**, private eye or gumshoe,
- the **prostitute** (see Wilson, 2001, for the debate about prostitutes as flâneuses),
- the **journalist**,
- and – later – the **supermodel**.

The first three were staples of modern fiction (the last had to wait for Helen Fielding's *Cause Celeb* (1995) perhaps). They were almost always encountered in cities – they were flâneurs. But their special purpose was as brokers of *knowledge* between different segments and sectors of society. The paradigm example of the licensed observer of the minutiae and banalities of modern life, who brought apparently unconnected trivia into significant and consequential knowledge, was Sherlock Holmes (see Richards, 1993). A later reincarnation of the cross-demographic boundary-hopper, who brought a very different kind of knowledge to a generation more impressed by inter-class affect than interdisciplinary knowledge, was Julia Roberts's character in the 1990 film *Pretty Woman*. She too was a flâneuse; a denizen of hotels not homes, communicating across demographic boundaries by shopping (on Rodeo Drive), observing the life of the 'other' (in this case her rich client) by getting into its bath.

As for journalists, not least in imaginative screen fiction from films such as *Watergate* to TV series like *Glasgow Kiss*, their disciplinary gaze ('vaguely sexualised', in Wilson's phrase) was, horror to them, remarkably similar to that of cultural studies. Both journalism and cultural studies were licensed by the nature of their task to:

- **explore** the full range of the social,
- **describe** other people's lives,
- **generalise** specialist knowledge for general readers,
- **interrogate** decisions and actions on behalf of 'governmental' discourses of appropriate behaviour (ethical and legal) and manageability (decision-making, policy),

- **textualise** the world in order to know it,
- **communicate** by appropriate idiom to target demographics.

That description of what journalists did was an exact match for what academic cultural studies claimed to do. Journalism and cultural studies were in fact *competitors* in the social production of knowledge about everyday life. They vied with each other for power to command in the name of truth. Perhaps journalists *walked* more, certainly in their own imaginations, and they definitely reached a wider public, as they followed their nose for news among the living agents of modernity. Cultural studies, for its part, was perhaps more likely to pursue its observations virtually, in the textual realm, loitering among media, gazing at screens and documents. But the converse could equally hold, since investigative journalism was predominantly a documentary pursuit, while even cultural studies scholars liked to go out on the raz once in a while, collecting data as participant observers of the urban mélange (an example in this context would be James Donald's *Imagining the Modern City*, 1999).

One thing that journalism and cultural studies shared was an attraction to the negatives of modern life, the human cost of progress. The flâneur was said to aspire to psychic possession of the sights beheld; to 'enjoy' them in an act of selfish and sexualised consumption. But there was a pathological side to flânerie, since some solitary observers of the urban scene wanted to consume more than the pleasurable sight of the anonymous crowd. Here were muggers, stalkers, kerb-crawlers, predators on urban mobility and anonymity, even serial killers such as the Yorkshire Ripper. The journalist would turn up, in the style of New York crime photographer Weegee, to record the costs of that possessiveness on the occasions when the flâneur took a step too far. Some journalists, who specialised in getting to the scenes of such violations faster than the police, in cities as varied as New York and São Paulo or Mexico City, became celebrities as a result.

On the next corner the investigating ethnographer from cultural studies would be stationed. Here the pathologisation of walking and loitering was observed as a gendered and racialised practice. Instead of flâneurs, they'd see women in danger, or a law-enforcement system that stopped and searched people walking on the streets for no other reason than that they were black. Even in Paris itself, it was hard to act the flâneur if you were *Algerian*. And judging by their own experience at the hands of police and other citizens, many African-Americans, Caribbean Britons and Aboriginal Australians would find the very concept of the flâneur hard to credit. According to *Policing the Crisis* and *The Empire Strikes Back*, among the most ambitious studies published by the Birmingham Centre, racialised surveillance and policing of the streets was part of the command strategy of modern hegemony (see Hall, et al., 1978; CCCS, 1982). But 'stop and search' was increasingly captured by the very surveillance cameras that were installed to make urban danger a 'sign of itself', with videotape capturing not felonious flâneurs but the forces of order themselves, laying into pedestrians of colour with night sticks, producing not knowledge but *difference*; reinforcing fear of difference.

And then, *resistive* walking in cities was always a popular method of counter-hegemonic answering back, making mischief, even mending fences. Michel de Certeau's pedestrian 'poachers' appropriated meanings and thence freedom from the very use of routes through city streets designed for purposes other than theirs. Protest marches and demonstrations evolved into different genres, from the barricade to the carnival. Women against violence marched together in 'reclaim the streets' or 'reclaim the night' events. Gay, lesbian and trans-sexual culture paraded in the kitsch spectacular of Mardi Gras parades. There were 'Walks for Reconciliation', where Indigenous and non-Indigenous Australians walked together in their hundreds of thousands, typically across city bridges. A quarter of a million walked across the Sydney Harbour Bridge in May 2000. Walking was put to *critical* use.

As a 'sign of itself', critical walking through potentially hostile streets could become compelling television, for instance in Darcus Howe's TV series on English ethnicity, *White Tribe*, as he (a Caribbean Englishman) ambled through white-bigot suburbs from Oldham to Dover, talking to racists in their door-ways, finding aliens on park benches, and making the English strange – and embarrassing – to themselves simply by walking among them. In another vein, but equally dependent on what might be termed critical walking, was a Channel 4 chat show of the 1980s, hosted by Muriel Gray, called *Walkie Talkie*, where she interviewed guests as the two of them took a walk, rather than doing it in a studio.

Walking was put to *aesthetic* use in fashion. The catwalk has been commented on without much enthusiasm by many critics, for whom parading apparel of little everyday utility on impossibly proportioned models was just another example of commercial exploitation and excess. There was less interest in what the catwalk was *for*. It demonstrated clothes and body in *action* – it was the aes-theticisation not of the body alone, nor of garments alone, but of *walking*. The fall of a garment over a walking body was the acid test of whether it worked or not. The exaggerated sashay of the model (each foot successively crossing in front of the other) was not so much, or only, a fetishisation of walking-to-be-looked-at, but also a *method* for *analysing* clothes.

As with tourism and flânerie, the fashion walk was postmodernised and democratised by mediation, as fashion broke out of its specialist, class and eco-nomic confines in the late 1980s, and began to 'address' a mass audience of increasingly sophisticated 'readers'. The supermodel especially was an agent through whose bodily displays cross-demographic communication became pos-sible – she joined, or possibly began to displace, the detective, prostitute and journalist as one who could connect the different worlds of the city. The anti-fashion or 'grunge' moment of the early 1990s, exemplified by the model Kate Moss and her Svengali-photographer Corinne Day, brought the opposites together most challengingly, as a gawky Croydon schoolgirl with a 'fuck you' attitude, photographed in nondescript suburban surroundings and trashed apartments, brought fashion to its knees, and thereby to millions (see Moss, 1995; Cotton, 2000: 78–85). Meanwhile, in carefully calculated campaigns, the supermodels of the day, led by Cindy Crawford, Linda Evangelista, Christy Turlington and Claudia Schiffer, began to allow their images to appear in cross-over media such as men's, 'lad' and sports magazines, extending the reach of fashion across the gender boundary for the first time via the fact that walking could at last, without reference to streetwalking, be seen as seriously sexy.

Walking – and fashion with it – became a *literacy*. The Parisian cable and Internet channel, FTV and FTV.com, took the process a stage further. Here, viewers could watch a literally endless succession of models walking, usually directly towards the camera. The information element of FTV was kept to the minimum – there was music but no voice-over or presentation, although there were captions and inter-titles. FTV could be used as wallpaper in any venue from a retail outlet to a rave party; and appreciated in many modes, from chemically induced euphoria delighting in repetition, to study aid, to 'that obscure object of desire'. This was the democratisation of the bodily sublime. For a vernacular definition of the sublime, as 'something treated *with admiration and respect* . . . as the cause of a feeling of shock, amazement, or simply of being "impressed"', see Meaghan Morris (1998a: 243). Ordinary walking, for everyone to see, was recruited to the display of bodies, couture and ideas-in-motion that had previously been held back from the vulgar gaze of the *hoi polloi*. And depending on whose collection, which model, and how shot, the result was quite frequently shocking, amazing and impressive, all at once: well photographed fashion models *were* the democratisation of the sublime.

Walking was part of public life in the city, a civic activity, and therefore part of civilisation. It was an expression of the individual's citizenship, and of the population's interconnectedness. In this it differed from what was previously thought of as a separate realm from civilisation, namely culture, which was made in the home, not the city. As Prato and Trivero put it, 'the city-fortress is the basis of modern civilization and the house is where culture is developed and preserved' (1985: 39). In this archaic schema, culture was human, while the city was technological. But under the pressure of mobility, 'domestic space preserves a purely reproductive function . . . The epoch of mass transport coincides with the decline of the significance of domestic, working and recreational spaces, intended as "places" where affectations accumulate and social identity is formed' (40).

Eating out

The 'separation between being and the home', and the shift of the centre of gravity of everyday life from home to mobility, from culture to civilisation, meant that another component of everyday life was radically transformed: food.

The old idea of culture referred to by Prato and Trivero was that of the hearth and home, kith and kin, where family, nation and identity were thought to be brought to mutual self-realisation – the home was the place where *being* was produced, and a central activity in that process was eating.

An exemplary bearer of such a concept of culture was Dorothy Hartley. Her name is the same as my own mother's, but this Dorothy Hartley was no relation. She was born in 1892 of an English father and Welsh mother, remained a spinster, signing herself as D. Hartley (Miss). She travelled the countryside in Britain and Africa, often alone as a proto-backpacker, wrote for the *Daily Sketch*, and died at 93 (see an appreciation of her by Adrian Bailey in *Gourmet*, December 2000: http://www.epicurious.com/g_gourmet/g06_feature/james_beard/indomitabl e.html). Dorothy Hartley published many books about England, including a six-volume account of the *Life and Work of the People of England*. She lived near Llangollen, 'on the Welsh border where the mutton is good, the beef bad, and the best fruits are the wild ones' (1999: 18).

From there this Dorothy Hartley, who styled herself 'the historian housekeeper' (1999: 578), wrote a much-praised book called *Food in England*, published in 1954. She introduced it as if welcoming a visitor: 'So please consider this book as an old-fashioned kitchen, not impressive, but a warm friendly place, where one can come in at any time and have a chat with the cook' (1999: iii). She imagined its pages as a meeting of friends, some reaching back to early medieval times:

> All are friendly together and make you very welcome in the kitchen they have all loved so long – the English kitchen. It is not a very tidy kitchen, because, like this book, it has been in use so long; and so many different people have worked therein, putting things into different places, so that the author does apologise to cooks – past and present – if anyone has slipped out in the blitz or turned up in the wrong recipe. (1999: v)

Miss Hartley invited 'any cook who enjoys our ancestral heritage' to 'begin at the material end and study the fuel and methods first', but the book itself began with a history of the English people going back to Saxons, Danes and Normans. A 'dark-headed, enterprising people of strong, warlike stock' mixed with a 'white-haired, stubborn people, at least half of whom were only one generation settled from sea raiding, and whose flanks were constantly beset by the resentful aboriginals that they had penned up in Wales' (1999: 27). Only once the people were 'planted' did she introduce the various kinds of hearth, the stoves, fires, fuels and gadgets that would make up the 'hearth and home' of English culture. She summed up the attractions of all that at the end of her description of the 'roasting jack and screen' (a vertical spit that turned meat by clockwork in front of an open fire):

> The jack was of polished brass, wound up with a simple key, turning clockwork that lasted about an hour. It didn't go round and round, but, like a circular pendulum, turned four times to the left, turn-turn-turn-click; then slowly back the other way, turn-turn-turn-click to the right, and so the pleasant fireside rhythm synchronised with the

ticking of the grandfather clock at the far side of the kitchen, and the sizzling of the meat, the bubbling and boiling orchestration of the pots, and the purring obligato of the kitchen cat. (Hartley, 1999: 51)

A nostalgic symphony perhaps, but in fact the book was clear-eyed as well as warm-hearted. The domestic down side was not neglected, with a good understanding of want and waste, poverty and plenty, medicines and potions. There were odd hints of domestic relations poking through the practicalities. 'Scottish Hot Pint', for instance, whose main ingredients were ale, heat and half a pint of whisky, was prepared by pouring the mixture 'rapidly from one jug to another till the hot pint is smooth, and the patient ready for it. It can be made in the time it takes to get a man's boots off on a cold night' (1999: 557). Or, more cryptically, this note on sloe gin: 'Sloes are best preserved in gin. Sloe gin, blended with Penny Royal and Valerian, has for years been used by country wives in connubial emergencies' (1999: 570). The nature of a 'connubial emergency' was not specified; on such subjects the book 'preserved an elegant reticence', just as, apparently, Victorian cookbooks had done on the subject of the cooking of winkles (1999: 278–9).

There was a chapter on the Industrial Revolution, headed 'Starvation and Plenty', that gave contrasting recipes and household accounts for orphans and rich people in London, Scottish farmers, English tourists to Wales, mill owners in Yorkshire and emigrants to Brisbane (1999: 578–606). The very flâneur himself made an appearance as 'the man about town'. Miss Hartley quoted a contemporary account that was all too well aware of the flâneur's need to cut a dash on limited cash: 'At a Coffee House you may dine for 2/6d, and there is also a Cigar Divan in the Strand or in Regent Street where you may lounge in the evening and have admirable coffee, a cigar and newspaper to read in a splendid well warmed room for 1/-' (1999: 604–5).

Hartley herself was certain that the effect of modernity was not so much that the new extremes of wealth and poverty translated into good and poor food. The connection was not direct. Pre-industrial poor people often fed healthily if simply. But:

> With the Industrial Revolution the people are driven off the land; they are cut off from their natural food supply, and are compelled for the first time to *buy* food. The cruelty of the Industrial Revolution was that it made money a necessity of *life*; it is not the crowding into towns, to work in the factories, nor the land, neglected, ceasing to provide food, *it is a dislocation of the food supply.* (1999: 578)

The industrialisation and commodification of food itself, then, was the cause of dislocation of that old notion of culture that included not just emotional succour and ideological self-realisation in the customs and practices of one's ancestral country, but also literal survival by means of self-sufficiency in food. Once food was brought within the cash nexus, culture itself had to yield to modernity, for people could not be self-sufficient, and had perforce to rely on large-scale social, industrial and state organisation to stay alive till payday. Food thereafter was part of urban civilisation – so much so that latter-day efforts to redress that industrial 'dislocation of the food supply' by DIY methods such as allotments and smallholdings seemed increasingly nostalgic or militantly 'alternative', and eventually fell over themselves laughing in the long-running BBC-TV sitcom *The Good Life*. The cook-housewife was converted from producer (of foods grown, taken or raised without money) to consumer.

   Once food entered the domain of consumption and mobility, it was open to a different kind of cultural studies. There was a connection between Dorothy Hartley's writing – as a kind of cultural studies in its own right – and the academic subject that grew up under that name. The link was Richard Hoggart. Hoggart was a generation younger than Hartley, but as a child he had experienced a culture that he had valued at his grandmother's kitchen table in Yorkshire. Some of it no doubt was the homeliness and creative making-do of Dorothy Hartley's English kitchen, but his was an urban and industrial, not a countryside experience. His own culture derived from the 'cruelty' of industrialisation itself, though of course he did not experience it as cruel. Quite the reverse. *The Uses of Literacy* famously recalls the sense of place, community, family and neighbourhood that characterised the back-to-back working-class houses of Leeds in Yorkshire after the First World War. Hoggart was concerned about what may have been lost when that culture in turn began to dissolve into a later phase of development, with the coming of popular media consumerism during the 1950s.

   But Dorothy Hartley was not nostalgic in any serious way; more grounded, bustling, curious. Her analysis of the effects of the Industrial Revolution did not prevent her continuing to tell the history of working-class, factory and trade foods with both insider knowledge and evident relish (1999: 233, 572). As Paul Gilroy pointed out (in a criticism of Richard Hoggart), the mode of writing in cultural studies that focused on personal experience of Englishness tended to exclude attention to racial and ethnic aspects of that culture (Gilroy, 1987: 12; 1996: 236; see also Carrington, 2001: 279–85, for a good account of these issues). Hartley's history of food did not neglect the fruits of empire. In a chapter on the 'new problems in the kitchen' consequent upon the discovery of the New World in Elizabethan times, she included a section on slave ships, and commented: 'those in England who knew the conditions of the "blackbirding" trade deplored it, but in the sixteenth century (as in ours) some wives troubled little how their husbands made money, provided they made enough!' (1999: 316–17). She noted the immigration of 'native princes' to England, and that they 'usually died – of the climate or the civilisation'. More to her purpose, she reported that the 'popular little "black slave boys"' were fashionable in the late seventeenth and eighteenth centuries, but that although pictures showed them holding tobacco or chocolate, 'we cannot find that they did any housework or had anything to do with the cooking' (1999: 317).

   Anthropology had a long history of inquiry into food and its preparation. Of the studies that crossed over from anthropology to cultural studies, perhaps Claude Lévi-Strauss's work on 'the raw and the cooked' was most prominent (Lévi-Strauss, 1969). Edmund Leach was also influential as an early Anglophone proponent of the structuralist method in anthropology and thence cultural studies, largely via a little book called *Culture and Communication* (Leach, 1976).

He also wrote a clever essay that demonstrated both the structuralist method and how food was structurally related to language, space and sex (Leach, 1972). It focused on the links between animal categories and verbal abuse in language. Leach wanted to explain why some animals' names (in English and other languages) were loaded terms (bitch, pig, ox, ass, 'cunny'), while others weren't (hart, elephant). He argued that the categorisation of spatial zones of increasing distance from the male self (1 to 4, below) corresponded to the categorisation of animals:

(self) → (1) house → (2) farm → (3) field → (4) remote
(self) → (1) pet → (2) livestock → (3) game → (4) wild animal

The same range and categories applied equally to marriageability:

(self) → (1) sister → (2) cousin → (3) neighbour → (4) stranger

and also to edibility:

(self) → (1) inedible → (2) edible if castrated → (3) edible/inedible → (4) inedible

So (Leach's argument went): (1) pets were inedible, as sisters were unmarriageable (to male self); (2) livestock were edible if castrated, as cousins were suitable for kissing but not marriage; (4) wild animals were inedible, as remote strangers were unmarriageable. Marriage partners tended to be sought among the category of (3) neighbour, which was also where enemies were selected (this being the logic of *Big Brother*, of course), and in this area sexually intact animals were edible, but only according to season (e.g. 'game' like deer/venison, etc.).

Leach argued that the border zones between the categories were most subject to shame and taboo, in terms of both animals and sex. These in-between zones were occupied by animals like the pig (between 1 and 2) – in the house but not a pet; the 'coney' or rabbit (between 2 and 3) – farm and field; and fox (between 3 and 4) – field and wild. The in-between animals were the creatures whose names were used as obscenities or as terms of abuse, not least, Leach argued, because the linguistic structure allowed no place for them. Leach's method linked language, culture, sex, food and economic organisation – just the thing for cultural studies.

On the Larsonian far side of 4 (wild animals), though Leach himself didn't venture here, would be found imaginary creatures, especially monsters (e.g. dinosaurs, or the wolf in Little Red Riding Hood), supernatural beings (e.g.

vampires in *Buffy*) and aliens (e.g. the ovipositor with attitude in *Alien*). These too were anomalous, in-between creatures, occupying the space *beyond* remote; the category *beyond* wild; the relation *beyond* stranger. No wonder they were all too frequently imagined also to be *beyond* edibility/inedibility, apt to turn the tables on the 'self' and eat that!

The cultural sectors categorised by Leach, based on the self as a male inhabitant of farming countryside, dissolved with urbanisation, industrialisation and mobility. What counted as 'far' or 'remote' (and therefore as inedible and unmarriageable) changed. Nor were rural customs in relation to cousins carried into cities. The language of obscenity and abuse lingered on, however. And it may even have transpired that through stories and media many urban people became more familiar with imaginary animals (monsters, vampires, aliens) than they were with those that lived on farm and field.

In due course, just as walking was aestheticised and virtualised via fashion, so food was emancipated from eating. This feat was achieved in media. Cooking shows on television became ever more popular, particularly with the rise of the celebrity chef (see Chapter 3), and the cook as eye candy (Nigella Lawson, Naked Chef Jamie Oliver, etc.). Sales of cookbooks burgeoned. Specialist kitchen retailers, selling everything from cute shiny gadgets through to complete kitchen design and installation, prospered. People ate out more; and they consumed more convenience foods. Both specialist gourmet restaurants and fast food outlets boomed. But all of this ran well ahead of the actual practice of cooking; people cooked less.

Cooking had been commodified, industrialised and then virtualised. Food migrated from unbought anthropological sustenance, via an industrial phase, the fast food industry, into a new interconnectedness with tourism and leisure, right through to the centre of entertainment culture. Food was now a 'sign of itself'.

One attempt to engage with eating as a project within cultural studies was Elspeth Probyn's truly strange book *Carnal Appetites*, which *appeared* to be arguing that cannibalism was a kind of civic ethics (Probyn, 2000: 97); while most other discourses on food seemed to be different species of racism or colonialism. Probyn was attempting to 'queer' food discourse into an aesthetic of disgust and shame, connecting the two ends of the alimentary canal in impolite messy bodily contact, almost drowning in its own toxins.

Naturally, there was a down side to the industrialisation of food, the postmodernisation of eating, the emancipation of appetite from need. Critical commentators lined up to count the human and environmental cost. Apart from what eating was doing to bodies – obesity (disease of plenty-beating-scarcity and therefore of modernity), anorexia (disease of image-control and therefore of postmodernity) – there were troubles further down the food chain. Food itself was out of control, scary. The era of genetically modified food, foot and mouth, salmonella, E.coli, listeria, culminated in the apocalyptic dread of the possible statistics of CJD after BSE ... what if *millions* had eaten those prion-laden burgers made of mad-cow spinal cords? Such fears not only added endless images of stumbling beasts, brutal abattoirs and burning carcasses to the nightly news, but new burdens of guilt and shame to the consumption of food. Especially in America, a country where, as Terry Eagleton pointed out, 'people of truly surreal fatness complacently patrol the streets' (2000: 91), food nevertheless began to be treated as *alien* – in the extra-terrestrial sense of that word:

> The pathological US fear of smoking is as much a fear of extra-terrestrials as it is of lung-cancer. Like the loathsome creatures of *Alien*, smoke and cancer are those dreadful bits of otherness which manage somehow to insinuate themselves at the core of one's being. So indeed are food and drink, which middle-class America now approaches with fear and trembling. Which bits of these perilous substances to shovel inside yourself has now become a national neurosis. (Eagleton, 2000: 89)

Neurosis or not, there was certainly cause for worry, especially as the aliens turned out to be close to home: agribusiness, abetted by a Ministry of Agriculture whose policy was entirely captured by producers' desire for productivity, rather than consumers' for safety. Until BSE, people hadn't properly understood that the beef they ate came from cattle that, in the words of one outraged observer at the height of the mad cow scare, had been fed their own arseholes. When the minister, John Gummer, attempted to demonstrate how safe British beef was by making his own young daughter eat it on television, the effect looked like vampirism, and the man very properly lost his seat at the ensuing election. The fate of his daughter remained unknown.

In fact, over on the other channel, the vampires were having a ball. These meat-eaters got their day in the sun courtesy of their slayer-*cum*-suitor Buffy, whose own relation to them was, in Edmund Leach's terms, precisely one of edibility in sexually intact form under certain circumstances, and therefore also marriageabilty. For Buffy, love and being eaten were coterminous. The pathologisation of food into a teenage nightmare was complete – consumption by the desired/feared object. Love, corporeality, death.

In a similar vein, so to speak, the tabloids weighed in against genetically modified crops as 'Frankenstein Foods'. Great slogan, but one that forgot that every improved strain of beast or bread since Pharaoh's time was genetically modified, in a process that was continuous from the discovery of agriculture. But the scene was now set for culture to defeat politics. No one could show that genetic modifications by bioscientists were any more dangerous than those performed by people in wellies out in the fields. But no one was willing to give scientists and government permission to make the decision in favour of science. Rational public policy was defeated by a weird alliance of intellectual newspapers (the *Guardian*), tabloid media, supermarket chains and eco-warrior activists. It seemed that mediated culture had produced a 'sign of itself' that worked almost as its own opposite: a *mediated image* of ordinary folk who sought maximum *unmediated* transparency. They trusted what they could see (and that included media images); they distrusted being fiddled around with by people in white coats. This image was the product of newspapers, retailers and advocacy groups, all spinning the message like mad. But it worked – public policy abandoned any immediate release of large-scale GM crops in the UK, though not in the USA, where the image of popular demand stressed germ-free sterility (immigrant America's fear of the other), rather than unmodified ancestry (ancestral Europe's fear of history).

New modes of resistive cultural studies began to form, some of them appearing to take the form of the street theatre version of the adolescent tantrum. The more activist down-siders homed in on a more public manifestation of what was thought to be pathological about food. The main quarry here was an organisation whose origins were seriously democratic – grounded in a 1950s streamlined-industrial desire to offer mass populations a good, balanced meal whose quality could be standardised at a level much higher than the greasy-spoon caffs and diners of the day, and whose product could be counted in the millions (and indeed was, for many years, as part of its logo). This was of course McDonald's, where juvenile comfort food fused with global corporate brand-name marketing. It attracted increasingly fierce opposition:

- **Politically**, it was accused of spreading American culture and conservative business practices around the world – it was part of cultural imperialism.
- **Environmentally**, it was accused of forcing farmers to produce standardised crops no matter what the local conditions. Its beef lots and French-fried potato varieties imposed monoculture on the land.
- **Economically**, its giant scale converted agriculture into agribusiness, and farmers into dependent satellites of an industry controlled by marketing, not production. It was also reputed to use up labour while it was young and cheap, finding workers who reached the threshold of adult entitlements suddenly hard to place.
- **Ideologically**, it was accused of 'replacing women with itself in the traditional triangle of food, femininity and the family' (Probyn, 2000: 50). It *deleted the mother* from the cooking equation.
- **Resistively**, a French nationalist farmer gained a conviction and worldwide celebrity status for trashing his local McDonald's restaurant in the name of 'authentic' French farming and food. Thereafter, a global craze took hold of anti-globalisation activists, and McDonald's restaurants were duly trashed for the benefit of the news media in Genoa, Stockholm and elsewhere.

This was *St Trinian's* politics – unruly teenagers chucking food about and making mischief generally, to demonstrate their disrespect for authorities they couldn't encounter directly. It was all part of culture-jamming – political activism as a 'sign of itself'.

Meanwhile, everyday life went on. In these unfolding conditions where different sectors dissolved into each other, bringing art and entertainment, culture and politics, industry and mediation together, it was hard to maintain the distinctions that had once sustained the economy of taste (Bourdieu, 1986). Bourdieu and Beethoven alike were dethroned. High art was a niche market in global entertainment; philosophy was a by-product of urban youth culture; ordinariness was sublime; critique and resistive practices were consumer choices. Travel, shopping, walking, eating – these everyday activities were suffused with globally mediated 'signs of themselves'. Everyday life would never be the same again.

6
Reading the Readers
From Marx to Market (desperately seeking adoption)

Cultural studies and teaching

Cultural studies was not just an intellectual enterprise created by those who taught and published in its name. It was also an imagined community of readers and students called into being by that activity. It was a reading public. The formation of a reader for cultural studies began outside the walls of formal academic knowledge, although certainly in their shadow. These early readers were assumed to be activist in some way. But over time the reader was institutionalised, as it were – readers were assumed to be students or their lecturers, and cultural studies became an academic discipline.

Creating a subject

The creation of a reading public as one of the achievements of cultural studies was itself of some interest as a cultural phenomenon. It conformed to, and was a case study of, the process of formation of imagined communities (Benedict Anderson's famous formula for nations) and also, using a more recent linguistic register, the formation of virtual communities. That is, the reader of cultural studies was to some extent a product of communicational strategies circulated in texts such as journals and books. Although readers of particular textbooks or articles were no doubt living, breathing (if occasionally sleepy) people, they were also themselves textualised by the writing that addressed them. Such textual activity was rarely a passive or neutral description of an existing relationship between known parties to a communicative act – the mode of address also often sought to *create* or call into being a particular kind of readership, imagined in particular ways.

And the act of reading such material connected each reader imaginatively or virtually with many others, unknown personally to each other, whose existence was nevertheless assumed (and required) in order for participation in cultural studies to be meaningful. When a reader, whether activist or academic, read a published work in cultural studies, the work itself and the way the reader dealt with it both differed from what would be the case if the writing were, say, an email, or a letter. The engagement was impersonal, public and purposive – it anticipated some outcome other than reading, whether that was the production of understanding, action, or a mid-term assessment. So the reader of cultural studies was an interesting work of collective imagination – the assumed, presumed, desired, admonished, humoured, hectored 'you' to whom a public rhetoric was addressed. Reading the reader is one way of tracing the historical shifts in cultural studies as a collective or social enterprise.

What kind of animals were those readers assumed to be, within the horizons of imagination of the writing addressed to them? And how did such creatures morph and evolve, over the years? At the outset, the reader of cultural studies was presumed to be adult, probably male, politically radical or already a social ist by conviction, and activist in some political or intellectual pursuit. Later, readers were juvenated, feminised, multi-raced, multiculturalised and institutionalised as students. They were no longer *presumed* to be radical or activist, but were still frequently *encouraged* to radical activism (of the pen usually, rather than of the sword). They were also internationalised – from England and Europe to America, and thence to that place publishers call ROW, the *rest of the world*.

In practice ROW meant English-speaking parts of it, or places with previous colonial connections to the US or UK. Thus, to show how these currents could work out (and over-simplifying), cultural studies arrived in two Chinese countries from opposite directions: to Taiwan via the USA, e.g. Kuan-Hsing Chen (trained in the USA), and to Singapore via the Anglo-educational tradition, e.g. Chua Beng-Huat. Later was it Asianised, for instance in the journal *Inter-Asia Cultural Studies* edited jointly by Chen and Chua, which was launched in Birmingham by Stuart Hall at a big 'Crossroads in Cultural Studies' conference in 2000.

Perhaps most peculiarly, the reader of cultural studies morphed from freedom to servitude. The relation between writer and reader originally was that of equal colloquy among co-subjects. But later it altered to one where the writer alone was understood to be a knowing subject. The reader on the other hand was subjected in a much more direct way – they were subject *to* examination; presumed to be preparing for assessment. The use of cultural studies to them was not emancipation but certification.

A power relation was instituted between writer and reader at the very place where one side sought to develop the literacy and to train the knowing-subjectivity of the other, in what was understood (by the writer) as a necessary preparation for 'emancipation into intellectual freedom' (in Quiller-Couch's phrase). Whether the reader saw things the same way, or instead encountered cultural studies as a necessary hurdle to be jumped, *en route* to another destination – completion of a degree programme, getting a job or, less instrumentally, understanding what was going on – was rarely tested.

This history of cultural studies can be traced via publications that addressed the free (activist) reader and the student (academic) reader respectively. The former was generally approached within the covers of small journals directed towards specific interest groups. The latter were increasingly rounded up by books that were themselves called *Readers* – books containing numerous essays or chapters by different writers, edited to represent cultural studies as an imagined whole. (I'll use the capital letter to refer to published anthologies; lower case to the persons, real and imagined, who use them: i.e. readers (persons) read Readers (books).)

As a matter of practical fact, it may be that the intended readers of Readers were not students directly, but their course co-ordinators and instructors; junior and middle-ranking academics whose job included setting texts for course units and recommending them for the library. To secure commercial returns, publishers offered free inspection copies of textbooks to hard-up instructors. Just as guided tours to Egypt used to offer a free place to teachers who could attract enough students to pay for the trip, so publishers offered free copies of Readers and other textbooks where course adoptions led to purchases of a dozen or more copies. More than that, the Reader offered a convenient course structure for unit co-ordinators, who could use a given set text to order the weekly sequence of topics, readings and even assessments. The emergence of the cultural studies Reader signalled a major move towards standardisation and commodification of the IP – the intellectual property – of what had been until then more of a conversation than a consumer good.

The Reader signalled the end of the R & D phase of cultural studies, if you like, and the commencement of its commercialisation, at least in publishing terms. But of course that success – for book, editor and publisher – depended upon its uptake within an academic context. And so both a collaborative and a competitive element entered cultural studies.

- **Collaboratively**, publishers worked with young teaching-immersed authors, and with more senior people who had authorial track records, to *assist* academic institutions in their endeavour to bring to the attention of ever-widening circles of the reading public the fruits of this once marginal discourse.
- **Competitively**, many publishers had a go, using many editors. Which books would gain supremacy, in both sales and repute (bearing in mind that reputation drove sales at least as much as did price, design, timing and luck)?

In this expansive, enterprising, international, collaborative, competitive, commercial context, the context where education for citizenship met learning services for profit, what became of the reader of cultural studies?

Activist readers (I)

The earliest imagined reader of cultural studies was not an academic at all; in 1957 Richard Hoggart addressed *The Uses of Literacy* to that since forgotten species, the 'intelligent layman'. Stuart Hall's first book (with Paddy Whannel) in 1964 was written for radical/reformist schoolteachers and social reform activists working with what were then called deprived youth, and working-class children, especially ethnic minorities in urban settings.

Meanwhile, what was eventually to flourish as cultural studies took root in journals such as the *Universities and Left Review* (*ULR*, edited in the later 1950s by a young Stuart Hall) and its better-known successor *New Left Review* (*NLR*, edited for a long time by Perry Anderson after Stuart Hall's initial stint), and in E.P. Thompson's *New Reasoner*. Later on specialist but still radical journals took up the thread, such as *Working Papers in Cultural Studies*, published by the Birmingham Centre for Contemporary Cultural Studies after Stuart Hall took over its direction, *Screen* and *Screen Education*, *Feminist Review*, the *LTP Journal* (LTP = Literature Teaching Politics), *New Formations* and others. These included the *Australian Journal of Cultural Studies*, founded in Perth, WA, in 1983, and handed over to Routledge (UK) to become *Cultural Studies*, an American journal, in 1987.

These journals may in point of empirical fact have been read mostly by people working and studying in the academy. However, that was not their initial purpose. They addressed not academic readers but radical ones, people interested in social and cultural change, who believed that certain causes (socialism), or even organisations (like one of the numerous communist parties), were the appropriate agencies to achieve it. In other words they thought that understanding social reality was not enough, nor was the point *simply* to change it. Readers needed to identify, and identify with, explicitly named projects of political identification (say Marxism), before they could be converted into effective *agents* of change toward 'progressive' goals. In Toby Miller's terms, they were 'journals of tendency', not 'journals of profession' (Miller, 2001: 8).

And the tendencies were *militant*. The word revolution was not unheard, although few people in cultural studies recommended the violent overthrow of the state by clandestinely organised armed class warriors . . . at least, not yet. However, some of them, the late Ian Connell for example, could be seen on the street corners of Birmingham of a Saturday afternoon trying to interest shoppers in the *Morning Star*. There was quite broad agreement that fundamental or structural change was needed before social equality for particular groups understood as oppressed could eventuate. Cultural studies took its place on the Left in a period of increasingly adversarial, ideological politics (the late 1960s at least to the 1980s – from Vietnam to Thatcher), where the goal was understood to be more ambitious than mere reform or amelioration of existing institutions and practices.

Tacitly often, and sometimes explicitly, cultural studies addressed a revolutionary reader. The radical journals looked to 'make socialists' (Hall's phrase), rather than teach students. Disciplinarily, they distinguished less than subsequently became familiar between (say) socialist theory and practice, sociology of deviance, radical social work (on the streets and in the housing estates), subcultural youth theory, and pop-music connoisseurship. They clearly worried about the boundary between *activism* and *academicism*. Here's *NLR* in November 1961, in an editorial comment on the occasion of Stuart Hall's departure from the editorship:

> What is *wrong* with the New Left? Everyone has an answer. The journal: too glossy, too detached, too Cuban, too much. The Board: too big, too windy, too incompetent. Raymond Williams' long involutions and Edward Thompson's long revolting replies. The Clubs [New Left Clubs]: too few, too gimmicky, too much talking-shops, too little hard organisation. Too much 'Old Left'. Too little 'culture'. You can take your pick. (*NLR*, 12, November–December 1961: inside covers)

One thing the *NLR* didn't seem to think was wrong with the New Left was Stuart Hall: 'Stuart has been at the centre of "the lot" since 1956, was one of the editors of *ULR* [*Universities & Left Review*], and edited *NLR* since its inception. More than this, he has *been* – at times almost single-handed – the New Left' (ibid.: inside covers).

It wasn't quite single-handed. Persons from across a range of disciplines, occupations and commitments might not only meet at conferences, but also bumped into each other at politico-cultural events. They were likely to meet at CND (Campaign for Nuclear Disarmament) marches; anti-war demonstrations such as that in Grosvenor Square in 1968 (Halloran et al., 1970). They may have taken (or offered) classes at the Communist University of London (CUL): a summer school run at the University of London Union by the Communist Party, not by the university authorities. It attracted students in their thousands through several successive decently hot metropolitan summers in the mid-1970s, turning a bland bit of Bloomsbury into something redolent of Paris in the 1960s, just as punk hit the streets. Certainly, CUL was way ahead of academic cultural studies at this time, in terms of its urgent attention to gender, race, sexual practice and urban-youth politics, not to mention a refreshing feel – among attendees as much as the organisers – of street-smart design, media savvy and intellectual self-confidence (see Wilson, 2001: 48, n. 2).

Eventually – though not as quickly as would have been good for them – the radical journals began also to imagine readers to include social activists in the new social movements – for peace, feminism, youth politics, gay & lesbian and other identity-based politics, environmentalism and the like. These movements were rarely revolutionary in the classic Marxist-modernist mould, but they were royally pissed off with existing institutions and practices, including socialism. A long dialogue ensued between different movements and factions, during which it became increasingly clear that there was no longer such a thing as 'the' Left, in the sense that socialist, feminist, Black-activist, environmentalist or gay/lesbian discourses could be assumed to address the *same* reader (never mind the long-standing splits between Trotskyist, Marxist, communist and non-aligned socialists).

At the very best, like ethnic Americans, the Left *hyphenated* (as in socialist-feminists). In Wales or Scotland there were socialist-nationalists (e.g. Cymdeithas yr Iaith Gymraeg, the Welsh Language Society). This was a formula literally unthinkable in metropolitan-socialist politics, where nationalists were *by defini-tion* racists, as Paul Gilroy thought, for instance, in his discussion of a painting by the English artist J.M.W. Turner: 'The New Left heirs to this aesthetic and cul-tural tradition compounded and reproduced its nationalism and therefore its racism (the former entails the latter) . . .' (Gilroy, 1992: 192). No such entailment would have been safe in national regions of unitary states, or within first-people nationalism. In practice you had to work out if you were being interpellated at all, and some texts were quite explicit about their desire *not* to include everyone among their readers.

But the culture of the broad Left persisted for a while at least. Occasionally its 'reading public' could still gather in serious numbers, for instance at Anti-Nazi League rally-concerts, where everyone bopped to Tom Robinson, UB40 or Ian Dury and the Blockheads – doing this *as* radical politics. Or it joined the throng at the Notting Hill Carnival; or braved November gloom to attend the opening of any post-1967 Godard film. It might even stand at the back at avant-garde event/installations at the Arts Lab or later the ICA (Lawrence Grossberg, for one, told his readers that he 'spent a number of years traveling and performing in Europe in an itinerant anarchist theatre commune'; Nelson and Grossberg, 1988: 725). Increasingly the stalwarts would frequent such events less to have their consciousness raised, more to support their soon-to-graduate daughters.

In the meantime the Left was less visible during traditional set-piece political struggles like the Miners' Strike of 1984–5, where activism took the form of flying pickets drawn from the industrial trade unions (railways, transport and mining). It was not prominent in the anti-poll-tax riots of the later Thatcher era; these were English rather than ideological riots – E.P. Thompson not Stuart Hall. The Left had, as the saying went, fragmented. Some activists were reclaiming the night, some were going feral in the forests, or digging in under motorway devel-opments. Some infiltrated the Labour Party in the form of the Militant Tendency. Some turned their back on straight politics, working in music, media or cyber-space. Some got high; some got hired.

Eventually, socialism changed its name entirely, becoming anti-globalisation, and took to the streets with a reinvigorated sense of collaboration among incom-mensurate groups, cemented by email, Internet and a compulsive desire to trash McDonald's restaurants all over the world. These activists trailed meetings of globalising corporations and governments, putting the theatre of the street battle on a global scale, in Seattle, Melbourne, Toronto, Switzerland, Stockholm, even Pakistan. As one of its earlier chroniclers noted, 'just as postmodernism was *the* concept of the 1980s, globalisation may be *the* concept of the 1990s, a key idea by which we understand the transition of human society into the third millen-nium' (Waters, 1995: 1). By the turn of the millennium, indeed, the key term was *anti*-globalisation, which became a kind of shorthand for intellectual radicalism in general.

An important signal of change in the public sphere of the Left occurred in the mid-1970s. Raymond Williams was one of the doyens of cultural studies, where his work was universally accepted as foundational. He himself was an academic, a Cambridge Welshman at Jesus College, but his work was also activist. He had been involved in *ULR* and *NLR* from the 1950s. He was a well-known speaker at Left forums. He also reached out for the 'intelligent lay reader' via a column in the *Listener*, a middlebrow weekly published by the BBC (O'Connor, 1989). Throughout, his work had been presented as socialist or leftist rather than as explicitly Marxist and therefore revolutionary. But in the mid-1970s he published a couple of articles in *NLR*, the leading forum for Left intellectual theory at that time, in which explicitly Marxist terms like 'base' and 'super-structure' appeared in Williams's analytical repertoire in their own right. Williams also published a book in 1977 that for the first time named his intellectual endeavour as Marxist – *Marxism and Literature*. Here the reader of cultural studies was pushed from Williams's earlier non-sectarian 'long revolution' (national history) frame of analysis to a Marxist one. Perhaps this matched Williams's own political drift to the margin (he gave up on parliamentary democracy during the Wilson Labour governments of the late 1960s and 1970s), or perhaps it was merely symptomatic of the increasing adversarialism of politically truculent times.

But an odd thing was happening here. Even as the politics of cultural studies became more explicitly Marxist and to that extent more extreme, so the enterprise retreated more decisively from party activism to academic institutionalisation. Raymond Williams took over Sir Arthur Quiller-Couch's old King Edward VII Chair of English at Cambridge University in 1974. And *Marxism and Literature* was about the subject English, not the English subject, as it were. Hyper-politicisation of the writing accompanied the academicisation of the reader. As academic cultural studies got under way, its rhetoric became more theoretical and abstract (Hall, 1992): it insisted upon politics while withdrawing from direct engagement with the political process of the day.

In one sense developing abstraction and theory merely followed other disciplinary histories – the liberal arts of painting and literature had both previously sought emancipation from 'servile' versions of themselves (see Chapter 3) by the same means. Of course the practitioners of cultural studies would have dismissed with outrage any suggestion that theoretical work was trying to elevate a mechanical subject to liberal academic status, and thus servile practitioners into gentlemen. Gaining honorific status in cultural or educational institutions was not the idea. Cultural studies was an avant-garde practice, designed not to join but to beat liberal institutions of knowledge.

Academic readers

The moment of abstraction took the form of what was called at the time Grand Theory. Meaghan Morris called 'meta-theory':

a fantasy about theory's power, not a description of what Marxism actually is or needs to be. . . . Here I'd agree with Ian Hunter, that this kind of Big Dialectic actually works to ensure that our idea of future society has no definite shape, so it's really a way of withdrawing from the sites where change can be negotiated. (Morris, 1992: 473)

Thus, while there may have been no *intention* to talk up politics while withdrawing from them, this certainly was an *outcome* of academic cultural studies. Abstraction had practical consequences. Cultural studies' intersection with academia took many forms, of course. Perhaps its main mode of academic existence was (and remained) as an innovative, critical (abstract) discourse and an interdisciplinary site of research, used by those interested in the interrelations of knowledge, power, meaning and various forms of artistic expression, especially contemporary popular media and everyday practices. It was an experimental gathering of previously trained disciplinary specialists in, say, anthropology, literary studies, political economy, sociology and media technologies (plus others) to exchange views and develop modes of understanding of the cultural field.

But at this very moment, and in this very place, another element came into decisive play, if you could call the United States of America an element. Whatever; cultural studies invented its own mass readership in the USA. In the UK and Australia cultural studies had already found fertile soil in nontraditional institutions of higher education; those with the longest association with mechanics' institutes, adult and workers' education, such as polytechnics and institutes of technology (see also Gibson, 2001). But these had neither the numbers of students nor the institutional prestige to fuel the invention of an entirely new academic subject as a global phenomenon. That kind of grunt came from only one place: the country where democratised mass education was established earliest and was most advanced. It all happened within coo-ee of O'Hare (see Chapter 1).

Some time during the 1980s it extended to widely *taught* programmes (taught, but not undergraduate – cultural studies remained a largely graduate discipline in the US). Only then could cultural studies appear in its own name as an academic subject. That process occurred first in British polytechnics but took hold in the USA. While in Britain and elsewhere such a development was centred on undergraduates (notoriously poor book-buyers), the giant scale of higher education in the USA allowed for it to remain a largely *postgraduate* enterprise there. This had the benefit of exposing cultural studies to motivated students of whom a good proportion were already committed to careers inside higher education; students who were very likely to buy books for their own use, and also to adopt them on courses they taught. Intellectual entrepreneurs, looking for ways to modernise the liberal curriculum of American mass education, found in cultural studies a powerful new engine for change *inside* the academy. Its writings needed to be made available to those motivated students in accessible form. The scene was set for the Reader.

Illini Cultural Studies (I) – Marxism

Naturally, the first Reader of any consequence was about *Marxism and the Interpretation of Culture*. Edited by Cary Nelson and Lawrence Grossberg and published in 1988, it was the outcome of a large conference and summer school that had been held at the University of Illinois in Urbana-Champaign in 1983. Urbana-Champaign was reachable in half an hour from O'Hare by a local airline using alarmingly small 'wind-up' aeroplanes, flying low over horizon-to-horizon Kellogg's corn and McDonald's cattle, staffed by attendants with impenetrable rural accents. Shaken about by this, delegates would arrive at a town so small that they had to join two of them together (Urbana and Champaign) to accommodate the giant university. The most notable features were a giant football stadium and the giant Illini Union building. Here conferees could go for spare ribs, a beer, ten-pin bowling and a sleep, before being awoken from their cosmopolitan Marxist slumbers at 7 a.m. by chanting Marine cadet-students marching at the run through the campus in lusty training for the continued maintenance, by whatever means, of global *pax Americana*.

Within those wide horizons, there assembled a mixed but formidable array of speakers on the theme of:

> our belief in emerging change in the discursive formations of intellectual life, a change that cuts across the humanities and the social sciences. It suggests that the proper horizon for interpretive activity, whatever its object and whatever its disciplinary base, is the entire field of cultural practices, all of which give meaning, texture, and structure to human life. Moreover, the title [*Marxism and the Interpretation of Culture*] situates Marxism at the center of such developments and thus suggests the need to transgress the line that has traditionally separated culture from social, economic, and political relations. (Nelson and Grossberg, 1988: 1)

There was a characteristic two-way movement here. The definition of *activism* was radically narrowed and hemmed in, referring only to textualised interpretive activity. But meanwhile the horizon scanned by cultural studies was widened to the *universal*: 'the entire field of cultural practices'. This was exactly what was needed to render cultural studies into *academic* cultural studies, practised 'across the humanities and social sciences'.

The practitioners who were collected into the Reader (with country of origin, country of residence; university affiliation at the time of publication) were, in this order:

- Cornel West (US; Yale),
- Stuart Hall (Jamaica, UK; Open),
- Henri Lefebvre (France; retired),
- Chantal Mouffe (Belgium, UK; London),
- Catharine A. MacKinnon (US; Stanford),
- Paul Patton (Australia; New South Wales),

- Belden Fields (US; Illinois),
- Étienne Balibar (France; Paris),
- Oskar Negt (USSR, Germany; Hanover),
- Gajo Petrović (Yugoslavia; Zagreb),
- Ernesto Laclau (Argentina, UK; Essex/Chicago),
- Christine Delphy (France; Centre National de la Recherche Scientifique – CNRS),
- Gayatri Chakravorty Spivak (India, US; Pittsburgh),
- Perry Anderson (UK; *NLR*),
- Franco Moretti (Italy; Salerno),
- Fredric Jameson (US; Duke),
- Andrew Ross (Scotland, US; Princeton),
- Fred Pfeil (US; Oregon State),
- Eugene Holland (US; Ohio State),
- Julia Lesage (US; Indiana),
- Michèle Mattelart (France; CNRS),
- Fernando Reyes Matta (Chile; UNESCO),
- Simon Frith (UK; Warwick),
- Michael Ryan (Ireland; Northeastern),
- Jack L. Amariglio (US; Franklin & Marshall College), Stephen A. Resnick (US; Amherst), Richard D. Wolff (US; Amherst),
- Jean Franco (UK, US; Stanford),
- Stanley Aronowitz (US; City University of New York),
- Sue Golding (US; Trent),
- Richard Schacht (US; Illinois),
- Armand Mattelart (Belgium, France; Upper Brittany),
- Iain Chambers (UK; Naples),
- Terry Eagleton (UK; Oxford),
- Michel Pêcheux (France; CNRS [deceased]),
- Hugo Achugar (Uruguay, US; Northwestern),
- Darko Suvin (Yugoslavia, Canada; McGill),
- Michèle Barrett (UK; City),
- Fengzhen Wang (China; Chinese Academy of Social Sciences, Peking).

Of these contributors, only two were not university teachers at the time – Anderson (Eton, Oxford, *NLR*) and Reyes Matta (journalist, UNESCO, New World Information Order). Only two were working in communist countries – Petrović (Yugoslavia) and Wang (China). Apart from Wang only one was from outside Europe and the Americas – Patton (Australia). All in all, nineteen taught at American universities, six in French, six in British and four in other European universities, plus one each from China and Australia. In other words, here was a convention of *academic* heavy hitters, concentrated in the USA and drawing inspiration from Europe, working on a series of questions about Marxism and culture that were about as far away from politics (traditionally understood) as could be.

Who even remembered – even then! – that the name of the General Secretary of the Communist Party and Chairman of the Praesidium of the Supreme Soviet of the Union of Soviet Socialist Republics at this time was . . . Yuri Andropov? Certainly his name was never mentioned in 740 pages. Clearly Soviet Marxism as, you know, dictatorship of the proletariat via a command bureaucracy, was no inspiration.

What was the Marxism that was placed at the centre of 'the entire field of cultural practices' by these writers?

> Marxism, of course, has long been at least implicitly involved in breaking down the barriers between these domains ['culture, social, economic and political relations'], making each of necessity a site of interpretive activity – by politicizing interpretive and cultural practices, by looking at the economic determinations of cultural production, by radically historicizing our understanding of signifying practices – from political discourses to art, from beliefs to social practices, from the discourse of psychology to the discourse of economics – and, of course, by continuing to revise and enlarge a body of theory with multidisciplinary implications. (Nelson and Grossberg, 1988: 1)

'Breaking down the barriers' was a metaphorical task for this Marxism, not to be confused with attacking the barricades; its purpose was to add political, historical, economic and theoretical dimensions to interpretive analyses of culture (the latter understood broadly as 'discourses . . . art . . . beliefs . . . social practices . . . psychology'). This was a *reading* praxis.

What work was the Reader itself intended to do?

> The very act of gathering these essays together challenges their self-sufficiency. . . . If the book undermines the traditional divisions between academic disciplines, it also, by its scope, by the juxtapositions it creates, of necessity calls many of the individual contributions into question. This book, then, is intended to be a collective intervention in the contested terrain it maps. (Nelson and Grossberg, 1988: 1–2)

And what work was the reader intended to do?

> To read the book, we think, is to be drawn to reorganize both it and the domain of culture itself, for any point of entrance will lead one to risk losing control of the disciplinary terrain one considered a secure possession. Reading the book involves continually recognising not only . . . relations that transgress traditional disciplines, but also multiple ways of structuring the book and thus of charting a path through the terrain in which the relations among power, signification and history are defined and debated. (Nelson and Grossberg: 1–2)

The *work* of reading the Reader, according to the editors, was to 'lose control' of a secure 'possession' while recognising transgression, disciplinarily at least, thence to head off, 'charting a path through the terrain', to 'secure' some new territory. This language of *colonising land* was quite explicit; the introduction was entitled 'The Territory of Marxism':

> The problem for Marxism is thus twofold: on the one hand, to deterritorialize its own discourse . . . and on the hand, to reterritorialize itself. . . . Indeed, as the reader reorganizes this volume to suit his or her own interests and commitments – deciding which patterns of alliance and opposition among the essays to credit – the territory of Marxism will thereby be redefined. (Nelson and Grossberg: 11–12)

After making the necessary alliances and creating the necessary foes to oppose, the *act of reading itself* would be a sort of dawn raid *on* Marxism (rather than *with* it, upon some existing bastion of class supremacy), and readers would thereby carve out a bit of their own 'territory'.

In this context, the word 'revolution' was not unheard; indeed its Marxist form was defined as 'something like a commitment to revolutionary identification with the cause of the oppressed' (12).

> Just what will *count* as revolutionary intervention is an issue that animates, defines, and challenges all the theoretical positions and cultural domains discussed in the book. One way of reading the book, in fact, is as a debate on that issue. (ibid.)

The editors conducted that debate on behalf of readers, by listing some of their contributors' versions of 'revolutionary intervention'. Namely: author *a* 'deconstructs a series of semantic oppositions and equivalences'; *b* is into 'altering cultural semiotics from an oppositional standpoint'; *c* writes of 'pop culture as resistance'; *d* has 'a theory that gives people an active role in political struggles within the consumption of cultural objects'; *e* tries out a 'new poststructuralist play on the semiosis of "revolution"'; *f* insists on 'the historical imperatives of sexism and racism'. Only then was Benedict's scary brother Perry Anderson revealed (he'd been behind the rhetorical arras all the time, poniard at the ready), 'stating firmly that revolution is *only* a specific, punctual, and convulsive event that radically transforms the political structures of a society' (ibid.).

On that party-pooping note, *revolutionary Marxism* was escorted politely to the door. It didn't even get past *first* reading. The very first readers of the Reader, presumably, were the big-name authors who were solicited to provide endorsements on the back cover. This interesting group comprised Hayden White, Ien Ang, John Fiske, Mark Poster, William Leon McBride, Dick Hebdige and Angela McRobbie. Ang liked the book for being 'radically undogmatic', Fiske because it 'never closes off issues', Hebdige because 'Marxism here is not . . . automatically accorded mastery of the field'. Indeed, he thought that the papers in it were 'on the cusp between the disintegrating certainties of an earlier moment and the new demands and questions posed by a fresh set of voices'. Angela McRobbie was pleased to find that 'where questions of race or gender are confronted most directly, Marxism, refreshingly, is forced to take a back seat'.

It wasn't exactly killing the father, or maybe it was exactly that, but Marxism was certainly retired, pensioned off with a bus pass to make room for clamouring youth, comprising, as it happened, 'a fresh set of voices' belonging to such as, well, Ang, Fiske, Hebdige and McRobbie. Two of the authentic Marxists invited to the conference embodied the point: the great Henri Lefebvre was in his eighties, and in any case had been thrown out of the French CP in the 1950s; and Althusser's student Michel Pêcheux died in the year of the conference (i.e. five years before the book appeared).

Illini Cultural Studies (II) – Fiskeism

Old father Karl out of the way, the scene was set for the full-scale transformation of cultural studies into a *teaching machine*. The next Reader on the scene was also edited by Larry Grossberg and Cary Nelson, this time joined by their colleague Paula Treichler. It too originated in a conference at the University of Illinois, this one held in April 1990, attended by 'about 900 people'.

The intellectual climate had changed between the 'Marxism/Interpretation' conference (1983) and the 'Cultural Studies' conference (1990). In terms of cultural studies in the USA, that change could be summed up in one name – academic cultural studies' first populariser, i.e. *teacher* – John Fiske. In 1983, few in the USA had ever heard of him. 1983 was the year when, on the basis of our book *Reading Television*, Fiske and I were invited to speak in the USA for the first time, at a mass-comm TV conference at the University of Michigan (see Rowland and Watkins, 1984). By 1990 Fiske had emigrated to the US, published three or four new books in quick succession, and was all over American cultural studies like a rash. Of him, more later.

(I should add here that I wasn't present at either of the Illinois conferences discussed in this chapter. I did go to a conference there, also featuring Larry Grossberg. This was a symposium on TV audiences held later in 1990, soon after the event described below was over (see Hay et al., 1994). My account of both of the Illinois events has been produced from documentary sources and what people who were there have told me, reinforced by personal acquaintance with the places and some of the participants involved.)

The Reader of the 1990 conference was simply (or was that land-grabbingly, as believed by some academics not invited?) called *Cultural Studies*, naming a discipline, not a problem as the earlier one had done. It was published by Routledge's US office at an aggressively low price for a 790-page book (£15 in the UK) – meaning that Routledge relied on high volume of sales, not high return per copy. The pages were big too, lots of words, and the book contained over forty chapters. It was dubbed 'gigantic' by Toby Miller (2001: 10) and 'most tombstone-like of all' the Readers (Curran et al., 1996: 4). It was intended to codify and order cultural studies in conditions of its 'material and economic promise':

> In the United States, where the boom [in cultural studies] is especially strong, many academic institutions – presses, journals, hiring committees, conferences, university curricula – have created significant investment opportunities in cultural studies, sometimes in ignorance of its history, its practitioners, its relation to traditional disciplines, and its life outside the academy. (Grossberg et al., 1992: 1)

These were the matters on which the Reader would put the reader straight: 'Here we introduce the field of cultural studies, describe the goals of the book and offer a "user's guide" to the essays it includes' (ibid.).

But first, a definition – 'it would be arrogant not to' identify the field:

> As a first step, we can try to offer a very general, generic definition of cultural studies. . . . Cultural studies is an interdisciplinary, transdisciplinary, and sometimes counter-disciplinary field that operates in the tension between its tendencies to embrace both a broad, anthropological and a more narrowly humanistic conception of culture. Unlike traditional anthropology . . . it has grown out of analyses of modern industrial societies. . . . Unlike humanism it rejects the exclusive equation of culture with high culture. . . . Cultural studies is thus committed to the study of the entire range of a society's arts, beliefs, institutions, and communicative practices. (Grossberg et al.: 4)

The editors went on to insist that 'practice does matter', but that 'cultural studies offers a bridge between theory and material culture', between intellectual work and political struggle. They stressed the limited portability of theory; i.e. it wasn't universally useful, but praised the concept of articulation, which they thought was pretty well universally useful (6–8).

The editors sought to include within the definition of cultural studies work done under its banner by writers in the Birmingham tradition (i.e. its own history: 8–9), in order to oblige others to acknowledge that intellectual history. In the context of its institutionalisation in the USA, they worried about 'what kind of work will be identified with cultural studies and what social effects it will have'. The problem wasn't 'institutionalization *per se*', but people who 'simply rename what they were already doing to take advantage of the cultural studies boom' (10–11). The problem, in short, was a turf war.

The 'Users' Guide' grouped different papers under thematic headings (each paper could appear under more than one). It amounted to a *syllabus*, for which no further reading would be required than the Reader itself, thereby establishing the book as a set text, and justifying Routledge's investment in it:

- The history of cultural studies
- Gender and sexuality
- Nationhood and national identity
- Colonialism and postcolonialism
- Race and ethnicity
- Popular culture and its audiences
- Identity politics
- Pedagogy
- The politics of aesthetics
- Culture and its institutions
- Ethnography and cultural studies
- The politics of disciplinarity

- Discourse and textuality
- Science, culture and the ecosystem
- Rereading history
- Global culture in a postmodern age.

The 'User's Guide' had the added benefit of allowing the editors to 'print the essays in alphabetical order', thereby escaping charges of operating a star system in the presentation of speakers. So where the previous ('Marxism/Interpretation') publication had opened with three star turns – Cornel West, Stuart Hall, Henri Lefebvre – this one hid the dynamics of inter-speaker prestige by running them from Bennett, Tony to Wolff, Janet (plus a postscript by Angela McRobbie).

This tactic masked the politics of the conference itself. However – to their credit – the organiser-editors included transcripts of some of the discussion sessions in which this issue had bubbled uncontrollably to the surface. Tension had built over a couple of days until an almighty row had broken out; Stuart Hall sitting with his head in his hands, unable to complete his presentation while young-Turk graduate students and identity-activist academics argued power principles with conference organisers. This triggered a critique of the 'cultural politics' of the conference as a whole and of the alleged bad faith of the organisers in crudely imposing the normal hierarchy of existing power relations of the American academy, while espousing the political rhetoric of liberation of the oppressed.

Just as Stuart Hall was using his paper to talk about how, at the Birmingham Centre, feminism 'broke in; interrupted, made an unseemly noise, seized the time, crapped on the table of cultural studies' (Hall, 1992: 282), the very same thing happened again, there and then at the conference. The hall may or may not have numbered among its 900 occupants some of Tom Wolfe's fantasy co-eds, rosy-cheeked and desirable in blue jeans (see Chapter 1). But if so, their attitudes and concerns certainly had changed in the intervening years. Their horizons were no longer limited to questions of car parking. Here at last was the *voice* of the reader, self-represented. Alexandra Chasin said:

> I have been anonymous up til now. Until, I suppose, the moment of speaking. I mean to be both courteous and constructive but I'm also quite serious and I think this stuff really matters. . . . In its structure, the conference most definitely privileges certain people, empowering them to speak while disempowering others. It also duplicates the traditional structures of power which practitioners of cultural studies almost uniformly claim to be committed to subverting. One or two rounds of applause for graduate student labor and for staff helping with conference 'mechanics' does not go very far towards changing a familiar and oppressive division of labor. (Chasin, 1992: 293)

The division of labour that downgraded mechanical activities in contrast to the freedom bestowed by intellectual work has a very long history as the underpinning of liberal humanism (it is detailed in Chapter 3). It was perhaps the very thing that most speakers at the conference could agree that they all opposed as a theory for cultural studies. But it was still silently running the class relations (divisions of labour) of the enterprise.

The 'Cultural Studies' conference was seeking to specify – and claimed special prowess in analysing – the relations among theory, culture and politics. The politics of the speech act was therefore a serious matter indeed. Who could (and who could not) be emancipated into freedom of speech within that context, as opposed to those who merely – mechanically – secured the material basis for the event by doing the washing up (as it were), went to the heart of the whole enterprise. This was a case of 'physician, heal thyself!'

Cultural studies was in the act of supplying itself with a very large-scale text – the Reader – to demonstrate its own emancipation as a discourse. To do this practically, to get clean recordings of interventions from important people in the field, it had to control who spoke. 'There is no scheduled place for a participant in this conference to say anything which is not to or from the podium' (Chasin: 293). The microphones seemed to pick up some (well-known) discussants but not others (grad students). This technology was required to record the *enunciation* of cultural studies, not least so that it could later be read by students. But this very technology – the room, the organisation, the microphones, the division of labour – had the effect of silencing, even 'terrorizing', the participants (readers) who were actually there. Bell hooks said:

> I am excited about [cultural studies] as a critical political intervention. And when I felt that I was being marginalised and silenced, I felt that as a terror. . . . I felt bad because I felt my comments got reduced to this question of the room and the microphones and things like that, which are important but which are not what I was trying to talk about. I was trying to talk about what kind of discourse was being produced here and its implications for political practice. (hooks, 1992: 294)

The last word went to Scott Cooper, who compared the 'Cultural Studies' event unfavourably with the 'Marxism/Interpretation' one, having attended Hall's presentations at both. He was concerned about 'what cultural studies is becoming in the American context. My fear is that cultural studies will . . . be denied its political meaning. American institutions of education are far more powerful even than all the people in this room' (1992: 294). He called for 'strategies by which we're going to intervene in those institutions'.

What was needed, perhaps, was a readers' liberation front.

The luminary who was already notorious for suggesting that just such a movement was needed – not for the conference but for the readers of popular media everywhere – had in fact already spoken. This was John Fiske. At his 'Cultural Studies' session Fiske argued the need to 'grant the concrete practices of subordinated ways of living a degree of importance in theory'. He also hoped that cultural theory itself would 'try to avoid the risk of implicitly granting its theoretical discourse a position of privilege which would reproduce in academic terms the process of subordination which is characteristic of the social order that we wish to criticize and change' (Fiske, 1992: 165). This latter point was taken up eventually by Henry Jenkins, Alan McKee and others who wanted to work as public intellectuals and not just as academics, to describe the 'vernacular theory' that they found being produced all around them in journalism, popular media and activist communities (see Lumby, 1999).

But fascinatingly it was Fiske's attempt to equalise the importance of academic theorising on the one hand and popular or everyday vernacular theorising on the other, that led to criticism of John Fiske himself, and of the conference. As someone who felt herself to be 'both working in the underclass in many ways and an intellectual', bell hooks thought that Fiske's separation of those domains (he saw each as a different 'habitus') seemed violent, rather than 'liberating' for the 'underclass' side. 'I feel all the more of an outsider here, at this conference that seems to me to be so much a mirroring of the very kinds of hierarchies that terrorize and violate', said hooks (1992; 171).

Fiske's point about academic privilege was used against himself, but it also triggered the critique of the academic politics of the conference. So in the end he got exactly what he had argued for: criticism of the position of privilege that reproduced subordination within academic-theoretical practices, including his own. What he probably hadn't bargained for was that the critique would turn inward, into the US academy, not outward, to the extra-mural buccaneers of media capitalism and sweatshop consumerism.

Fiske's session attracted a series of unusually sharp questions, some of them not even attempting to disguise their hostility, from Meaghan Morris, Paula Treichler, Bill Warner, Homi Bhabha, Rosalind Brunt, Elspeth Probyn, bell hooks, Linda Charnes and Tara McPherson (Grossberg et al., 1992: 165–73). This was a peculiar kind of reader's liberation, though, because it took the form of critique by astute readers, who weren't novices to be taught, but who were about as astute as readers could get. Many of them had a major investment in theory. The sting that could still be felt in some of the questions, even on the highly edited printed page, was directed towards someone who had never made any great claims as an original theorist. Fiske wrote teaching texts; he interpreted and simplified theory for new readers. The affront he seemed to cause his colleagues may not have been about the details of his argument. In the final analysis it may have been about Fiske's own status.

Fiske was an example of what would have been called in the days of Hoggart and Allen Lane a *populariser*, in the pedagogic sense. He was trying to bring together academic, theoretical and intellectual work, on the one hand, and popular culture, everyday life and 'embodied' practices, on the other. The *way* he did this was characteristic of a teacher, not a theorist. He simplified (sometimes overly). He illustrated (sometimes causing the single case to stand for a whole class of evidence). He introduced great theorists (sometimes getting them wrong). He tried to convey the excitement and utility of doing things with ideas (sometimes he opposed ideas too binarily). He wore his progressive heart on his sleeve (sometimes his positions were quite conservative). Rhetorically, he was running a class, not an idea, and he often spoke without notes – he behaved like a performer, rather than reading out a theory. Like any performer, he didn't mind speaking other people's lines, so he'd explain the work of founding theorists, of his colleagues and students. And he was doing all this to popularise *cultural studies* – to recruit to that discourse more *readers*.

Criticising John Fiske for bad theory was always going to be poor sport. It was like kicking the dog for not being a cat. It was simple category error that didn't address what he was undoubtedly good at. This was teaching relative newcomers to cultural studies, i.e. students (including, judging by dog-eared and heavily annotated Fiskes on many a current luminary's back shelf, grad students who went on to make their own mark in it), why it was worth bothering with. Fiske gathered readers for other writers while he was at it.

So at the conference that marked the institutionalisation of cultural studies into American academic politics, the contribution of John Fiske, actor-teacher *par excellence*, was given short shrift by his intellectual critics, who were affronted by the fact that they were more astute as readers than he was. But meanwhile those potential readers, the students, were up in arms about the institutional politics of the event.

'Eros', 'appetite' and supply side cultural studies

This became something of a theme in cultural studies thenceforward. Teachers weren't hailed as popularisers but denounced as populists. Entertaining readers wasn't praised as a good device for keeping them on board, but deplored as a populist or celebratory depoliticisation of the field. Students continued, as was already traditional, to be seen but not heard. Disproportionate attention was given to the supply side of cultural studies. Readers (the books) obsessively focused on what people *wrote*; not on what they *read*. Since the condition of being a student was understood as transient, their job was to read the discourse of the free citizens they aspired to become. Reading cultural studies was not understood to be an end in itself, for that would make it mere consumption; reading was part of the process of emancipation *into* the public sphere of critical colloquy that was being conducted by those whose work was collected into Readers. Until then, students were not emancipated, could not speak, precisely because they were students, not readers understood as equal co-subjects in a republic of letters.

Ironically, one of the earliest practices of cultural studies *was* teaching, in the years after the Second World War, since its founding parents had all been associated in various ways with adult education – with the effort of emancipating people from working-class (etc.) backgrounds into intellectual freedom. And still many radical practitioners were attracted to cultural studies because it allowed politicised practice in the classroom (Chasin and hooks both mentioned this, 1992: 293–4). But once cultural studies had crossed the Rubicon from activism to academe, teaching could no longer be the *foundational* practice of its written performance. That had to be about ideas and theories; intellectual not communicative work. Those like Fiske whose performance was teacherly not theoretical, communicational not canonical, polemical not philosophical, were subject to rather stringent quality-control techniques by their peers, as if they were somehow devaluing the currency.

This set the stage for the next phase of cultural studies Readers. Designed for reading by students, they concentrated on theoretical work produced by figures regarded, by their editors at least, as seminal (or, less mannishly, as germinal). One of the best of the cultural studies Readers from this point of view was Simon During's *The Cultural Studies Reader*, first published in 1993, with a revised edition in 1999. It too came from Routledge, perhaps the leading publisher in this field (but I would say that, wouldn't I? – I have half a dozen books with them).

Of course the first thing to be found in During's Reader was a critique of John Fiske's 'cultural populism' in the editor's introduction, but no selection from his work in the anthology (During, 1999: 17–18). Instead, During pursued a relentless history of ideas approach to the development of cultural studies. In this narrative, a succession of theoretical, conceptual or methodological innovations was followed by discovery of 'limits' or difficulties associated with each new approach, followed by further innovation. The reader of the Reader was not mentioned, nor given any advice about their own role in the business, beyond a valedictory 'There remains much work to do' – perhaps implying that readers themselves might go forth and do some of it (During, 1999: 25). The only concession to the reader was an 'extensive guide to further reading', which took the form of four or five references appended to each selection.

During offered his collection as 'representative essays in cultural studies as an introduction to this increasingly popular field of study' (1999: 1). The 'representatives', gathered under thematic headings, with second-edition additions in **bold** and deletions from the first edition in brackets (so that you can trace the historical trends), were:

- *Theory and Method:* Theodor Adorno and Max Horkheimer; Roland Barthes; Carolyn Steedman; James Clifford; Angela McRobbie; Stuart Hall; (Teresa de Lauretis; Renato Rosaldo; Michele Wallace)
- *Space and Time:* Edward Soja; Michel de Certeau; Michel Foucault; Jean-François Lyotard; Ackbar Abbas
- *Nation* **(2nd edn: Nationalism, Postcolonialism and Globalization):** Gayatri Chakravorty Spivak; Homi K. Bhabha; David Forgacs; Arjun Appadurai
- *Ethnicity and Muliculturalism:* bell hooks; Eric Lott; Cornel West; (Gayatri Chakravorty Spivak and Sneja Gunew)
- **2nd edn: Science and Cyberculture**: Donna Haraway; Andrew Ross
- *Sexuality:* Teresa de Lauretis; Eve Kosofsky Sedgwick; Judith Butler; Lauren Berlant and Michael Warner; (Andrew Ross)
- *Carnival and Utopia:* Richard Dyer; Peter Stallybrass and Allon White
- *Consumption and the Market:* Meaghan Morris; Raymond Williams

- *Leisure:* Pierre Bourdieu; Dick Hebdige; Will Straw; Rey Chow
- **2nd edn: Culture – Political Economy and Policy**: Tony Bennett, Nicholas Garnham
- *Media* **(2nd edn: Media and Public Spheres):** Stuart Hall; Nancy Fraser; Hamid Naficy; Janice Radway; (Ien Ang; Armand Mattelart, Xavier Delcourt and Michèle Mattelart)

The only concession to the existence of readers in the second edition was the last sentence of the revised introduction. Readers were invited to make judgements: 'Whether or not engaged cultural studies accommodates to globalization and managerialism in quite the way I am proposing is up to readers of this book as much as anyone else' (During, 1999: 28). Go forth and *engage*, in other words.

Many other Readers were published. They soon tended to specialise. Specialisation could be:

- **Geographical**: John Frow and Meaghan Morris edited a Reader in *Australian Cultural Studies* in 1993, as did Graeme Turner in the same year. Krishna Sen and Maila Stevens edited a collection on *Gender and Power in Affluent Asia* in 1998, with contributions on Indonesia, Malaysia, Singapore, China, Vietnam, Thailand and the Philippines. Kuan-Hsing Chen edited *Trajectories: Inter-Asia Cultural Studies* in 1998, with contributions on the Philippines, Japan, Hong Kong, China, Singapore, Thailand, East Timor, Taiwan and Korea, as well as a number of identity-based contributions (see below). Barry Jordan and Rikki Morgan-Tamosunas edited one on *Contemporary Spanish Cultural Studies* in 2000. John Hartley and Roberta E. Pearson edited *American Cultural Studies: A Reader* in 2000.
- **Disciplinary**: Ann Gray and Jim McGuigan edited a Reader that represented a 'comparatively sociological "take" on cultural studies', making a selection that 'slightly marginalizes the textual in favour of the lived' (Gray and McGuigan, 1993: x). In 1997 Marjorie Ferguson and Peter Golding – both sociologists unsympathetic to cultural studies as they found it – edited *Cultural Studies in Question*. It was a kind of reverse raid on cultural studies from some of its critics in the empirical and social sciences. Richard Hoggart told me in conversation that year that Todd Gitlin's critical chapter in this Reader represented Hoggart's own views on the state of cultural studies at that time. This view brought his literary and Gitlin's sociological perspective together to *criticise* a field in which both had important investments; it also took Hoggart out of cultural studies as it had evolved since his retirement.
- **Identity-based**: Houston Baker, Manthia Diawara and Ruth Lindeborg edited *Black British Cultural Studies* in 1996. Kwesi Owusu edited *Black British Culture and Society* in 1999. Jacqueline Bobo edited *Black Feminist Cultural Criticism* in 2001. There were collections within cognate areas of inquiry, such as feminism (see Thornham, 2000), or gay and lesbian studies, that were co-badged as cultural studies – e.g. Terry Lovell's big reference

collection, *Feminist Cultural Studies* (1995), or *Out in Culture: Gay, Lesbian and Queer Essays on Popular Culture*, edited by Corey Creekmur and Alexander Doty in 1995.

Gray and McGuigan thought that their Reader was shaped by *teaching*: their 'particular version' of cultural studies was 'shaped by educational considerations derived from our own experiences of studying and teaching cultural studies over several years' (1993: vii). Their bias in favour of the 'lived' (social) and against the 'textual' (as ever, implying that textuality can't be lived) was itself a version of a growing current in cultural studies, as for instance represented by *Cultural Studies in Question* (Ferguson and Golding, 1997). This saw not only a shift towards sociology, but also a directly expressed hostility towards the literary-critical strand of cultural studies, which was held responsible for cultural populism, celebrating rather than critiquing popular culture, forgetting the economy, postmodern excess, abandonment of political critique in the public sphere, and hyper-theorisation.

In the light of all that, it was no surprise that an enterprising publisher decided to have a Reader that brought everyone back to reality. *Back to Reality? Social Experience and Cultural Studies* was edited by Angela McRobbie and published by Manchester University Press in 1997. McRobbie was herself a senior figure in cultural studies from its Birmingham days, noted for her own partly textual analyses of magazines aimed at girls and young women. So this was no young-Turk assault on the ivory tower of anything-goes relativism. Indeed, *Back to Reality* was an interesting mix of senior position pieces (by Lawrence Grossberg, Meaghan Morris, Graham Murdock and bell hooks) and a series of articles designed to answer those critics 'who imagine cultural studies as virtually incapable of touching ground. . . . Can cultural studies answer its critics by proving itself more than capable of doing the empirical groundwork. . .?' (McRobbie, 1997: 3). The affirmative answer was supplied by Paul Gilroy, Dave Laing, Vron Ware, Maria Pini, Sean Nixon and Angela McRobbie herself.

Interestingly, the McRobbie Reader made almost no song and dance (in the blurb, or in the introduction) about what was most challenging within its pages. While seeking to showcase a 'grounded' cultural studies, it succeeded in producing an innovative version, compared with other Readers to date, that was both *sexualised* and *feminised*. It had interesting new perspectives on cultural studies and:

- **Women**: Unusually, exactly half of the contributions were by women. And – also unusually – the contributions by the men were also alert to issues of feminisation and sexualisation.
- **Men**: Contributors drew attention to the 'predominantly masculine cast' (as Meaghan Morris phrased it: 1997: 40) of 'canonical' cultural studies to date.
- **Feminisation**: Many drew attention to the feminisation and/or sexualisation of aspects of the culture under discussion. Thus (among numerous

examples in the book), Maria Pini concluded her study of women in early rave culture in the UK with this: 'Rave can be seen as indicating an important shift in sexual relations, and indeed might suggest (with its emphasis on dance, physicality, affection and unity) a general "feminisation" of "youth"' (Pini, 1997: 168).

- **Eroticisation**: Most interestingly for present purposes, the contribution by bell hooks concerned the eroticisation of the relationship between teacher and student in cultural studies.

hooks's point was simple:

> Given that critical pedagogy seeks to transform consciousness, to provide students with ways of knowing that enable them to know themselves better and live in the world more fully, to some extent it must rely on the presence of the erotic in the classroom to aid the learning process. (hooks, 1997: 76)

Believing that a transformative, critical and 'passionate' field like cultural studies (or African-American studies, or women's studies) 'must rely' on erotic force in the classroom, hooks argued that it should not be disavowed, not least because that gesture would confirm a mind/body distinction that was untenable in principle, although harder to deal with in practice. Traditional academic practice required that professors were 'expected to *publish*' but not to 'care about *teaching*'.

Similarly, in the Readers at least, cultural studies concentrated on perfecting its speaking position without much regard for the question of who was there to listen, how they did that, and what sort of a relationship was required. Unusually, bell hooks sought to actualise the lesson of this theoretical insight within the classroom itself, and even more unusually she then used that classroom practice as the basis for her theoretical intervention in the Reader:

> When eros is present in the classroom setting then love is bound to flourish. Well-learned distinctions between public and private make us believe that love has no place in the classroom. . . . As professors we are expected to publish, but no one really expects or demands of us that we really care about teaching in uniquely passionate and different ways. (hooks, 1997: 79)

Of course, as hooks noted, 'teachers who love students and are loved by them are still "suspect" in the academy' (ibid.).

This was a new issue for cultural studies, not least because (like other academic enterprises) it had seemed thus far to rely on an almost obsessive over-investment in the *writer*, not the *reader* of its developing discourse. Despite their name, 'Readers' were of course anthologies of writing, and were understood in their editorial introductions as particular slices of (or contributions to) a canon. In the Readers (and for the writers collected therein), it was the accumulation of writing that *constituted* cultural studies as an academic subject.

A reading became a performance in print by one theorist to or about another. For instance, a Reader called *Cultural Studies and Communications* was edited by James Curran, David Morley and Valerie Walkerdine in 1996. They were senior figures who at that time were colleagues at Goldsmiths College (University of London). Most of the dozen contributors were also people associated with Goldsmiths, though perhaps significantly they did not include Richard Hoggart, its former Warden. One of the contributions was by Angela McRobbie – a version of the same essay she published in her own Reader a year later (by which time she had taken a post at another university). Since all the contributors knew each other there was plenty of room for debate. Indeed, the job of the reader was to follow these debates between the writers: 'We can, and do, disagree, sometimes passionately: theoretically, empirically, politically. During the course of this book, the reader will become familiar with debates. . .' (Curran et al., 1996: 1).

The editors explicitly refuted the idea that their Reader might be 'an authoritative definition (or "canon")' of cultural studies. There were, 'in our opinion, quite enough texts in existence' of that sort, including 'most tombstone-like of all, Grossberg et al. (1992)' (Curran et al.: 4). Instead, they sought to produce a 'genuinely introductory' and 'more hybrid' text that 'indicates how a *range* of cultural studies perspectives might be applied to the study of issues in the field of media and communications. It is for our readers to judge how far we have (or have not!) succeeded in that endeavour' (ibid.).

Navigating the 'passionate', avoiding the 'tombstones', readers would have noticed eight individual chapters by the editors themselves. Four of these staged an unfolding debate between Curran and Morley, the last of which was a contribution by Morley called 'Media Dialogue: Reading the Readings of the Readings . . .' (300–5). Here he recognised the 'potential absurdities' of 'embattled polemic with my "opponent"'. But debates 'necessarily involve my querying James's reading of my reading of his reading of my reading' (Morley in Curran et al., 1996: 300). In the end, presumably addressing the book's actual readers directly, Morley closed the 'reading' debate with this:

> PS: And if, minimally, all of this encourages more people to go back and read (or re-read, even with new eyes) the history of audience research, then so much the better for the field. (304)

That seemed to be about as far as cultural studies could go in thinking about 'audience research' into itself. Cultural studies was *something to read*. Its own 'audience' was exhorted in a postscript to read or re-read the 'readings of the readings of the readings'.

Like other talent-based professions such as acting or art, cultural studies was focused obsessively on the supply side. Questions about the *uses* to which literacy in reading – including cultural studies – might be put had not been asked since Richard Hoggart in 1957. Even writers like Morley, famous for championing the cause of empirical audiences in research, showed no interest in a move across from the supply to the demand side of cultural studies' own enterprise. None of the Readers investigated the readers of cultural studies as such. Nor, apart from bell hooks, did they investigate their own relationships with students. No curiosity was expressed about readers as empirical persons engaged in the activity of doing cultural studies. What might have happened to the fruits of their reading was ignored altogether. Did they go on to successful graduate outcomes? Were astute readers likely to end up as workforce or wealth-creators? Did they make use of their readings of cultural studies in other contexts? Did they take up the activist political positions recommended to them?

What were readers' consumer preferences, among different Readers? Here there may have been some evidence, in the form of sales figures. But even if these had been readily available (like newspapers' audited circulations), they would have been at best only an indirect measure of demand by any actual readers of Readers, since the best-sellers reflected institutional or professorial adoption policies, not readers' own *love* for this or that Reader.

It seemed, in the end, that cultural studies was prey to one of the tendencies it had criticised most persistently in those media and cultural institutions that it analysed. That tendency was to over-privilege the supply side (i.e. writing, understood as production), and to under-value the demand side (i.e. reading, understood as consumption). Indeed, Ben Carrington criticised histories of cultural studies for their tendency to 'highlight the publication of academic *texts* as "producing" cultural studies as an academic discipline taught within universities, rather than seeing such texts themselves as being the outcome of wider sociopolitical processes of education . . . aimed at social transformation' (Carrington, 2001: 277). The Readers, in short, began to focus more on the academic production of cultural studies, which took the form of published debate among themselves, rather than seeking to know and to service the needs, demands or thoughts of their own readers.

The latter were construed as incomplete academic subjects, their incompleteness consisting precisely in what they did *not* know, which the Readers purported to supply. In such an economy, there was no demand side – readers could not demand what they did not know. So they got what the producers thought they needed, which often included histories of academic publishing (not unlike the present chapter), or a blow by blow account of disputes among academic producers of cultural studies. This tendency for discursive professionals to supply an imagined lack in an unknown audience without direct reference to that audience was just what cultural studies criticised in canonical media. While much passion was expended on insisting that media audiences needed to be known, usually by means of empirical ethnographic investigation of the kind associated with David Morley, little energy seemed to go into making similar inquiries into cultural studies' own audience of readers.

The real appetite for cultural studies on the demand side could perhaps be gauged by the popularity of websites devoted to it. These have attracted analytical attention in, for instance, articles that appraised their impact on cultural studies by Will Brooker (1998) and Eva Vieth (2000). Book sales, both current best-sellers (ratings) and stalwarts of the backlist (reach), could also be used as evidence. However, they were not published in a reliable league table, and in any case the reader of Readers was never a *sovereign* consumer, but was subject to guided choice about what to buy in an academic-capitalist funny-mirror distortion of Stalinist democratic centralism. In other words, students bought what their instructors thought was good for them, perhaps including, what luck, this book. Here cultural studies was following a tradition it had itself critiqued. As was noted in Chapter 2, above, John Carey coruscated twentieth-century intellectuals who 'believe in giving the public what intellectuals want; that, generally speaking is what they mean by education' (Carey, 1992: 6).

Perhaps the affinity between teacher and student glimpsed by bell hooks was only a passing infatuation; everyone soon got over it, at least in print, and perhaps that was just as well for all concerned. Certainly by the time Toby Miller came on to the scene the reader had pretty well disappeared entirely, even though Miller's own Reader, *A Companion to Cultural Studies*, was billed by the publisher's blurb as a 'stimulating Companion' – i.e. an object of desire for readers new and old:

> The volume offers a gritty introduction for the neophyte who is keen to find out what all the fuss is about, and it also covers debates that will satisfy the appetite of the advanced scholar. Hence, it will stimulate debate as well as providing an accessible introduction. (Miller (ed.), 2001: cover blurb)

Unusually for a Reader, many of the essays in Miller's *Companion* were specially commissioned. Many of the contributors were 'companions' (or, Australian style, mates) of the editor. Miller drew attention to his contributors' disciplinary and geographical diversity:

> This volume is designed to show where cultural studies exists and what it does there, reflecting a significant diversity of interests and methods. We reach across disciplines, places, issues, and sources, in keeping with the postdisciplinary project of cultural studies – and do so in the interests of deprovincialization [sic] (contributors reside in five different continents). (Miller, ed. 2001: 12)

Affect in cultural studies had migrated from classroom to peer group. 'Passionate engagement' was an *editorial* strategy, not a *pedagogical* one. But the 'we' of cultural studies was thereby extended beyond the previously charmed circle of British and American witnesses to a new generation of non-canonical voices.

Of course, questions of teaching and therefore of students did surface within the 580 pages of the *Companion*, and not just in the fact that its essays were addressed to an imagined student reader. Justin Lewis on the 'purpose and pitfalls of teaching popular culture', centred his chapter on the experience of teaching, and confessed that his 'main concern is one of being taken seriously' (Lewis, 2001: 317). He argued that universities were hostile environments for teaching cultural studies, a fact that required its proponents to be 'more forceful and less opaque' about 'advocating the importance of teaching popular culture' (Lewis: 318). In that context, he drew attention to the need both to 'address the politics of pleasure' and, contrariwise, to 'acknowledge the awkward pedagogy' involved when the 'frames of reference' of teacher and student would be quite different because of the age gap between them. In short, thought Lewis, cultural studies had to face the fact that from the point of view of the neophyte undergraduate the teacher was hardly a locus of eros. More likely they would be seen as 'a boring old fart' (Lewis: 317–18). But students remained the object of the exercise: Lewis concluded with this sentence: 'And if students are to feel that they can have any part in shaping these [historically enabled range of] possibilities, then cultural policy must be enmeshed into the pedagogy of teaching popular culture' (Lewis: 328).

In Miller's own introduction to the collection, the 'boring old fart' was yet to make an appearance, and the grit-seeking neophyte of the cover had already faded from view. The closest Miller himself came to any reader was a recollection of *himself* as that neophyte. He concluded his introduction to what cultural studies 'is, and isn't', thus:

> I recall my excitement when I first saw the cover of the Birmingham Centre's *Working Papers in Cultural Studies* 4 of 1973 . . . the bottom center-left read like this:
>
>
>
> LITERATURE – SOCIETY
> MOTOR RACING
>
>
>
> It seemed natural to me for these topics to be together. . . . But of course that is not academically 'normal.' To make them syntagmatic was *utterly sensible* in terms of people's lives and mediated reality, and *utterly improbable* in terms of intellectual divisions of labor and hierarchies of discrimination. Bravo. (Miller, 2001: 13–14)

'Bravo' – Miller's last word was a gesture of applause for cultural studies as an outcome of *reading*, albeit his own.

Activist readers (II)

Miller's position on reading by readers other than himself was expressed outside the conventions of the Reader as discussed in this chapter. In *Global Hollywood*, Miller and his co-authors Nitin Govil, John McMurria and Richard Maxwell argued for a mixture of cultural studies (interpretation, semiotics, consumption) with political economy (policy, intellectual property, production). Within such a hybrid mode of analysis, the role of the reader could be reinterpreted. Miller et al. argued that reading should be regarded not as consumption but as *labour*. Readers' rights (for instance of access to images of their own region, to copyrighted material, consumer rights) should be subject to 'constitutional protection' (Miller et al., 2001: 202–5). They concluded their study with a fascinating rewriting of the image of the reader:

> We have endeavoured to write for filmgoers whose identities rival the ones generated for and about them by global Hollywood. In doing so we envisaged a filmgoer with capacious interests that take into account the ethical and political problems of the contemporary political economy of culture: the Americanisation of production, distribution and exhibition with its persistent vision of separate spheres of work and consumption; the bureaucratisation of national policy and the privatisation of global policy; the impact of deregulated markets, including television; the dominance of the 'Washington Consensus'; the spread of the NICL [New International Division of Cultural Labour]; the co-optation of resistive national cultural policy by bourgeoisies and Hollywood itself; the continued power of the US domestic audience as a marketing site; and the force of DEM/GEM [Domestic Effects Model/Global Effects Model] logics of citizenship and consumption. (Miller et al., 216)

In short, Miller and his colleagues were proposing to fuzzy the line between producers and consumers of cultural studies itself, to get away from the idea that the role of readers was simply to consume what their teachers thought was good for them, or what would help them to pass exams (i.e. successfully to subject themselves to a *regime* of knowledge). Instead they wanted their reader – the 'filmgoer' – to carry their interests with them directly into the cultural field. They even proposed that the political economy approach would benefit if it addressed issues of ownership not at the level of production (Murdoch) but instead started with the act of consumption (203). Their 'reader' was an *agent*.

Miller et al. foresaw a situation where such 'capacious interests', duly processed and reworked to accommodate to readers' own situations, would once again support activism. The reader, the consumer of culture, the 'filmgoer', would be 'literate' in the issues dear to academic writers, but also facing 'cultural citizens' (however defined) at large. They would certainly watch movies in this knowledge, but there was scope, argued Miller and his colleagues, for much more thoroughgoing activism organised around the concept of culture as work. And they wanted both their own and 'Hollywood' knowledge to be readily available. They quoted John Frow, who had asserted that 'knowledge actually increases when it is shared' (Frow, 2000: 182), to argue for readers' rights to access to knowledge, and to claim that in that space, reception was 'an *act of creative labour*' (Miller et al., 2001; 209).

Cultural studies was poised on the brink of a new adventure that in many ways resembled the one it had been through during the latter part of the twentieth century. But cultural studies for the twenty-first century provided analyst and activist alike with some new perspectives that went well beyond what had animated the pioneers. Active, imaginative, resistive and creative reading practices were, however, still at its centre. It was still a *philosophy of plenty*, wishing to increase knowledge as it shared its own insights, the better to bring consumers, producers, analysts and activists into the *same* cultural commons, at least for the purposes of dialogue.

As the creative industries began to demonstrate their economic clout in a period of new investment in the 'copyright' sector of the global economy, the time was ripe for cultural studies to enter a more public phase. As a 'literacy' in which the 'capacious interests' of readers – who were newly aware of their rights – were widely shared and understood, cultural studies could engage with producers, policy-makers, regulators, R&D and technical innovators, *and* the consumer-citizens of those industries. It was no longer required to produce a *winner* out of the perennial arguments among critical outsiders, political economists, postmodern textualists or cultural activists, not to mention the users of culture. The new cultural studies was a hybrid, global, post-disciplinary conversation, whose differing participants could mutually recognise that 'knowledge increased when it was shared'. But while conceding that culture – the latest service industry – was plentiful, cultural studies was still finding that there was real work to be done on the question of how it was shared.

References
Cites to Behold

Cultural studies and publishing

Cultural studies was a publishing enterprise . . .

Abercrombie, Nicholas and Brian Longhurst (1998) *Audiences: A Sociological theory of Performance and Imagination*. London: Sage.

Althusser, Louis (1969) *For Marx*. London: Allen Lane.

Althusser, Louis (1971) *Lenin and Philosophy and Other Essays*. London: New Left Books.

Arnold, Matthew ([1869] 1993) *Culture and Anarchy and Other Writings*. Cambridge: Cambridge University Press.

Baker, Houston A. Jr., Manthia Diawara and Ruth H. Lindeborg (eds) (1996) *Black British Cultural Studies*. Chicago: University of Chicago Press.

Barker, Chris (2000) *Cultural Studies: Theory and Practice*. London: Sage.

Barrell, John (1986) *The Political Theory of Painting from Reynolds to Hazlitt: 'The Body of the Public.'* New Haven: Yale University Press.

Barthes, Roland ([1953] 1967) *Writing Degree Zero*. Trans. Annette Lavers and Colin Smith. London: Jonathan Cape.

Beeton, Mrs [Isabella] (1909) *Mrs Beeton's Every-day Cookery*. New edition. London: Ward, Lock.

Beeton, Isabella ([1861] 2000) *Mrs Beeton's Book of Household Management*. Abridged edition, edited by Nicola Humble. Oxford: Oxford World Classics.

Bennett, David (ed.) (1998) *Multicultural States: Rethinking Difference and Identity*. London: Routledge.

Bennett, Tony (1979) *Marxism and Formalism*. London: Methuen.

Bennett, Tony (1992) 'Useful Culture.' *Cultural Studies*, 6(3): 395–408.

Bennett, Tony (1995) *The Birth of the Museum: History, Theory, Politics*. London: Routledge.

Bennett, Tony (1998) *Culture: A Reformer's Science*. Sydney: Allen & Unwin.

Bennett, Tony and David Carter (eds) (2001) *Culture in Australia: Policies, Publics and Programs*. Cambridge: Cambridge University Press.

Berger, John (1972) *Ways of Seeing*. London: BBC/Penguin.

Berry, Sarah (2001) 'Fashion.' In Miller (ed.), 454–70.

Bethell, S.L. (1944) *Shakespeare and the Popular Dramatic Tradition*. London: Staples.

Bethell, S.L. (1951) *The Cultural Revolution of the Seventeenth Century*. London: Dobson.

Bhabha, Homi (1998) 'Culture's In Between.' In David Bennett (ed.), 29–36.

Blair, Tony (2001) 'Foreword by the Prime Minister.' *Culture and Creativity: The Next Ten Years* [Green Paper]. London: Department of Culture, Media and Sport.

Bobo, Jacqueline (ed.) (2001) *Black Feminist Cultural Criticism (Keyworks in Cultural Studies)*. Malden, MA: Blackwell.

Bourdieu, Pierre (1986) *Distinction*. London: Routledge.

Bowlby, Rachel (19850 *Just Looking*. London: Methuen.

Brooker, Will (1998) 'Under Construction: Cultural Studies in Cyberspace.' *International Journal of Cultural Studies*, 1(3): 415–24.

Brunsdon, Charlotte (1996) 'A Thief in the Night: Stories of Feminism in the 1970s at CCCS.' In Hall, Morley and Chen (eds).

Brunsdon, Charlotte, Julie D'Acci and Lynn Spigel (eds) (1997) *Feminist Television Criticism: A Reader*. Oxford: Oxford University Press.

Buck-Morss, Susan (1986) 'The *Flâneur*, the Sandwichman and the Whore: The Politics of Loitering.' *New German Critique*, 39 (Fall): 99–140.

Burchell, Graham, Colin Gordon and Peter Miller (eds) (1991) *The Foucault Effect: Studies in Governmentality*. Hemel Hempstead: Harvester Wheatsheaf.

CCCS (1982) *The Empire Strikes Back*. London: Hutchinson.

Carey, John (1992) *The Intellectuals and the Masses*. London: Faber & Faber.

Carrington, Ben (2001) 'Decentering the Centre: Cultural Studies in Britain and its Legacy.' In Miller (ed.), 275–97.

Caves, Richard (2000) *Creative Industries*. Cambridge, MA: Harvard University Press.

Chasin, Alexandra (1992) Discussant. In Grossberg, Nelson and Treichler (eds), 293.

Chen, Kuan-Hsing (ed.) (1998) *Trajectories:Inter-Asia Cultural Studies*. London: Routledge.

Cheskin (January 2002) *Media Content: The Place Where We Live*. Cheskin Market Insight Series: www.cheskin.com.

Cohen, Phil (1972) 'Subcultural Conflict and Working Class Community.' *Working Papers in Cultural Studies*, 2, Spring: 5–51.

Cooper, Scott (1992) Discussant. In Grossberg, Nelson and Treichler (eds), 294.

Cotton, Charlotte (2000) *Imperfect Beauty: The Making of Contemporary Fashion Photographs*. London: V&A Publications.

Couldry, Nick (2000) *Inside Culture: Re-imagining the Method of Cultural Studies*. London: Sage.

Creekmur, Corey and Alexander Doty (eds) (1995) *Out in Culture: Gay, Lesbian and Queer Essays on Popular Culture*. Durham, NC: Duke University Press; London: Cassell.

Culler, Jonathan (1981) 'Semiotics of Tourism. '*American Journal of Semiotics*, 1: 127–40.

Culture, Media and Sport, Department of (2001) *Creative Industries: Mapping Document 2001*. London: HMSO (http://www.culture.gov.uk/creative/mapping.html).

Cunningham, Stuart (1992) *Framing Culture: Criticism and Policy in Australia*. Sydney: Allen & Unwin.

Curran, James and Jean Seaton (1987) *Power without Responsibility*. London: Routledge.

Curran, James, David Morley and Valerie Walkerdine (eds) (1996) *Cultural Studies and Communications*. London: Arnold.

Darnton, Robert (1997) *The Forbidden Best-sellers of Pre-Revolutionary France*. New York and London: HarperCollins.

De Certeau, Michel (1984) *The Practice of Everyday Life*. Berkeley: University of California Press.

Donald, James (1999) *Imagining the Modern City*. London: Pippin Publishing.

Donzelot, Jacques (1980) *The Policing of Families*. Trans. Robert Hurley. London: Hutchinson.

During, Simon (ed.) ([1993] 1999) *The Cultural Studies Reader*. London: Routledge.

Eagleton, Terry (2000) *The Idea of Culture*. Oxford: Blackwell.

Enzensberger, Hans Magnus (1976) *Raids and Reconstructions: Essays in Politics, Crime and Culture*. London: Pluto.

Evans, Harold (1998) *The American Century: People, Power and Politics*. London: Jonathan Cape; New York: Alfred A. Knopf.

Felski, Rita (1995) *The Gender of Modernity*. Cambridge, MA: Harvard University Press.

Ferguson, Marjorie and Peter Golding (eds) (1997) *Cultural Studies in Question*. London: Sage.

Fielding, Helen (1995) *Cause Celeb*, London: Picador.

Fiske, John (1983) 'Surfalism and Sandiotics: The Beach in Oz Popular Culture.' *Australian Journal of Cultural Studies*, 1(i): 120–49.

Fiske, John (1992) 'Cultural Studies and the Culture of Everyday Life.' In Grossberg, Nelson and Treichler (eds), 154–73.

Fiske, John and John Hartley (1978) *Reading Television*. London: Methuen [Routledge].

Foucault, Michel (1980) 'Two Lectures.' In Colin Gordon (ed.), *Power/Knowledge: Selected Interviews and Other Writings 1972–77*. New York: Pantheon.

Foucault, Michel (1984) *The Foucault Reader*. Ed. Paul Rabinow. New York: Pantheon; London: Penguin.

Foucault, Michel (1991) 'Governmentality.' In Burchell, Gordon and Miller (eds), 87–104.

Frow, John (1997) *Time and Commodity Culture: Essays on Cultural Theory and Modernity*. Oxford: Oxford University Press.

Frow, John (2000) 'Public Domain and the New World Order in Knowledge.' *Social Semiotics* 10(2).

Frow, John and Meaghan Morris (eds) (1993) *Australian Cultural Studies: A Reader.* Sydney: Allen & Unwin.

Gallacher, William (1949) *The Case for Communism*. Harmondsworth: Penguin Special.

Garnham, Nicholas (1987) 'Concepts of Culture: Public Policy and the Culture Industries.' *Cultural Studies*, 1(1): 23–38.

Garnham, Nicholas (1990) *Capitalism and Communication: Global Culture and the Economics of Information*. London: Sage.

Gibson, Lisanne (2001) *The Uses of Art: Constructing Australian Identities*. Brisbane: University of Queensland Press.

Gibson, Mark (2001) 'Monday Morning and the Millennium: Cultural Studies, Scepticism and the Concept of Power'. PhD thesis. Perth, Australia: Edith Cowan University.

Gilroy, Paul (1987) *There Ain't No Black in the Union Jack: The Cultural Politics of Race and Nation*. London: Routledge.

Gilroy, Paul (1992) 'Cultural Studies and Ethnic Absolutism.' In Grossberg, Nelson and Treichler (eds), 187–98.

Gilroy, Paul (1996) 'British Cultural Studies and the Pitfalls of Identity.' In Baker, Diawara and Lindeborg (eds).

Golding, Peter and Graham Murdock (eds) (1997) *The Political Economy of the Media* Cheltenham, UK and Brookfield, VT: Edward Elgar.

Gorbachev, Mikhail (1996) *Memoirs*. London: Doubleday.

Goulden, Holly and John Hartley (1982) '"Nor should such topics as homosexuality, masturbation, frigidity, premature ejaculation or the menopause be regarded as unmentionable": English Literature, School Examinations and Official Discourses.' *LTP Journal: Journal of Literature Teaching Politics*, 1(April): 4–20.

Gramsci, Antonio (1971) *Selections from the Prison Notebooks*. London: Lawrence & Wishart.

Gray, Ann and Jim McGuigan (eds) ([1993]1997) *Studying Culture: An Introductory Reader.* London: Arnold.

Grossberg, Lawrence (1995) 'Cultural Studies vs Political Economy: Is Anybody Else Bored with This Debate?' *Critical Studies in Mass Communication*, 12(1): March: 72–81.

Grossberg, Lawrence, Cary Nelson and Paula Treichler (eds) (1992) *Cultural Studies*. New York: Routledge.

Hall, Stuart (1959) 'The Big Swipe: Some Comments on the "Classlessness Controversy".' *Universities and Left Review*, 7: 50–2.

Hall, Stuart, Charles Critcher, Tony Jefferson, John Clarke and Brian Robert (1978) *Policing the Crisis*. London: Hutchinson.

Hall, Stuart (1981) 'Notes on Deconstructing the Popular.' In Samuel (ed.).

Hall, Stuart (1992) 'Cultural Studies and its Theoretical Legacies.' In Grossberg, Nelson and Treichler (eds), 277–94.

Hall, Stuart and Paddy Whannel (1964) *The Popular Arts*. London: Hutchinson.

Hall, Stuart, David Morley and Kuan-Hsing Chen (eds) (1996) *Stuart Hall: Critical Dialogues in Cultural Studies*. London: Comedia [Routledge].

Halloran, J.D., Graham Murdock and Philip Schlesinger (1970) *Demonstrations and Communications: A Case Study*. Harmondsworth: Penguin.

Harbage, Alfred (1941) *Shakespeare's Audience*. Chicago: University of Chicago Press.

Hartley, Dorothy ([1954] 1999) *Food in England*. London: Little, Brown.

Hartley, John (1992) *The Politics of Pictures: The Creation of the Public in the Age of Popular Media*. London: Routledge.

Hartley, John (1996) *Popular Reality: Journalism, Modernity, Popular Culture*. London: Arnold.

Hartley, John (2000a) 'Communicative Democracy in a Redactional Society: The Future of Journalism Studies.' *Journalism: Theory, Practice & Criticism*, 1(1): 39–47.

Hartley, John (2000b) '"Cultural Exceptionalism": Freedom, Imperialism, Power, America.' In Hartley and Pearson (eds), 1–20.

Hartley, John and Roberta E. Pearson (eds) (2000) *American Cultural Studies: A Reader*. Oxford: Oxford University Press.

Hartley, John and Catharine Lumby (2002) 'Working Girls or Drop-Dead Gorgeous? Young Girls in Fashion and News.' In K. Mallan and S. Pearce (eds), Chapter 4.

Harvard Business Review (2001) 'A Reading List for Bill Gates – and You: An Interview with Literary Critic Harold Bloom.' *HBR* 79 (5) May: 63–8.

Hauser, Arnold ([1951] 1999) *The Social History of Art*, 4 vols. New York and London: Routledge.

Hawkes, Terence (1969) 'Postscript: Theatre against Shakespeare.' In David Galloway (ed.) *The Elizabethan Theatre*. Canada: Macmillan, 117–26.

Hawkes, Terence (1973) *Shakespeare's Talking Animals: Language and Drama in Society*. London: Edward Arnold.

Hawkes, Terence (1977) *Structuralism and Semiotics*. London: Routledge.

Hawkes, Terence (1986) *That Shakespeherian Rag*. London: Routledge.

Hay, James, Lawrence Grossberg and Ellen Wartella (eds) (1994) *The Audience and its Landscape*. Boulder, CO: Westview Press.

Hebdige, Dick (1979) *Subculture: The Meaning of Style*. London: Methuen.

Hebdige, Dick (1988) *Hiding in the Light: On Images and Things*. London: Comedia/Routledge.

Hermes, Joke (1995) *Reading Women's Magazines: An Analysis of Everyday Media Use*. Cambridge: Polity.

Hobbes, Thomas ([1651] 1968) *Leviathan*. Ed. C.B. Macpherson. Harmondsworth: Penguin.

Hoggart, Richard (1957) *The Uses of Literacy*. London: Chatto and Windus.

Hoggart, Richard (1992) *An Imagined Life (Life and Times, Volume III: 1959–91)*. London: Chatto and Windus [Oxford University Press, 1993].

hooks, bell (1992) Discussant. In Grossberg, Nelson and Treichler (eds), 171; 293–4.

hooks, bell (1997) 'Eros, Eroticism, and the Pedagogical Process.' In McRobbie (ed.), 74–80.

Hughes, Robert ([1981] 1991) *The Shock of the New*. New York: Knopf.

Hunter, Ian (1988) *Culture and Government: The Emergence of Literary Education*. London: Macmillan.

Jordan, Barry and Rikki Morgan-Tamosunas (eds) (2000) *Contemporary Spanish Cultural Studies*. London: Arnold.

Klein, Naomi (2000) *No Logo: Taking Aim at the Brand Bullies*. Toronto: Vintage Canada.

Leach, Edmund ([1964] 1972) 'Anthropological Aspects of Language: Animal Categories and Verbal Abuse.' In Maranda (ed.), 39–67.

Leach, Edmund (1976) *Culture and Communication*. Cambridge: Cambridge University Press.

Leadbeater, Charles (1997) *Living on Thin Air: The New Economy*. London: Viking.

Leadbeater, Charles and Kate Oakley (1999) *The Independents: Britain's New Cultural Entrepreneurs*. London: Demos.

Leavis, F.R. (1952) *The Common Pursuit*. Harmondsworth: Penguin.

Leavis, F.R. and Denys Thompson (1933) *Culture and Environment: The Training of Critical Awareness*. London: Chatto and Windus.

Leavis, Q.D. (1965) *Fiction and the Reading Public*. London: Chatto and Windus.

Lévi-Strauss, Claude (1969) *The Raw and the Cooked*. Trans. D. Weightman. London: Jonathan Cape.

Lewis, Justin (2001) 'Let's Get Serious: Notes on Teaching Youth Culture.' In Miller (ed.), 317–30.

Lotman, Yuri, M. (1990) *Universe of the Mind: A Semiotic Theory of Culture*. Bloomington & Indianapolis: Indiana University Press.

Lovell, Terry (ed.) (1995) *Feminist Cultural Studies*. London: Edward Elgar.

Lucy, Niall (1995) *Debating Derrida*. Melbourne: Melbourne University Press.

Lucy, Niall (1997) *Postmodern Literary Theory: An Introduction*. Oxford: Blackwell.

Lumby, Catharine (1999) *Gotcha! Living in a Tabloid World*. Sydney: Allen and Unwin.

McGuigan, Jim (1992) *Cultural Populism*. London: Routledge.

McKay, George (1998) *DiY Culture: Party and Protest in Nineties Britain*. London: Verso.

McRobbie, Angela (ed.) (1997) *Back to Reality? Social Experience and Cultural Studies*. Manchester: Manchester University Press.

Mallan, Kerry and Sharyn Pearce (eds) (2002) *Youth Cultures: Texts, Images and Identities*. Westport, CT: Greenwood.

Manguel, Alberto (1996) *A History of Reading*. London: Flamingo, HarperCollins.

Mansbach, Steven A. (2000) 'A Universal Voice in Russian Berlin.' In Railing (ed.), 159–84.

Maranda, Pierre (ed.) (1972) *Mythology*. Harmondsworth: Penguin.

Marcus, George E. (2001) 'The Unbalanced Reciprocity between Cultural Studies and Anthropology.' In Miller (ed.), 169–86.

Mathieson, Margaret (1975) *The Preachers of Culture*. London: Unwin Education.

Mayakovsky, Vladimir , El Lissitzky [book constructor] (2000) *For the Voice*. Facsimile edition and English translation. Cambridge, MA: MIT Press.

Metz, Christian (1978) *Film Language*. Oxford: Oxford University Press.

Michaels, Eric (1994) *Bad Aboriginal Art: Tradition, Media and Technological Horizons*. Sydney: Allen and Unwin.

Miller, Daniel (1998) *A Theory of Shopping*. Cambridge: Polity.

Miller, Toby (1993) *The Well-Tempered Self: Citizenship, Culture and the Postmodern Subject*. Baltimore: Johns Hopkins University Press.

Miller, Toby (1998) *Technologies of Truth: Cultural Citizenship and the Popular Media*. Minneapolis: University of Minnesota Press.

Miller, Toby (2001) 'What It Is and What It Isn't: Introducing … Cultural Studies.' In Miller (ed.): 1–19.

Miller, Toby (ed.) (2001) *A Companion to Cultural Studies*. Malden, MA and Oxford: Blackwell.

Miller, Toby, Nitin Govil, John McMurria and Richard Maxwell (2001) *Global Hollywood*. London: British Film Institute Publishing.

Morris, Meaghan (1988) *The Pirate's Fiancée: Feminism, Reading, Postmodernism*. London: Verso.

Morris, Meaghan (1992) 'Discussion: Meaghan Morris.' In Grossberg, Nelson and Treichler (eds), 473–78.

Morris, Meaghan (1997) 'A Question of Cultural Studies.' In McRobbie (ed.), 36–57.

Morris, Meaghan(1998a) *Too Soon Too Late: History in Popular Culture*. Bloomington: Indiana University Press.

Morris, Meaghan (1998b) 'White panic or Mad Max and the Sublime.' In Chen (ed.), 239–62.

Morrison, David E. (1998) *The Search for a Method: Focus Groups and the Development of Mass Communication Research*. Luton: University of Luton Press.

Moss, Kate (1995) *Kate*. London: Pavilion.

Nava, Mica (1998) 'The Cosmopolitanism of Commerce and the Allure of Difference: Selfridge's, the Russian Ballet and the Tango, 1911–1914.' *International Journal of Cultural Studies*, 1(2): 163–96.

Nelson, Cary and Lawrence Grossberg (eds) (1988) *Marxism and the Interpretation of Culture*. Urbana: University of Illinois Press.

Nowell-Smith, Geoffrey (ed.) (1996) *The Oxford History of World Cinema*. Oxford: Oxford University Press.

O'Connor, Alan (ed.) (1989) *Raymond Williams on Television: Selected Writings*. New York and London: Routledge.

Owusu, Kwesi (ed.) (1999) *Black British Culture and Society*. London: Routledge.

Paine, Thomas ([1793] 1938) *The Age of Reason*. Ed. Hypatia Bradlaugh Bonner. London: Watts.

Philo, Greg and David Miller (1999) *Cultural Compliance*. London: Longman.

Picardie, Justine (May 2000) 'Creating Kate.' British *Vogue* (whole number 2422 Vol 166): 158–71.

Pini, Maria (1997) 'Women and the Early British Rave Scene.' In McRobbie (ed.), 152–69.

Prato, Paulo and Gianluca Trivero (1985) 'The Spectacle of Travel.' *Australian Journal of Cultural Studies* 3(2): 25–43.

Probyn, Elspeth (2000) *Carnal Appetites: Food Sex Identities*. London and New York: Routledge.

Quiller-Couch, Arthur ([1916] 1946) *The Art of Writing*. London: Guild Books.

Railing, Patricia (2000) 'A Revolutionary Spirit.' In Railing (ed.), 15–33.

Railing, Patricia, ed. (2000) *Voices of Revolution: Collected Essays*. Cambridge, MA: MIT Press.

Richards, Thomas (1993) *The Imperial Archive: Knowledge and the Fantasy of Empire*. London: Verso.

Ross, Andrew (1999) *The Celebration Chronicles: Life, Liberty and the Pursuit of Property Value in Disney's New Town*. New York: Ballantine.

Rowland, Willard D. and Bruce Watkins (eds) (1984) *Interpreting Television: Current Research Perspectives*. Beverly Hills: Sage.

Samuel, Raphael (ed.) (1981) *People's History and Socialist Theory*. London: Routledge and Kegan Paul.

Sartelle, Joseph (1996) 'Dreams and Nightmares in the Hollywood Blockbuster.' In Nowell-Smith (ed.), 516–26.

Saul, Marianne (1990) *Perestroika: The Dinner Party*. Berlin: Benedikt Taschen.

Saussure, Ferdinand de (1974) *Course in General Linguistics*. London: Fontana.

Schiller, Herbert (1989) *Culture, Inc: The Corporate Takeover of Public Expression*. New York: Oxford University Press.

Seldes, Barry (2000) 'Sensibilities for the New Man. Politics, Poetics and Graphics.' In Railing (ed.), 138–58.

Self, Will (1991) *The Quantity Theory of Insanity*. Harmondsworth: Penguin.

Sen, Krishna and Maila Stevens (eds) (1998) *Gender and Power in Affluent Asia*. London: Routledge.

Shaw, George Bernard (1937) *The Intelligent Woman's Guide to Socialism, Capitalism, Sovietism and Fascism*, 2 Vols. Harmondsworth: Pelican Books.

Shuttleworth, Alan (1966) *Two Working Papers in Cultural Studies – A Humane Centre* and *Max Weber and the 'Cultural Sciences.'* (Occasional Paper No. 2). Birmingham University: Centre for Contemporary Cultural Studies.

Spender, Dale (1980) *Man Made Language*. London: Routledge and Kegan Paul.

Stevenson, Nick (1995) *Understanding Media Cultures: Social Theory and Mass Communication*. London: Sage.

Storey, John (1999) *Cultural Consumption and Everyday Life*. London: Arnold.

Tester, Keith (ed.) (1994) *The Flâneur*. London: Routledge.

Thompson, E.P. ([1963]1968) *The Making of the English Working Class*. Harmondsworth: Pelican Books.

Thornham, Sue (2000) *Feminist Theory and Cultural Studies*. Tester: Arnold.

Turner, Graeme (1990) *British Cultural Studies* New York: Unwin Hyman. (2nd edn 1996; 3rd edn 2002). London: Routledge.

Turner, Graeme (ed.) (1993) *Nation, Culture, Text: Australian Cultural and Media Studies*. London: Routledge.

Urry, John (1990) *The Tourist Gaze: Leisure and Travel in Contemporary Societies*. London: Sage.

Veblen, Thorstein (1899 [this edn 1953]) *The Theory of the Leisure Class: An Economic Study of Institutions*. New York: Mentor.

Vieth, Eva (2000) 'Epilogue: The Future is Present: American Cultural Studies on the Net.' In Hartley and Pearson (eds), 427–36.

Waters, Malcolm (1995) *Globalization*. London: Routledge.

Whitford, Frank (1987) *Understanding Abstract Art*. London: Barrie & Jenkins.

Williams, Raymond ([1958] 1961) *Culture and Society 1780–1950*. Harmondsworth: Penguin.

Williams, Raymond (1968) *Drama from Ibsen to Brecht*. London: Chatto and Windus.

Williams, Raymond (1974) *Television: Technology and Cultural Form*. London: Fontana.

Williams, Raymond (1977) *Marxism and Literature*. Oxford: Oxford University Press.

Willis, Paul (1978) *Learning to Labour: How Working Class Kids Get Working Class Jobs*. London: Routledge & Kegan Paul.

Wilson, Elizabeth (1999) 'The Bohemianization of Mass Culture.' *International Journal of Cultural Studies*, 2(1): 11–32.

Wilson, Elizabeth (2001) *The Contradictions of Culture: Cities, Culture, Women*. London: Sage.

Wolfe, Tom ([1969] 2000) 'What If He Is Right?' In Hartley and Pearson (eds), 22–31.

Wolfe, Tom (1999) *The Painted Word*. New York: Bantam Books.

Women's Studies Group of the CCCS (1978) *Women Take Issue: Aspects of Women's Subordination*. London: Hutchinson.

Woolf, Virginia ([1929] 1945) *A Room of One's Own*. Harmondsworth: Penguin.

Woroszylski, Wiktor (1972) *The Life of Mayakovsky*. London: Victor Gollancz.

Index